AF511682

Pastoral Care and Counselling

Pastoral Care and Counselling

Towards Cultural Fidelity Among Naga Youth

Boholi Z. Sema

Christian World Imprints

© Boholi Z. Sema

First Published in 2020 by

Christian World Imprints
Christian Publishing & Books from India
C-3, Wazirpur Industrial Area
Delhi-110052
cwidelhi2017@gmail.com
www.ChristianWorldImprints.com
Phone: +91 11 41526079

ISBN: 978-93-5148-445-5 (HB)
ISBN: 978-93-5148-446-2 (PB)

All rights are reserved. No part of this publication can be reproduced, distributed, performed, publicly displayed, stored in a retrieval system, made into a derivative work, transmitted or utilized in any form or by any means; electronic, mechanical, photocopying, recording or any information storage system, without the prior written permission of the copyright holder(s), as indicated, and the publishers.

Jurisdiction: Any conflict or dispute in relation to this publication shall be adjudged in accordance with the laws of India and the matter shall be subject to the jurisdiction of the Courts, Tribunals or any other Forums of New Delhi, India, only.

Disclaimer: The views, facts, contents, any copyright material used and analysis arrived at in this publication are solely of the Author(s) who assert/s the right to be identified as Author(s); the Publisher does not take any responsibility for the same in any manner whatsoever.

Printed in India.

DEDICATION

THIS BOOK IS DEDICATED TO MY LOVING MOM,
KUHOLI ZHESHITO AYE
&
MY SIBLINGS

Contents

Foreword

I am extremely honored to write a foreword on the book *Pastoral Care and Counselling: Towards Cultural Fidelity among the Naga Youth*, authored by my colleague Boholi Z. Sema. At the very outset, I would like to congratulate her on authoring such a profitable and valued book with many rich insights. Many scholars have attempted to look at the issues related to Naga youth staying outside of Nagaland from different perspectives. However, the present book stands out more powerfully because the author has looked at the issue of cultural fidelity with special reference to migrant Naga youth from the counselling perspective. The author has methodically adopted a comparative study between Naga youth living in and outside of Nagaland in order to ascertain cultural fidelity. Such a comparative study makes this book a very absorbing read and helps us understand the real situation in relation to cultural fidelity among migrant Naga youth.

For centuries, the tribal people of northeast India particularly the Nagas, lived in isolation from the outside world and with little inter-tribal contact. According to sources, it was from the early part of the 19th century that the Nagas started to interact with the so called "culture-producing organizations" or "agents", marking the beginning of a new era in their history. Generally, it is believed that the advent of British colonial administration in the Naga Hills in 1832 and the introduction of Christianity by American Baptist missionaries in 1872 resulted in the interaction of the Nagas with western culture. This interaction impacted the Naga culture, which resulted in many changes and eventually led to the disappearance of many Naga cultural elements. Today, after more than a century of Christianity in their homeland, Nagas have started to re-evaluate the changes which occurred in their culture. This awareness is making the Nagas reflect critically on and assess the consequences of change in their culture. Nagas in general assume that these changes distorted their original culture and led to its disintegration and the disappearance of cultural values and elements.

The present Naga society is becoming increasingly modern and urbanized. The present complex socio-cultural shift is leading to unprecedented psychological problems and conflicts, especially among the youth. It is a reality that many Naga youth, both educated and uneducated prefer to go outside of their homeland.

Naga youth are flocking towards cities in search of better education and job opportunities. It is a known fact that they go through different challenges after migrating to cities. They encounter different sections of people from all walks of life and from different cultures altogether. Although there are many different tribes in Nagaland and while there may be slight differences in each tribal culture, the Naga culture is common to all. Once in a foreign land, an individual experiences an unfamiliar way of life and is forced to adapt to the new culture. The old cultural patterns are no longer applicable, and the individual experiences change in all aspects of life – be it food, language and social roles. Herein lies the problem- in order to fit in and become a part of the new cultural group, one is tempted to adopt the new culture and way of life completely, ignoring their original culture. There is a tendency for a large number of Naga youth to abandon their culture completely and no longer give importance to their culture. However, they should learn the importance of their culture and respect it.

The Naga society today is at the crossroads between tradition and modernity. In the name of modernity, the strict rules and discipline of traditional norms are fading away among the Naga youngsters. Modernity has also brought with it many social problems which have affected the life of the Nagas adversely, especially the young people. The youth are exposed to the modern culture and reject their own culture. It is vital for parents to educate and instruct their children before they venture out to cities. They should be trained to respect their culture since a young age and despite their exposure to the modern lifestyle, they should not forget the importance of their cultural values and elements. Rather, they should elevate their culture wherever they are and introduce their culture to other people. It is vital that we understand and respect other cultures and also adapt to changes wherever we go, in order to live in harmony with different groups, but ignoring one's culture completely should be corrected and changed.

One's culture is one's identity. The migrant Naga youth should be encouraged and trained to develop a positive approach towards their culture. The persistent conviction in the minds of the Nagas that their culture is "devilish, heathen and outdated" is biased and this needs to be changed since not all elements in a culture should be interpreted negatively. No matter how a person and society continues to modernize and develop, Nagas need to respect their culture and must work to preserve it. The people should break free and rid themselves of stereotypes, misinterpretation, and negative concepts that they have towards their culture.

This book contains rich wisdom on how to deal with the fidelity to Naga culture among the migrant Naga youth and you will be enriched by reading this book.

Mar Pongener
Clark Theological College

Abstract

Youth today stand in a unique place in the history of Naga society; they live among people whose character and ways of perceiving life were formed in very different ways from their own. The youth's exposure to outside Nagaland in search of education and job opportunities has a major influence on their lifestyles, language, and dress code etc. They are more likely to abandon traditional customs and ways of thought. It also has a major impact on the spirit of dignity of labor, social and moral, norms and values and the rich old family values. Often it is forgotten that the present day youth adopt the patterns and lifestyles of other societies. The process of urbanization, modernization, and globalization however has degraded the lives of the people especially in the breaking up of social norms and practices and of the family. Though a semblance of it still exists, the kind of group feelings which used to exist and a sense of belonging are fast vanishing.

Thus, the researcher has intended to study fidelity to culture among the youths staying outside of Nagaland in different cities in India. To ascertain about fidelity to culture, a comparative study between Naga youths living in and outside of Nagaland is important to look at whether the place of stay has influential factor upon the fidelity to one culture. Variables studies like dignity of labor, education and language, family system, generation gap between parent and youth, present Naga youth style, equality and respect, dresses and ornaments, music and dances, behavior and attitude, hospitality, communitarian spirit, folklore and art crafts, information technology age, church and youth are important to analyse the problem.

The present study on the fidelity to Naga culture and Naga youth is undertaken in the context of extensive migration. Migrants usually have a tendency to organize themselves into a group with a view to retain or preserve their socio-cultural characteristics. In other words, they intend to retain or reproduce the structure and culture of their native origin at the place of migration. The retention of structural and cultural identity to some extent solves the problem of adjustment in the new surroundings. The present generation is integrating indigenous culture with modernity; they must also understand that there is huge responsibility for them to transmit what they received from their foreparents in order not to make their culture extinct. Many people still have not come to the realization that to be someone in a society one has to be rooted in one's own culture.

There are cultural features of the Nagas which were highly organized and well established, which explain the ancient Naga traditions that were imprinted in the social, religious and political structures. These cultural features controlled every individual in his/her total life existence be it social, religious, political and economic life. One must realize that Nagas had concrete ideas, theories and beliefs rooted in their history. Nagas should clearly see through various cultural features like equality of all people and respect towards fellow humans, strong customary laws that govern every individual; joy in community living; hospitality and truthfulness blend with honesty and hardwork; strong morality blend with free life. Also, in spite of not having written language, Nagas could communicate and preserved their tradition, history, norms and values, and their practices and beliefs through songs, dances and poetry. More than that, their dresses and ornaments speak who they are. It also speaks about one status, clan, tribe, and history. Therefore, the Naga youth should made an attempt to understand and return to at least some of distinct features of the Naga culture, which have gone unappreciated and devalued.

Today, concern over the disappearance of the cultural features is one of the most complicated and challenging issues facing by the Nagas. Nagas has been created out of the adjustments in the lives and the minds of the people. This is the consequence of the influence to which the Nagas have been exposed to Metropolitan cities. Serious consideration is now being given to restore Naga cultural elements virtually non-existent in the recent past. The researcher has undertaken the theoretical framework on culture and its interdisciplinary studies such as anthropology, psychology, sociology, social media, factors of migration, and youth in the present scenario to explore on the growing awareness among Naga youth today and the need to employ the traditional cultural elements in order to use them meaningfully in current Naga society.

The culture of modernism is such that the very idea of 'culture' is venerated as the 'final' arbiter of human experience. Naga youth are left lacking in a complex set of rules, norms, beliefs, habits, and values. The ongoing influence of migrating to urban areas being exerted by modern medias, technology and other trends of globalization. Consequently, the greater the loss of culture and diminishing identity the Nagas suffer, and unless the Naga youth makes a concerted and determined effort to reclaim what is left of their culture, they will soon be left with no cultural roots or identity from the past.

In the light of the above, the research work was designed with the aim of investigating the fidelity to Naga culture among Naga youth living in and outside Nagaland. The research method used in this work is a quantitative method. A structured questionnaire developed by the researcher as primary tool was prepared and given to the Naga youth to collect data. The tools used for data collection were personal data sheet and cultural fidelity scale for Nagas and the socio-demographic data. The scale was framed with statement representing favourable and unfavourable item mixed up. The researcher had dealt with the analysis and discussion of the study and the relationship among the variables used in the study.

The research revealed that place of stay had a highly significant effect on cultural fidelity. Analysis of variance of different sub-scores comparing place of stay of respondents showed a highly significant difference between different places of stay. dignity of labour, family system, generation gap, present Naga youth style, dress and ornaments, music and dance, folklore and art, information technology, church and youth were found to be highly significant. Total cultural fidelity score found to be very highly significant. Even though education and language, equality and respect, behaviour and attitude, hospitality, community spirit showed no statistical difference between place of stay. It was found higher Mean scores for many sub-scores. The analysis revealed that cultural fidelity scores have a very highly significant relationship among the Naga youth living in and outside Nagaland. Results suggest that Naga youth lives in Nagaland withhold almost all cultural aspects with traditional importance. But Naga youth who migrate to other cities, lose the original cultural loyalty and merge with the urban life.

It has found that there seems to be a diminishing of cultural values among contemporary Naga youths. This highlights the need that the Naga youths may be helped to improve their coping ability to Naga culture. Tradition, continuity and change should happen in a balance way among the Naga migrant. Significant elements of the old will remain necessary in the modern society; also cultural continuity along with cultural change. New customs are likely to be more readily adopted if they represent what is viewed as socially desirable and useful and if they do not clash with pre-existent and still-valued customs. Few counselling theories/approaches are suggested in order to help the youth to retain important culture. Following are person-centered theory, cognitive-behavioral theory, gestalt therapy, reality therapy, behavior therapy, and group counselling. With a view to eliciting significant insights that will be help for presenting implications for care and counselling to Naga youths.

Boholi Z. Sema

Acknowledgement

I praise God and thank God, the author and creator of the whole universe for enabling me to come thus far, giving me the strength and opportunity to complete this research work. I also acknowledge to all those who have been the source of support and inspiration in my theological journey.

I express my feelings of gratitude and thanks to my mentor and guide, Rev. Dr. O. Thomas, Professor of Christian Ministry, FFRRC, OTS, Kottayam, Kerala, for his unflinching support, guidance and patients, suggestion and encouragement through the period of my research work.

I am profoundly indebted to Rev. Dr. Limatula Longkumer, Rev. Dr. Abraham Kuruvilla, and Rev. Dr. Ezamo Murry, for their invaluable time and constructive comments that help me to bring this research into shape.

I am grateful to Prof. Mar Pongener, Principal, Clark Theological College for reading through my manuscript and writing the foreword for this humble book, as a worthy contribution in the field of Pastoral Care and Counselling.

I want to express my appreciation and acknowledge the graceful assistance received from the principals, Librarians and Staffs of Mar Thoma Theological Seminary, Kottayam; Orthodox Theological Seminary, Kottayam; Kerala United Theological Seminary, Thiruvananthapuram; United Theological College, Bangaluru; Bishop's College, Kolkata; Clark Theological College, Mokokchung; Eastern Theological College, Jorhat; Trinity Theological College, Dimapur for availing every possible access to me and making this research a reality.

I also extend my sincere thanks to the publisher, Christian World Imprints (CWI) for designing the cover, and for publishing this humble work.

I express my sincere thanks to the Academic Committee of the Senate of Serampore College (University) for granting me the permission to publish my dissertation which was originally entitled "Fidelity to Naga Culture Among Migrant Naga Youth." I am solely responsible for the changed title and the opinions expressed in it.

Boholi Z. Sema

List of Abbreviations

2nd ed., 3rd ed.	second edition, third edition
ACE	American Council on Education
ANOVA	Analysis of Variance
CBCE	Catholic Bishops' Conference of India
CLC	Christian Literature Centre
CSS	Christian Sahitya Samithy
CTC	Clark Theological College
ed., eds.	editor, editors, edition, editions
eg (*exempli gratia*)	for example
et al. (*et alii*)	and others
ETC	Eastern Theological College
etc. (et cetera)	and others of the same class and so forth
fig., figs.	figure, figures
i.e. *(id est)*	that is to say
ICSSR	Indian Council of Social Science Research
ISPCK	Indian Society for Promoting Christian Knowledge
n.d.	no date of publication given
n.p.	no place of publication given, no publisher given
NBYF	Nagaland Baptist Youth Fellowship
NBCC	Nagaland Baptist Churches Council
NCCI	National Council of Churches in India
NMM	Nagaland Missions Movement
RCID	Racial-cultural identity Development Theory
REBT	Rational Emotive Behaviour therapy
SNSWK	Society for Naga Students' Welfare Kerala
SPCK	Society for Promoting Christian Knowledge
TDCC	Tribal Development and Communication Centre
vol., vols.	volume, volumes

List of Tables

List of Figure

Chapter 1

Introduction

1. Introduction

There is no individual who has no culture.[1] Cultures will therefore include such dimensions as ways of living, thinking, language, arts, and crafts, eating habits, patterns of social relationships, political organizations, and notions of leadership, authority, power and rule. Religious and moral values, things deemed acceptable and unacceptable, are all elements of culture. They affect how particular persons and their social groupings understand themselves, how they understand the world, how they think to relate to their natural or physical environment; how they relate to the departed and how they deal with ancestors. These are all dimensions of culture.[2]

Naga[3] youth expose to several conflicting, distracting, difficult and stressful situations. In the past, youth generally tended to rely on the advice, wisdom and judgment of their elders. In modern times, owing to their exposure to other cultural milieu through migration to other metropolitan cities, they might

---

1 Etymologically, the word culture is derived from the latin *cultura*, from the verb *colere*, with the meaning of 'tending' or 'cultivation.' Until the modern definition of culture, which is relativistic, culture was used to mean the perfection of the individual, the values of the elite.

2 Kwame Bediako, "Gospel and Culture: Some Insights for Our Time from the Experience of the Earliest church," *Understanding Tribal for Effective Education*, edited by Joseph Anikuzhikattil, George Palackapillil, Joseph Puthenpurakal (New Delhi: Commission for Education and Culture, CBCI Centre, 2003), 301.

3 The term "Naga" refer to a tribal community comprising of sixteen tribe and various sub- tribes, having a strong sense of belongings and communitarian spirit. They embraced Christianity in the later part of 19th century nonetheless; today Nagas are proud to claim Christian state with 90 percent Christianity.

often tempt to imitate and emulate other modes and patterns of behavior. Such influence sometimes creates distressing problems of adjustment. They appear to be increasingly groping for a meaning in life consonant with their ideas and expectations. Due to several socio-economic and political factors, a significant section of Naga youth is becoming estranged and alienated from the Naga culture. Hence, the book "Fidelity to Naga Culture among Naga Youth" from pastoral care and Counselling perspective is taken to explore in this research.

1.1. Statement of the Problem

Fidelity to Naga culture among the youth who are staying outside Nagaland seems to be declining. Therefore, this research is an attempt to explore the problems in order to retain cultural practices more meaningfully through pastoral care and counselling perspective.

1.2. Elaboration of the Problem

The problem of youth among the Nagas failed to understand the Youth within their culture. One of the factors is migrating to other geographical regions, which have been influenced by the life style of other people's thinking, attitude, behavior, and their pattern of living. Certain cultural factors influence the intensity and an important one is the rapidity of change is the breakdown of traditional values. Many migrant youth today have failed to understand the norms and values, and the implication that the past lives with the present, and the present inseparable from the past, thus have failed to understand the deep rooted philosophy and ethos of the Nagas.

The present-day Naga youths are going through a period where their dreams and visions do not seem attainable. They talk alike, dress alike and even think alike. They no longer live in the world of elders who once lived as youth. They are living in an "Information Technology Age" where everything they want is at their finger tip. They have learned new knowledge and were taught to do things differently. In many ways, they are living in the world of the present much more than the elders. The experiences in their own world have developed into a recognizable subculture, with its own language, symbols, dress, and values.[4]

Youth today stand in a unique place in the history of Naga society; they live among people whose character and ways of perceiving life were formed in very different ways from their own.[5] The youth's exposure to outside Nagaland in search of education and job opportunities has a major influence on their lifestyles, language, and dress code etc. They are more likely to abandon traditional customs and ways of thought. It also has a major impact on the spirit of dignity of labor, social and moral, norms and values and the rich old family values. Often it is

4 Zelhou Keyho, "Church and Naga Youth," *Doing Youth Ministry in a Naga Context*, edited by Soren Oestergaard & Adelo Mero (Dimapur: NBYF, 2004), 129.

5 Zelhou Keyho, "Church and Naga Youth," 130.

forgotten that the present day youth adopt the patterns and lifestyles of other societies.[6] The process of urbanization, modernization, and globalization however has degraded the lives of the people especially in the breaking up of social norms and practices and of the family. Though a semblance of it still exists, the kind of group feelings which used to exist and a sense of belonging are fast vanishing. In the cities they face new problems such as identity crisis, housing, earning and spending, alcoholism, drug abuse, prostitution, and corruption.

With the growth of literacy, the unemployment problem has become one of the fastest growing crises of the modern Nagaland. Hence, many youth go outside Nagaland, also without the dignity of labor, many youth are involved in theft, robbery, extortion, and criminal activities.[7] The present youth are slowly losing the spirit of dignity of labor. They have started to assume that it is below their dignity to engage in manual labor, hence the value and dignity of work became a thing of the past. Gradually, Naga youth has began to live an easygoing life. They preferred "to eat better food, want to dress in better clothes, but they do not like the hard work, especially manual work." The educated Naga youth have tended to think that only sitting and eating jobs are suitable for them, the jobs carrying status but not involving manual work.[8] A generation ago, the Naga society was characterized by its hard work, communality, sense of justice, equality, integrity, and honesty. These are rapidly forsaken or modified beyond description.

The present educational system in Nagaland is exam-oriented and characterized by memorization. It is deficient in the sense that the theoretical aspect is emphasized but the practical is left out. Education has been a contributory factor for modernization among the Nagas but it has failed to bring about a sense of self-reliance among the youth.[9] It does not seem to prepare them for life, job and social milieu. For youth who want to pursue their life-goals, inability to secure a seat can be frustrating. The educational milieu itself should provide not merely learning but should have a forum for life orientation.[10] Influence of city life upon the migrant is noticeable in a way migrant youth desire to have good education

---

6 Social change as "transformation of culture and social institutions over time that is reflected in the life patterns of individuals." And *Modernity* as "… a profound transformation of tradition, pre-industrial societies, at once providing solutions to ago-old problems and creating problems beyond the imagination living centuries ago." John J. Macionis, *Sociology* (Eaglewood Cliffs: Prentice Hall Inc., 1980), 612.

7 Inato Yekheto Shikhu, *A Rediscovery and Rebuilding of Naga Cultural Values* (New Delhi: Regency Publications, 2007), 91.

8 Mar Pongener, *Morung Speaks* (Jorhat: Barkataki and Company Private Limited, 2011), 124.

9 V. K. Nuh, *My Country, My People: Focus in Nagaland* (Kohima, Nagaland: Vision Press, 1988), 28.

10 Dominic Jala, "Youth and the Challenges of the Twenty-First Century," *Society and Culture in North-East India: A christian Perspective*, edited by Saral K. Chatterji (Delhi: ISPCK, 1996), 60.

which produces better employment. However, there are problems connected with psychological tensions created in the urban environment.

The social pressures which helped greatly in the past in the moral wellbeing of the youth are now lacking. The Nagas were well-knit with social cohesion and solidarity, holding fast to the values of their community and capable of strong action for any community cause.[11] Nagas were known for their loyalty and respect towards the elders as well as obedience to the established authority. People always respected a person who was honest and truthful. It was also an honor to be called a hard working person.[12] The spirit of companionship in the caring, sharing, fellowship and goodwill shown to one another, maintained and practiced became a model for the Naga community.[13] But today, the unique traditional culture has been distorted. It has affected the young generation in many ways. They now behave differently and look at things from a different point of view. The moral values and the living standards have completely changed. People have become more selfish and individualistic. Nagas were known for their loyalty, simplicity, hospitality, truthfulness and honesty. But now, such things have become history.[14] New conventions, customs, and modes of behavior become conscious of the new urban milieu.

The Naga family has the most powerful influence on a youth's life.[15] The period of youth often becomes a time of crises in the family. As the social process continues to affect traditional home settings, the roles of various members of the family need to be re-defined. Further, youth today are the pillars of the families of tomorrow.[16] The Naga family is going through a time that seems uncertain and overwhelming. The present state of affairs is neither normal nor healthy for the Naga young generation to grow up in. The present situation seems to be uncertain, negative, frightening, and hopeless.[17] By the time a young person reaches higher secondary school age he/she wants to go outside the state to form impressions and ideas of outside world. In most Naga homes, conflict between parent and the youth comes out of favor to go outside Nagaland. This is because the expectation on the part of the parents and youth clash. Conflicting behaviors between the parents and the youths are due to differences in age and time, i.e., the

11 Mar Pongener, *Morung Speaks*, 119.

12 L. Imsutoshi Jamir, *Communication in Action, the Pattern of Naga Cultural Shift*, (Mokokchung: Tribal Religion and Communication Centre, 2000), 42.

13 Mar Pongener, *Morung Speaks*, 119.

14 C. Alitemjen Longkumer, "Impact of Rock Music Culture towards Naga Culture," *Communication and Naga Culture*, edited by L. Imsutoshi Jamir & C. Alitemjen Longkumer (Dimapur: The Tribal Development and Communication Center (TDCC), 2007), 155.

15 Wati Aier, *Alcohol and Alcoholism: A Better Guide for the Nagas* (Dimapur, India: Book House, n.d.), 43.

16 Dominic Jala, "Youth and the challenges of the twenty-first century," 61.

17 Renthy Keitzar, *Triumph of Faith in Nagaland* (Kohima, India: NBCC, 1987), 29.

generation gap. The traditional Naga tribal culture and society has been changing fast with the emergence of modernization.[18] This change has affected both the old and young alike. The older generation is trying to maintain the past values, at the same time making adaptations with the change. Misunderstanding arises when the old people, while maintaining the traditional customs and values, try to enforce the same upon the younger generations.[19] The word "generation gap" has a worldwide usage. Describing the generation gap among the Nagas, M. Horam in his lamenting tune writes, with all the impact of the urban environment upon the present Naga youth,

> One can also find the beginnings of the defiance of parental authority and rejection of their advice as old fashioned, but mostly among the modern homes impatiently dismissing their parents with the withering comments: "You don't know anything; you are too old fashioned." These young people tend to blame all family discord on the "generation gap." The results are unhappiness in the families.[20]

The social change and the urban influence have brought a totally new outlook in the way youth look at life. They stand discontented with what life has to offer and they look for ways to make life interesting and befitting to the change of time. Their vision for good life is often shaped by what they see from the outside world. The adopted life style through diffusion is considered by the youth as evil and against the norms and values of the society. They need to understand that they cannot avoid the influence from the outside world and maintain "Naga youth culture," but recognize Naga youth culture as part of the social change. Since the culture is dynamic, the social change will continue. When this is not understood, there is a possibility of youth becoming the victim of misunderstanding in the society and their new life style is viewed as a protest against the established norms and values.[21] In the midst of the changed scenario with the social changes taking place around them, the youth struggle to find meaning and purpose in life.

Today, there is also an erosion of values which has caused a vacuum in the shape of cultural and religious values and morality. These tend to create an atmosphere of brutal competition. Unfortunately, the individual's quest for a "better life" has become more narrowly defined in materialistic terms. The result

---

18 Modernization refers to the rapid changes taking place in Naga society with the expansion of development projects, such as a hydro-electric system, schools, colleges, hospitals, and roads; introduction of modern media such as radio, television, movies, computers, internet, western fashions, western music; inaugurating of industries, and rapid changes in the mode of transportation.

19 Adelo Mero, "The Naga Home and Youth," *Doing Youth Ministry in a Naga Context*, edited by Soren Oestergaard & Adelo Mero (Dimapur: NBYF, 2004), 140.

20 M. Horam, "Naga Religion: A Case Study," *In Religion and Society of the North-East India* (New Delhi, India: Vikas Publishing House, 1980), 17.

21 Zelhou Keyho, "Church and Naga Youth," 132.

is a crisis of cultural identity and values of honesty, respect for one's neighbor and social responsibility. Hence, it is very necessary to understand the youth and the efficacious ways of ministering them from different perspectives especially at the turn of a new millennium.[22]

1.3. Importance of the Problem

With the impact of social change and urban environment upon the present Naga youth, it is important to explore the issue of fidelity to their own culture. Thus, the researcher has intended to study fidelity to culture among the youths staying outside Nagaland in different cities in India. To ascertain about fidelity to culture, a comparative study between Naga youths living in and outside Nagaland is important to look at whether the place of stay has influential factor upon the fidelity to one culture. Variables studies like dignity of labor, education and language, family system, generation gap between parent and youth, present Naga youth style, equality and respect, dresses and ornaments, music and dances, behavior and attitude, hospitality, communitarian spirit, folklore and art crafts, information technology age, church and youth are important to analyse the problem.

The importance of the research is also to create awareness among the churches and families in Nagaland regarding youth's life styles and ways of living. Another area of importance is to facilitate the counsellors and therapist in formulating a model to help Naga youth to keep their good culture. Further, it also aims to provide pastoral care and counselling to become conscious of the role of youth in cultural, moral, and religious aspects of their lives.

1.4. Hypotheses

1. There will be no significant relationship between socio-demographic status and fidelity to Naga culture. (Age, Gender, Profession, and Family monthly income).
2. There will be no significant relationship between fidelity to Naga culture and the locale of migration. (Nagaland, Kolkata, Bengaluru, Delhi, Hyderabad, Pune, Chennai, and Kochi).
3. There will be no significant relationship between Naga youth living in and outside Nagaland in their fidelity to Naga culture. (Dignity of Labor, Education and language, Family System, Generation Gap between Parent and Naga Youth, Present Naga youth style, Equality and Respect, Dresses and Ornaments, Music and Dances, Behavior and Attitude, Hospitality, Communitarian Spirit, Folklore and Art crafts, Information Technology Age, and Church and Naga youth).

22 M. Antony P. Rajan, *Pastoral care of Adolescents and Young Adults* (Bangalore: Asian Trading Corporation, 2004), 8.

1.5. Scope and Limitations

A research work on "Pastoral Care and Counselling: Towards Cultural Fidelity Among Naga Youth" has immense scope to rediscover the old Naga cultures among the youth of the present day. This would positively facilitate to Naga youth both living in and outside Nagaland to know more of the norms and values of the Naga society.

The research is limited (within Nagaland) to the rural areas, metropolitan cities, and the medium sized cities in India. The age group is also limited to only the youth, who falls under the age group between 20-30.

1.6. Previous Research

As far as the researcher's knowledge is concerned, there has been previous research done on the Naga Culture and study on Naga Youth such as:

Communication and Naga Cultures, edited by, L. Imusutoshi Jamir & C. Alitemjen Longkumer, It is a collection of articles by different writers in the study of culture. It gives the clear picture of different dimensions of Naga culture and its varied effects. It also brings out a methodological issues and challenges on cultural studies, the development of shift in cultural values and practices, and the impact of mass media which is primarily intended from the communication perspective.

Doing Youth Ministry in Naga Context, edited by, Soren Oestergaard & Adelo Mero, It presents the youth ministry and the church, addressing the crises and needs of the present Naga youth culture. It takes seriously the revitalizing youth ministry and youth leadership development in the church.

Christian Education for Adults in Tribal Context by, Limatula Longkumer, it delves into the understanding of young adults in the tribal society, by defining three important classifications of adults, young, middle, and old adulthood. Also it includes the influence of modernity and mass media among young adults, and calls for an implication from a Christian educational perspective.

Thus, the works cited have contributed significantly toward the Naga/tribal people and their society. However, a detailed research particularly on this topic "Pastoral Care and Counselling: Towards Cultural Fidelity Among Naga Youth" has not been done.

Therefore, a critical study on the cultural fidelity among Naga youth would be beneficial to the Naga Society.

1.7. Operational Definition

1.7.1. Culture

E. B. Tylor provided the earliest definition of culture as "that complex whole which includes knowledge, belief, art, moral, laws, custom and any other capabilities and habits acquired by a man (sic) as a member of society."[23] Clyde Kluchohn who together with Alfred Kroeber made a critical review of concepts and definitions of culture, defined culture as "the total way of life of a people which included ways of thinking, feeling, believing and learned behavior." In a similar way, Hiebert defines culture as "the more or less integrated systems of ideas, feelings, and values and their associated patterns of behavior and products shared by a group of people who organize and regulate what they think, feel, and do."[24] The above definitions touch on various basic components which make up the culture of a people.

Based on the above definitions, culture can be explained as 'inclusive' and 'connected' way of life of a particular group of people. Therefore, the researcher would define culture as the total way of a specific group of people including their behavioral as culture is shared, learned human behavior, a way of life, normative as culture is ideals, values or rules for living, and functional as culture is the way humans solve problems of adapting to the environment or living together.

Therefore, 'Naga Culture,'[25] mean the way of life of the Nagas, it includes distinct customs characterizing a social group; social heredity of a particular community; meanings, values, norms, their actions and relationships; beliefs, laws, traditions and institutions; religion, ritual, language, song, dance, feast,

---

23 The word 'culture' with its modern technical or anthropological meaning was established in English by Edward Tylor in 1871 although it didn't penetrate any general American or British dictionary until more than 50 years later. Tylor, after hesitating to use the term 'civilization', borrowed the word culture from German, where it had acquired the modern (i.e. anthropological) meaning, and was an outgrowth of the older meaning of civilization-to cultivate, to grow, to tend, to develop in a positive, productive way.

24 As Quoted by L. Imsutoshi Jamir, "Methodological Challenges for the Tribal Cultural Studies," *Communication and Naga Culture*, edited by L. Imsutoshi Jamir & C. Alitemjen Longkumer (Dimapur: The Tribal Development and Communication Center (TDCC), 2007), 6.

25 Naga is a generic term used for about thirty tribes (including sub-tribes) of the eastern hill frontier in the states of Nagaland, Manipur, Arunachal Pradesh and Assam. The Angami, Ao, Chakhesang, Chang, Khiamungan, Konyak, Lotha, Phom, Pochury, Rengma, Sangtam, Sema, Yimchunger and Zeliang reside in the state of Nagaland. B. B. Kumar, *Naga Identity* (New Delhi: Concept publishing Company, 2005), 23. Though the Nagas are geographically isolated due to imposition of alien powers for their administrative convenience, they belong to one family and one blood. They have common history of origin, common culture, common self-governing institution, common birth right and common heritage of territory. This is the pride of the Nagas. Infact, every Naga tribe has distinct characteristics of their own. Speaking different tribal dialect is the greatest barrier between them. Though they all belong to the Naga ethnic family, they do not understand each other's dialect. This is the one of the major handicaps amongst them. N. Talitemjen Jamir & A. Lanunungsang, *Naga Society And Culture* (Jorhat: Nagaland University Tribal Research Centre Department of Sociology, 2005), 15. They also have their own unique norms, values, and practices however, inspite of the certain differences, there are many common characteristics of the Nagas as they belong to the same family and same blood having common origin, common birth place, common history, and common culture though they live in different geographical regions due to circumstances. Therefore, the researcher would be referring Naga culture in common.

living habits, dress and ornaments, crafts, and equipments, which passed on to the new generation, through oral traditions, and day to day practices, and the lifestyles of fore parents.

1.7.2. Youth

The age-group for this research work is limited only the youth.[26] This period extends from the end of adolescence[27] to the thirties. Youth is the time of peak physical abilities (e.g., strength, agility, speed, fertility). In the cognitive domain, it is a period of acquiring and mastering new skills and roles. Perry suggests that youth's transition from dualistic (black and white) thinking to acknowledging the relativism exists and finally to make a commitment to personal beliefs while accepting that others may come to a different conclusion. It is also a time of conflict between the motivation to leave home to go to the work, Institution; and the motivation to stay home to be with the parent or spouse.[28] The youth now constructs an initial life philosophy that guides decision-making and personal behaviors. The youth's interest and time are[29] increasingly future-oriented. A career, the possibility of future commitment, and future roles all take center stage for the youths.[30]

Numbers of scholars and psychologists have given different age category of youth. Some of which are referred here for consideration:

Erikson's psychoanalytic Ego Psychology has developed the eight stages of ego development. The classification are, birth-1year (Basic trust vs Mistrust), 2-3 years (Autonomy vs Shame and Doubt), 4-5 years (Initiative vs Guilt), 6-12 years (Industry vs Inferiority), 13-19 years (Identity vs Role Confusion), 20-24 years (Intimacy vs Isolation) 25 – 35 years (Generativity vs Stagnation), and 36- 60

---

26 Youth is the stage of life in which a person begins to take responsibility for his/her own commitments, lifestyle, beliefs, and attitudes. Tensions emerge: that between the individual and the community; between acknowledging the relative and hoping for the absolute. Self (identity) and outlook (worldview) come into view and are distinguished from those of others. This is a "demythologizing" stage: reflection can go too far and the person begins to believe too much in his or her own capacity to understand everything in the universe. Simon Hall, "Discipleship-Making: A Practical Theology of Adolescent Spirituality," *Doing Youth Ministry in a Naga Context*, edited by Soren Oestergaard & Adelo Mero (Dimapur: NBYF, 2004), 52.

27 The term adolescence is derived from the Latin word *adolescere*, meaning "to grow into maturity." Rolf E. Muuss, *Theories of Adolescence* (New York: Random House, 1964), 4.

28 As Quoted by K. A. Gathercoal, "Life span development," *Baker Encyclopedia of Psychology & Counseling*, edited by David G. Benner & Peter C. Hill (Grand Rapids: Baker Books, 1999), 690-694.

29 Charles M. Shelton, *Pastoral Counseling with Adolescents and Young Adults* (New York: The Crossroad Publishing Company, 1995), 8.

30 Charles M. Shelton, *Pastoral Counseling with Adolescents and Young Adults*, 9.

years and above (Ego integrity vs Despair).[31] Erikson's judgement on youth stems from role confusion concerning who they are and what they will become. The successful resolution of the crisis of youth leads to a sense of fidelity, which Erikson called "the ability to sustain loyalties freely pledged in spite of the inevitable contradictions of value system" they are ready to take their place in a technological society not just as guardians of traditions and customs but as rejuvenators and innovators of the culture. Youths who have not adequately resolved their conflicts may develop a negative identity, in which they act in scornful and hostile ways toward roles offered as proper and desirable by the community. Their loyalties are to groups, people, and ideologies that are destructive to them and to society.[32] Erikson has marked the age group 19-35 as 'young adulthood' which comes under developmental task 'Intimacy vs. Isolation' youth who have established a stable identity during adolescence that makes it possible for them to enter into intimate relationships with others, and they are ready to strengthen their personal identity. He has also covered this period with three stages namely young adulthood, middle age, and later life, each of which has developmental tasks.[33]

Lawrence Kohlberg's moral development has developed three levels on moral development; with each level having two stages, stage one (3-7 years) - punishment and obedience orientation, stage two (8-11 years) - naive reward orientation, stage three (12-17 years) - good boy/good girl orientation, stage four (18-25 years) - authority orientation, stage five (25 years plus) the social contract orientation, stage six- universal ethical orientation.[34] The youth stage can be considered under stage four and five where, one depends on upon the law and order of the society and the whole judgement depends on whether a person violates the law and order of the society. Also, here a person is able to make autonomous decisions. The person is well aware that the laws and rules may be changed for the benefit of the society.[35]

Carl Gustav Jung's analytical therapy has developed four stages: Children (Birth to Puberty), Youth (Puberty to 35 -40 years), and Middle Age (35-40 years to extreme old age. During the youth stage puberty to 35-40 years, the human mind's growth keeps pace with a widening range of consciousness and each step forward can be an extremely painful and laborious achievement. During youth the demands of life put an end to childhood. The essential feature of the problems of youth is a clinging to the childhood level of consciousness. Achievement,

---

31 As Cited by Richard M. Ryckman, *Theories of Personality*, 5th edition (Belmont, California: Cole Publishing company, 1993), 186.

32 Richard M. Ryckman, *Theories of Personality*, 194.

33 As cited by D. John Anthony, *Psychotherapies in Counselling* (Tamil Nadu, India: Anugraha Publications, 2003), 67.

34 As cited by Limatula Longkumer, *Chirstian Education For Transformation: Foundations, Approaches and effective Teaching*, (Kolkata: ESPACE, 2017), 154.

35 Limatula Longkumer, *Chirstian Education For Transformation,* 156.

usefulness and getting established are ways of proceeding out from the problems of the period of youth.[36]

In the tribal society, Limatula Longkumer describe 'adulthood' covers five groups or stages, each with its own physical, social, spiritual and psychological characteristics. The stages are: about 26-34 years, about 35-45 years, about 46-55 years and about 56-65 years and about 66 years above. All these five stages come under the general category of three stages of young, middle and old adulthood.[37]

The United Nations for statistical purposes defines 'youth', as those persons between the ages of 15-24 years, without prejudice to other definitions by member states. Hence, under the age category 15-24 years (introduced in 1981) are defined as youth. Apart from the statistical definition, the meaning of the term 'youth' varies in different societies around the world and may understood in a more flexible manner. However, United Nations in the year 2000 also reinforced same age group as a period of transition to adulthood's independence, particularly in relation to education, and finding their first job.[38]

Based on the above definitions, the researcher has identified the age category 20 -30 years as 'youth' in Naga context. Because, many youth at this stage wanted to leave their homes to find new opportunities, a path to participate in higher education, and in search of better and decent job. There are also many youth who wanted to satisfy their desire for adventure or experience a different culture. Therefore, in this study 20-30 years of age is considered as the term 'youth.'

1.7.3. Migrant Naga Youth

The term 'migrant' refers to a person who moves from one place to another in search of work. Migration is also defined as "the change of the place or abode permanently or when temporarily, for an appreciable duration, as for example in the case of seasonal workers. It is used symbolically in the transactions from one surrounding to another in the course of human life."[39] According to Choudhury, "Migration is a phenomenon observed down the ages. But in modern times it has changed much of its form and structure and has adapted to the needs and likings of the society. Migration is mainly due to a constant search for better livelihood."[40] The immediate problems faced by the Naga youth in Nagaland are

36 As Cited by Richard Nelson-Jones, *Theory and Practice of Counseling and Therapy*, 5th edition (New Delhi: Sage Publications India Pvt Ltd, 2006), 65.

37 Limatula Longkumer, *Christian Education for Adults in Tribal Context* (Jorhat: Published by the Author, 1998), 33.

38 www.un.org/esa/socdev/documents/youth/fact-sheets/youth-definition, on (Accesses December 26, 2017).

39 A. A. Weingberg, "Migration and Belonging: A Study of Mental Health and Personal Adjustment in Israel," *In People in the Move: Studies on International Migration*, edited by Laszek A. Kosinsk and R. Mansell Brothers (London: Methuen and Co Ltd, 1075), 3.

40 Nabanita Choudhury, "Women Migration in Asia and the Pacific: A Portrayal," *Migrating Women: Opportunities and Vulnerabilities*, edited by Asis Kumar Pain (Agartala: The Icfai

education and unemployment. A decade ago employment was not a problem even for a matriculate or under matriculate but the present time portrays graduates being left wandering in the streets, not knowing where to go and what to do.[41] Migration to big cities and towns, especially among the youth, is a common phenomenon in Nagaland. The inability to find good quality education in the rural areas drives the youth to study in urban areas. Skilled and adequate technical training personnel from outside the state are employed to fit the job of modern technology and science.[42]

Vikheho Swu, minister for Roads and Bridges in Nagaland asserted that Nagaland's greed for government jobs has led 40,000 excess of government employees. This has seen a huge urban population migrating from the rural areas and accumulating 9000 to 10,000 individuals annually in government sectors.[43] The huge number of Naga youth migrating to other cities and abroad from Nagaland for better job opportunities, educational or social event. The main push factor leading to migration is lack of educational infrastructure, and private companies in Nagaland. The notion of Naga migration as a way finding, which they have conceptualize for youth migrants, is not static.

Therefore, for the purpose of this study, the researcher refers 'migrant Naga youth' who has capacitated an urban consciousness, resulting in migration from rural areas to the towns in search of education, employment, and other related occupation on optimal migration duration. It can be for a shorter or a longer period of time, not capturing as permanent settlers.

1.7.4. Fidelity

According to the Chambers Dictionary, the term "Fidelity" refers to faithfulness; honesty; firm adherence; continuing faithfulness to a person, cause, or belief. It is therefore indispensable for anyone who wants to start upon the immense work of moral reconstruction which is necessary, to strive to re-establish this same value in the place which rightly belongs to it. That is to say in the very centre of human life, of life no longer degraded, alienated or prostituted, but lived in all fullness of its true significance. As a matter of fact the code of ethics which is the beginning to take shape in youth culture is necessarily based on fidelity.[44] Naga youth is increasingly flagrant disrepute in which the value of fidelity has been held.

University Press, 2008), 84.

41 Wati Aier, "Reconstructing A Theology For Naga Youth," *Doing Youth Ministry in a Naga Context*, edited by Soren Oestergaard & Adelo Mero (Dimapur: NBYF, 2004), 114.

42 Coppe Mero, "Current Social Issues Among The Naga Youth," *Doing Youth Ministry in a Naga Context*, edited by Soren Oestergaard & Adelo Mero (Dimapur: NBYF, 2004), 115.

43 www.easternmirrownagaland.com/thinkers-reason-why-naga-youth-areleaving -Nagaland, (Accesses on December, 27, 2017).

44 Gabriel Marcel, "Obedience and Fidelity," *On Being Responsible*, edited by, James M. Gustafson and James T. Laney (Great Britain: SCM Press Ltd, 1969), 75.

Therefore, an attempt will be made to look at the current Naga youth of fidelity in their culture. The researcher here refers "fidelity" to make a concerted effort to firm adherence to the Naga cultural practices, norms and values especially among Naga youth. Most Naga youth have almost lost the will-power to reassert their indigenous identity, culture and history. Therefore, there is an urgent need to identify the bedrock principles rooted in the Naga traditional culture and reclaim and practice them.

1.8. Method of Research

The design of the research adopted, method of collecting through Quantitative data,[45] the locale of the study, the sample and sampling procedure, inclusion and exclusion criterion, the tools used for analysis, scoring, and statistical technique for analysis are explained under the following heads.

1.8.1. Design of the Study

The Design of the exploration is Quasi-experimental in nature. A Quasi-experimental design is a type of research design for conducting studies in field or real life situations where the researcher cannot randomly assign subjects to control and experimental groups. It is explorative in nature. In this study, 50 questions were prepared and distributed among the Naga youth for responses. The questionnaire includes questions covering various dimensions on the Naga cultural practices and the present living such as Dignity of Labor, Education and language, Family System, Generation Gap between Parent and Naga Youth, Present Naga Youth Style, Equality and Respect, Dresses and Ornaments, Music and Dances, Behavior and Attitude, Hospitality, Communitarian Spirit, Folklore and Art crafts, Information Technology Age, Church and Naga Youth.

1.8.2. The Locale of the Study

The locale of the research is among 300 Naga youth, 150 Naga youth from Nagaland, and the other 150 Naga youth residing outside Nagaland, i.e., Kolkata, Bengaluru, Delhi, Hyderabad, Pune, Chennai, and Kochi.

1.8.3. Sample and Sampling Procedures

The sample consists of 300 respondents, out of which 150 are from the state of Nagaland and 150 are the Naga youth residing outside Nagaland. The random sampling method is adopted for the data collection. Naga youth were identified from the state of Nagaland, Kolkata, Bengaluru, Delhi, Hyderabad,

---

45 Quantitative research is the systematic empirical investigation of observable phenomena via statistical, mathematical, or computational techniques. The researcher analyses the data with the help of statistics and hopes the numbers will yield an unbiased result that can be generalized to some larger population. https://en.wikipedia.org/wiki/quantitative-research, (Accesses on December 26, 2017).

Pune, Chennai, and Kochi. Brief systems through Questionnaires are given in the appendix.

Data were analyzed using computer suitable software. Data are expressed in its frequency and percentage as well as mean and standard deviation. To elucidate the associations and comparisons between different parameters, Chi square (c^2) test was used as non-parametric test. Student's t test was used to compare mean values between two groups. Analysis of variance (One Way ANOVA) was performed as parametric test to compare different variables. For all statistical evaluations, a two-tailed probability of value, < 0.05 was considered significant.

1.8.4. Inclusion Criteria and Exclusion Criteria

1.8.4.1. Inclusion Criteria

1. Naga youth belonging to the age group of 20-30 years.
2. Naga youth residing in Nagaland, metropolitan cities, and the small sized cities.
3. Naga youth members belonging to both genders.
4. Students, and employed Naga youths are being included.

1.8.4.2. Exclusion Criteria

1. Naga youth who come below age group of 20 and above 30 years.
2. Naga youth who are illiterate.
3. Naga youth who are unemployed.
4. Married couples are excluded.

1.8.5. The Tools

1.8.5.1. Personal Data Sheet

1.8.5.2. Socio-Demographic Status Scale

1.8.5.3. Cultural Fidelity Scale for Nagas

The tools used for data collection were Personal Data Sheet; socio-demographic data consist of personal age group, gender, profession, place of stay, and their family monthly income and cultural fidelity scale for both the Naga youth living in and outside Nagaland. The researcher has prepared a questionnaire and distributed among the youth.

1.8.6. Scoring

The scale was framed with statement representing favourable and unfavourable item mixed up. Five level of direction-intensity description were used. Their responses were scored on five point scale. Schedule is given in the appendix.

Strongly agree = 5
Agree = 4
Don't know = 3

Disagree = 2
Strongly disagree = 1

1.8.7. Statistical Techniques

The tools of analysis such as analysis of variance – test (ANOVA), 't' test, and chi-square were used in this research.

a. Anova: Analysis of variance is a statistical tool used to the test the equality of variables of more than two categories. Since the present study is considering fourteen of the independent variables at a time to investigate their combined effect on the dependent variables, this analysis of variance was used.

b. 'T' Test: 'T' test is one of the statistical methods of testing the hypothesis about difference in mean especially when it involves twine studies. In this research, 'T' test is used to compare the mean score of age, gender and profession.

c. Chi-square: Chi-square test of independence is a non-parametric test of statistical significance for bivariate tabular analysis. It is used to examine the association between two categorical variables. In this research, chi-square was employed to identify the association between different independent variables of cultural scale as well as their fidelity to the Naga culture.

1.9. Structure of the Research

The structure of the research comprises five chapters:

Chapter one presents the statement of the problem, elaboration of the problem, importance of the problem, definition of terms, hypotheses, method of the study and procedure for data collection, scope and limitation of the study, previous research and structure of the research.

Chapter two lays out the understanding of Naga culture in relation to Naga thought form, factors influencing the loss of Naga culture such as handicrafts and woodcarvings, music and folktales, feast and festivals, traditional costumes, loss of community spirit and dignity of labor.

Chapter three presents the impact of migration on fidelity to Naga culture. Its multidimensional influence on the concept of culture, relation with cultural anthropology, psychology, sociology, urbanization, globalization, modernization, social media, Christianization, education, migration and the process of enculturation, and how these factors have affected the present Naga youth.

Chapter four deals with analysis, interpretation, findings adopted for the study, and suggestions for further research.

Chapter five presents pastoral care and counselling towards fidelity to Naga culture providing six important counselling theories/approaches to cultural fidelity such as person-centered approach, cognitive-behavioral approach, gestalt therapy approach, reality therapy approach, behavior therapy approach, group counselling, and general conclusion.

Chapter 2

Understanding of Naga Culture

2. Introduction

Culture[46] is the normative consciousness of a community inherited from the past and transmitted, with or without modifications, to coming generations. Culture may be described as the organic whole ideas, beliefs, values, and goals, which condition the thinking, and acting of a community or people. Culture is a complex of factors that makes a person what he/ she is an individual and as a member of a community. In this second chapter, the researcher explores dimensions of Naga culture, and its origin, cultural practices and loss of aesthetic components of Naga culture in the context of Naga youth today.

2.1. Naga: A Brief Historical Background

Nagas are divided into various tribes, sub-tribes and clans with differences in costumes, traditions, dress, language, and polity, etc., the Nagas are a people whose unit can be found in its diversity. They had been living in relative isolation for centuries. It was only from the first quarter of the last century that they were brought into real contact with the outside world by several agencies, the most prominent of which are British rule and Christianity. The British rule over the Nagas virtually began with the occupation of Samaguting (Chumukedima) in 1866 and continued till the transfer of power to Indian hands on 15 August

46 Culture is a human-made environment, brought into existence by the ability to symbol. Once established, culture has a life of its own, so to speak; that is, it is a continuum of things and events in a cause and effect relationship; it flows down through time from one generation to another. Since its inception 1,000,000 or more years ago, this culture- with its language, beliefs, tools, codes and so on- has an existence external to each individual born into it..... Thomas Menamparampil, *The Challenge of Cultures* (Bombay: St Pauls, 1996), 10.

1947. So the British occupation of the Naga Hills extended for a short period of eight decades which was also nominal in character. Therefore, the traditional life pattern of the Naga tribes remained unchanged, but inter-tribal warfare and headhunting diminished due to British intervention. However, along with the British rule came the introduction of currency, western education and Christian[47] religion. While the introduction of western education and Christianity inculcated liberal ideas and national consciousness in the Naga mind, monetization helped the formation of a middle class in the hitherto classless Naga Society.[48]

The origin of the word 'Naga' has been a source of much debate among different scholars. The two largely accepted viewpoints are taken from the etymology of the word 'Naga' and its varying connotations in the Burmese and the Assamese languages, in Burma, the Naga tribes are called Na-Ka, which, in Burmese means people or men or folk with pierced ear-lobes, piercing of the ear-lobes is a widespread practice among the Naga tribes. Most of the Naga tribes migrated to India from Burma, therefore the name Naka or Naga was given to them even before they reached India. Moreover, it was from Burmese that the British first came to know about the Nagas soon after their earliest wars with Burma during 1795-1826.[49] However, the places of the origin of the various Naga tribes remain an unsolved mystery till today. Different scholars, basing their surmises on the Naga art, material culture, language tonal, etc., have theorized that the Nagas have had some links with Indonesia and Malaysia; they belong to the Tibeto-Burman family; are the first stage migration groups from North-West China; they constitute a return group of migrant from the Polynesian islands, etc. however, these theories are remotely inferential theories and in the absence of substantive evidence these theories remain inconclusive.[50] To this contrary, V. K. Nuh opines that, the Naga people belong to the Mongolian family as a race which spread all over the world from China to as far as South America.[51] P. D. Stracy in his book mentioned, "The biggest mystery is the origin of various tribes of Nagas, because different tribes have their own version of their origin." However, a general consensus has been agreed upon by all scholars that the Nagas are Mongoloid by race.[52]

47 B. Pakem, ed., *Nationality, Ethnicity and Cultural Identity in North-East India* (Guwahati: R. Kumar for Omsons Publications, 1990), 309.

48 B. Pakem, ed., *Nationality, Ethnicity and Cultural Identity in North-East India*, 310.

49 Hokishe Sema, *Emergence of Nagaland: Socio-Economic and Political Transformation and the Future* (New Delhi: Vikas Publishing House, 1986), 3.

50 Hokishe Sema, *Emergence of Nagaland: Socio-Economic and Political Transformation and the Future*, 4.

51 V. K. Nuh, *A Theological Reflection On Naga Society* (Kohima, Nagaland: Research Wing, Council of Naga Baptist Churches, 1996), 15.

52 As Quoted by V. K. Nuh and Wetshokhrolo Lasuh, eds., *The Naga Chronicle* (New Delhi: Regency Publications, 2002), 17.

In India, the Nagas occupy the whole of the State of Nagaland,[53] stretching till Manipur valleys in the south, the Brahmaputra valleys in the west and till Tirap and Changlang of Arunachal Pradesh in the north. Towards the east in Myanmar, the Nagas inhabit all regions till the Chindwin River valley. Altogether the Nagas cover an area of about 47,000 square miles.[54] The mountains ranges "run in a general north-south direction and from west to east with the highest ranges- those patkai mountain ranges forming a natural boundary between India and Burma. The highest non-Himalayan peak of the Indian sub-continent (Saramati-3840m/ 12, 598ft.) is in this range."[55]

The Naga tribal traditions and cultures are existing from time immemorial. The western civilizations viewed Nagas as primitive and semi-human beings; to Indians, the tribal people are uncivilized and backward people. Most of the writers branded Naga people as naked people; but most anthropologists are of the view that Nagas form a very distinct race from time immemorial.[56] Nagas are by nature hardy and warlike for which they are feared by the neighboring people. And yet, the Nagas are known by their inherent qualities of honesty, truthfulness, maturity, simplicity, generosity and courage. History tells us that the Nagas are from a higher civilization, which once flourished in the South East Asia and is believed to have migrated from there to the present hilly region of North-East India and Northern Myanmar. Before the advent of Christianity the Nagas practised primal religion. Headhunting was one of the most honorable games for the Naga people in the ancient days. In the midst of such darkness, ignorance, and backwardness, the marvelous light of the Gospel of Christ brought new hope of life, civilization and education. This historic and dramatic change happened because of the American Baptist Missionaries and the British Imperial Power. Today, 90% of Naga populations are Christians, and Baptists are the pre-dominant denomination.[57]

---

53 Nagaland is one of the seven states of the Indian Union in the North Eastern region. Nagaland has a total area over 16500 square kilometers and is hill country. Nagaland is divided into seven districts-Kohima which is the home of the Angami tribe; also of Rengma and Zeliang. Mokokchung is the home of the Ao tribe, Mon of Konyak, Phek of Chekhesang, Twensang of Sangtam, Phom, Chang, Yimchunger and Khiamungan, Wokha of Lotha and Zunheboto of Sema. M. M. Thomas, *Nagas Towards A.D. 2000 and Other Selected Addresses and Writings* (Madras: Centre for Research on New International Economic Order, 1992), 5.

54 V. K. Nuh and Wetshokhrolo Lasuh, eds., *The Naga Chronicle,* 17.

55 V. K. Nuh, *Nagaland Church and Politics,* (Kohima, Nagaland: V. K. Nuh & Bros, 2002), 54.

56 V. K. Nuh, *A Theological Reflection On Naga Society,* 12.

57 V. K. Nuh, *A Theological Reflection On Naga Society,* 15.

2.2. Structure of the Naga Society

2.2.1. Social System

By the nature of their habitat, Naga society was basically rural in character. They remained isolated from the rest of the world thus keeping their culture intact until the arrival of British and Western Christianity in the 19th century. Though considered primal society, community spirit bound with high moral, honesty, sincerity and truthfulness. The Nagas were fond of social and community life. They were singing and dancing people in times of both joy and sorrow. Their social life was marked with feasts of merit, traditional games and festivals. The Nagas till date keep up many of their traditions preserved and passed on for ages together.[58]

Naga society represented a true socialist pattern of society and thus, every individual, family community, etc., their behavior; action and beliefs were guided by that ideology.[59] An individual who brought home a hunted wild animal distributed the meat to all the houses, no matter how small the piece of meat might be. Even when vegetables were brought home from the fields, the neighbors had a share in it. More than that, when one was fortunate to become rich, he or she was never selfish to keep the fruits of his or her blessing to oneself or to his/her own children, but sought to share the fortune with the entire population by performing the feast of merit. Because of this system of public,[60] sharing of the income and property of the rich people, disparity in riches was not found among the Nagas. During those days, there were no selfish people who saved everything to oneself. So also, there was no corrupt way of becoming rich.[61]

2.2.2. Economic System

Nagas lived in traditionally independent villages each of which may be called a village-state. They practiced the barter system with the plain people of Assam. They traded salt with their produce such as chilli, ginger, mustard seed, and decorated spear. The salt that was collected from Assam was in turn not only used for domestic consumption, but also was traded among the Nagas for land, animals, and household things.

Till the emergence of modernization, the main livelihood for the Nagas was mainly agriculture. They were self-sufficient people, contented with what they had. They cultivated their own food and manufactured most of their domestic requirements and social needs. Their other source of income was trading their finished goods and products through activities like spinning, weaving and dyeing,

58 V. K. Nuh and Wetshokhrolo Lasuh, eds., *The Naga Chronicle*, 16.

59 R. R. Shrimray, *Origin and Culture of Nagas*, (New Delhi: Somsak Publication, 1985), 153.

60 L. Imsutoshi Jamir, *Communication in Action: The Pattern of Naga Cultural Shift*, 50.

61 L. Imsutoshi Jamir, *Communication in Action: The Pattern of Naga Cultural Shift*, 51.

cane, wood and bamboo work, pottery, and leather work.[62] The ideology of consumerism has developed in the Naga society since the past few years. Hence, the money economy and the culture of consumerism brought about hegemony over the poor and the uneducated by the rich and educated in the Naga society.[63] One can now discern that over the centuries, the Nagas had established a region-wide barter system where an elaborate traditional channel of communication and standardized demand existed. This economic structure catered to the requirements of a specific cultural belt that has now crystallized into a composite Naga culture. Their practice of headhunting was rather a stimulus to its growth and ensured a regular circulation of wealth and increased demand for specific goods. For instance, the beads and brass gongs were imported from Tibet and Burma respectively. Such articles were essential for flaunting their statuses.[64]

2.2.3. Political System

The real political unit for the Naga tribes is the village. Each village was independent and had their own administration that represented the community in all the areas such as politics, society, economy and even religion. They maintained their own institutional system settled their own disputes and were self-governing under the leadership of the elected people, the village-states were governed by a Council of Elders representing each clan, and the representation depended on the population of the clans. This representative character of the council and the selection of the Chief is proof of democracy.[65] Though democratic and republic by nature, the pattern of administration and chieftainship were different among the Naga tribes. It was neither through appointment nor election, but on the basis of his capability, i.e., being powerful and influential. Thus, being powerful and superior, he could invade the neighboring villages resulting in enmity, vengeance or complete breakdown of inter-village relationships. The village under his administration was well knitted together and customs and discipline were rigidly maintained and adhered to by every member. They could not be removed or impeached by the general public unless their capability disproved them.[66] The Naga system of independent village sovereign states and isolation has made the Nagas determination of self rule, self identity and self protection against foreign

---

62 Inato Yekheto Shikhu, *A Rediscovery and Rebuilding of Naga Cultural Values*, 23.

63 L. Imsutoshi Jamir, *Communication in Action: The Pattern of Naga Cultural Shift*, 73.

64 C. L. Imchen, "The Nagas and the Legacy of Civilizing Mission of the Western World," *Understanding Tribal Cultures for Effective Education*, edited by Joseph Anikuzhikattil, George Palackapillil, Joseph Puthenpurakal (New Delhi: Commission for Education and Culture, CBCI Centre, 2003), 48.

65 R. R. Shrimray, *Origin and Culture of Nagas,* 240.

66 Inato Yekheto Shikhu, *A Rediscovery and Rebuilding of Naga Cultural Values*, 17.

rule.[67] However on the other hand, women are completely absent in this form of government. A woman is not allowed to become a village administrator under any circumstances. Only men are eligible to attend and take part in a public meeting. Deliberations and decision making, planning, administration, and policy framing belong to men,[68] where the total life of the community centers on the male perspective and male power in the traditional culture of the Naga society.

2.2.4. Religious System

Religion would generally mean living in spontaneous awareness of, an encounter with, acknowledgement of, and obedience to, the active reality of the presence of the Supreme Being. Religion permeates all aspects of life. In traditional tribal societies such as the Nagas, there were no irreligious people. Though they did not have written creeds to be recited, it was contained in their hearts and minds and therefore each individual, family, clan and village was the living creed. For them, religion existed within the whole system of their being because to be truly human was to belong to the whole community, and to do so involve active participation in the beliefs, ceremonies, rituals, and festivals of the community.[69]

The early Naga religion unlike other religions of the world had neither a founder nor a great historical person to be centered around. Rather, it was centered on earth and creations. Also unlike modern Christian belief in the dichotomy of the 'sacred' and the 'secular' or the 'spiritual' and the 'material', the traditional Naga religion did not have such a dichotomy. For them the 'sacred' and the 'secular' were one. In order to express their awe towards the supernatural being, their fascination with the mystery of existence, and in fear, pain and terror, the early Naga tribes practiced primal religion in the form of animism.[70] The patterns to belief of the early Naga show definite signs of being animistic in nature. These beliefs were expressed through their worship of nature and natural phenomena and through their faith in the power of magic and omens.[71]

2.2.5. Family System

The family was the basic social institution in the Naga society. The family was usually closely knit with bonds of affection and respect. Children loved and

---

67 Joseph S. Thong, *Head-Hunters Cultures* (Kohima, Nagaland: Khinyi Woch, Chunlika Tseminyu, 1997), 131.

68 Limatula Longkumer, *"Christianity and Naga Women," in Transforming Theology for Empowering Women,* ed. R.L.Hnuni (Jorhat: TSC, ETC, 1999), 56.

69 Inato Yekheto Shikhu, *A Rediscovery and Rebuilding of Naga Cultural Values*, 11.

70 The word "animism" is derived from the Latin word "anima" literally meaning "breath"' hence carries the idea of soul and spirit. Animism thus can be defined as a belief that objects and natural phenomena are inhabited by souls or spiritual beings.

71 Hokishe Sema, *Emergence of Nagaland: Socio-Economic and Political Transformation and the Future*, 35.

respected their parents, the father exercised authority over the entire family without consciously appearing to be authoritative. He chided and even beat his children but relationship of love and respect was least disturbed. Husband and wife respected each other and that mutual respect was the secret of domestic harmony in the Naga traditional society.

But today, one can find beginning of the defiance of parental authority and rejection of their advice as, old fashion an outdated.[72] One purpose for maintaining boundaries within a family is to ensure proper differentiation between parents and children. Families are likely to become troubled if parental authority is not clearly executed. That is not to say that all authority in a family resides with the parents. Nor does it imply that the way to same families is to reinstate rigid parental authority. What is most important is that parental roles be clearly defined and consistently executed. Where there is clarity about parental roles, and permeable boundaries exist between the executive and sibling sub-system, the family is likely to function well and children will be free to be children.[73]

Adela Mero in her research on 'The Naga Home and Youth' opines that with the drastic transition from tribalism to modernism, individualism has crept in not only in society but also in the family. In the past, parents were mainly responsible in instructing their children concerning social ethics and behavior as they sat around the kitchen fire for eating or relaxing. The authoritative discipline and teaching of the parents are becoming less acceptable. With the influence of the mass media and easy access to communication, families are disintegrating. The close fellowship carried out in the kitchen is moving to the television set, the computers, and night outings. Parents face tensions in their styles of parenting as they move from tribalism to modernism. The Nagas have a close-knit family tie. The Naga family being patriarchal, the father is the head; yet the mother plays an equally important role in the family. In such an environment, the authoritarian pattern of parenting is dominant. The authority in this pattern is both destructive and constructive. They attempt to mould, control, and evaluate the behavior and attitudes of their children according to their own criteria of evaluation. Youth fail to become independent and responsible for their actions when parents try to run their lives and overprotect them. Naga parents should make the family unit a place where they teach, mould, correct and provide the right type of influence. Parents of youth should realize that different generations have different needs and interest.[74]

---

72 L. Imsutoshi Jamir, *Communication in Action: The Pattern of Naga Cultural Shift*, 77.

73 Boholi Z. Sema, *Parent-Children relationship among the Naga Society Towards Family Enrichment* (Dimapur: Shikhu Scholastic Press, 2012), 100.

74 Adela Mero, "The Naga Home and Youth," *Doing Youth Ministry in a Naga Context*, 143.

2.3. Naga Thought Form

Dozo, a well known church leader and a writer in his book, "The Cross over Nagaland" wrote: By birth and by nature the Nagas are sociable people, sociality, hospitality, humor, geniality, honesty, bravery, reciprocity, hard work and self-reliance are the major ethnic characteristic noted in the Nagas by the outsiders.[75]

They are vigorous, honest, straight-forward and patriotic. Written about them, J. H. Hutton said,

> "Nagas have fine qualities. They are simple, cheerful, colorful, humorous, courteous and hospitable people." And further he added that the Nagas are people "with sense of humor and generosity at home, work, and at gathering. Laughter is the food of the society and hospitality is overwhelming......Nagas are honest and truthful people, stealing is not common... And have respect for elders. Nagas are generous; to them begging is an abomination. They are healthy, active, vigorous and brave people. The Nagas are well built and enthusiastically looking for a true God and are also religious."[76]

J. P. Mills, one time Deputy Commissioner also once remarked, "Naga people never lie." Those comments were given by non-Nagas after careful observations and therefore are not flattery. They have no written document of codes, regulations or procedures: the things needed to be done will be done. They depend only on the wisdom of the village elders who look into all cases. In their past life there were no police to enforce the law.[77] But there was no disorder in the village, doors were never locked. No army, but only a few patriotic people to guard the village from external danger. There was no established institution to teach the youngster to do things, they learned as they came by. They learned to cultivate the field, to do right things, to face nature and to stand up for life. Most Nagas are distinguished by some noble qualities- their pledge, word can be trusted. They are ever ready to devote themselves for common safety.

2.3.1. Equality

The Nagas never experienced and also never believed in the ideology of hegemony nor accepted the philosophy of subjugation and oppression. Every individual had their own freedom to express, share, think, etc. In the midst of the freedom they also knew that they belonged to a certain community and therefore they lived and worked for that particular society.[78] Every Naga believed that one was equal to the others. So also they considered fellow members of the community as equal to

75 P. Dozo, *The Cross over Nagaland* (Guwahati, Assam: Christian Literature Centre, 1983), 3.

76 J. H. Hutton, *The Sema Nagas* (London: Oxford University Press, 1967), 28.

77 As Quoted by V. K. Nuh, *Nagaland Church and Politics*, 50.

78 L. Imsutoshi Jamir, *Communication in Action: The Pattern of Naga Cultural Shift*, 38.

themselves[79] there was respect for every individual, whether young or old, rich or poor, male or female, all were accepted as equal members of the clan and village. Verrier Elwin, An outstanding anthropologist who worked among the people of the North East India wrote: Each village amongst the Naga is a small republic, and each man is as good as his neighbor, indeed it would be hard to find anywhere else more thoroughly democratic communities.[80]

It is important to note that in the Naga society, there was no difference between the village chief's children and the commoners in competition. The same was applied to everybody without distinction. Each had a right and equal opportunity to climb the social ladder of recognition by dint of merit. It was not possible for anyone to get a social distinction to any stroke. Society had only one class which the capitalist may call it 'the working class. For Naga society, it was primarily a body of farmers, because all the Nagas[81] were farmers, each having a farm and paddy fields to toil for living.

2.3.2. Respect

The Nagas were known for their loyalty and respect towards their elders as well as obedience to the established authority. A Naga was known for showing loyalty to elders, at the same time a Naga always have a sense of independence and freedom of speech. They did not contradict each other because there were always working together in harmony without causing rebellion or disobedience to authority. Every person knew for sure that once a point of decision was arrived after contradiction, arguments and questions, it was to be obeyed without boycott or declining.[82]

It is here, that one notices a wonderful blend of freedom of expression with the obedience to authority. In fact, though a Naga is known for the sense of independence and individualistic attitudes, no Naga will dare to take the law into his or her own hands. No Naga will dare not to respect the elders.

2.3.3. Honor

In the Naga fold, honor was life's most desired characteristic. This can be achieved through honesty, humility, truthfulness and hard work. Beggary was not only looked down upon, but was also considered a crime. Unlike the so called advanced societies, there was no one who lived on alms, there were no beggars, if because of some reason a person has fallen into misfortune, he or she was looked after by the relatives or clan or the whole community. The Nagas were happy, free and friendly, their friendliness was universal, but their truly human behavior during illness and misfortune was both touching and inspiring. It was an honor to care

79 L. Imsutoshi Jamir, *Communication in Action: The Pattern of Naga Cultural Shift*, 39.

80 Verrier Elwin, *Nagaland* (N.P: RDAS, 1961), 324.

81 L. Imsutoshi Jamir, *Communication in Action: The Pattern of Naga Cultural Shift*, 40.

82 Panger Imchen, *Ancient Ao Naga Religion and Culture* (New Delhi: Har-Anand Publication, 1993), 87.

and show concern to others, especially to the one who had fallen into misfortune like sickness, death, fire etc. it was also an honor to show hospitality to the guest especially to those who needed help and shelter. As a result of this care and concern for each other, loneliness was unknown among them and consequently there were no psychological cases as in the so called civilized society. Every Naga knew that it was better to die hungry than to acquire wealth and food through unjust means. Because for a Naga it was an honor to be truthful, people always respected persons who were honest and truthful. Moreover, it was honor to be called a hard working person and people admired such person.[83]

2.3.4. Etiquette

Nagas also had a high sense of etiquette and courtesy. If a person lacked those norms, they were looked down upon by the community. It is obvious that Nagas were people who always judge and weigh a person in the light of a set of etiquette.[84] Youth do accept the demands of discipline and authority. Though youth experience problems such as lack of self-confidence, immaturity and cultural disapproval in the area of boy-girl relationship, they perceive the importance of this element. They have an underlying desire and need for healthy mixing of boys and girls. The reaction of youth to the social situation of caste shows again the turmoil into which they are thrown. The values that tradition has ingrained into the mentality of youth leave these youth in a quandary.[85] Discipline is corrective and authority is directive. But a sizable group of youth today critically challenges the inconsistent value system of society which demands discipline and respect for authority.

2.3.5. Customary Laws and Ethics

Both for individuals as well as for the community, Nagas held certain unwritten laws which they kept in their hearts, which were handed down from time immemorial and from generation to generation. These laws and ethical value systems were universal among the Naga society to which they always gave the first importance in all their doings.[86] If a customs is broken, the entire system is in danger. Hence, those who break tested and time-honored customs are given heavy penalties and punishments. The system of the customs and laws was a monument in the history of the Nagas constructed out of human action, wisdom, belief and experience. These customs and laws which were unwritten, but written in the hearts of every individual reflect the way of life, maturity, intellectual power and the strength of the Naga society. These customary laws and ethics were related to individual and societal behavior which they always considered as the guiding principle for survival in their society. In other words, an accepted value system

83 Panger Imchen, *Ancient Ao Naga Religion and Culture*, 171.

84 L. Imsutoshi Jamir, *Communication in Action: The Pattern of Naga Cultural Shift*, 43.

85 Dominic Jala, "Youth and the challenges of the twenty-first century," 59.

86 Panger Imchen, *Ancient Ao Naga Religion and Culture*, 105.

centered on all activities of a person in relation to his or her community, the Naga customary laws provided every individual the opportunity to climb the social hierarchy. They were open to all. Hence, in the Naga community law there was no scope for class struggle of any kind. The customary law provided every individual equal freedom and right to live. It also provided various ways in which every individual was expected to behave, think, survive, etc.[87] Having said above on the other side, Naga women had not known, nor heard any past or lost golden age for women, one that they could long to reclaim, revive or mourn for today. In other words, they had not known any form of matricentricism either in the past or present.[88]

The customs and laws were considered to consist of truth, justice and public utility and were observed by people as the moral, religious and social codes. A memorandum issued in 1998 by the Land Revenue Development of the Government of Nagaland, under No. Lr/1-1/94 states its concern for the development of women in securing them justice and making them equal participants, yet it also mentions that the government will not interfere in the traditional customary law concerning land and its transfer.[89] As such, all Nagas in general believed and accepted culture as the right way of life as nature-intended. This clearly pictures that though people seems to be aware that women particularly in the practice of customary laws and ethics needs social, political, and religious upliftment; the customary law remains unchanged and unchallenged.

2.3.6. The Community Life

There is a vibrant social relationship in Naga villages. Whatever an individual does have an impact on the members of the village. If a person behaves well she/he bring laurel to the village. If a person misbehaves she/he brings bad name to the village. Hence, every citizen of the village tries to live a life acceptable to the society. They place the name of the village above individuals.[90] And so this nature of the community is understood as communitarians. Obviously, one of the most colorful ingredients of the Naga village state was its community life. A Naga individual knows no other life except that of a community life. They worked in groups, ate in groups, danced in groups, and also slept in groups. There was no individual cultivation or harvest, no individual house building or feast of merit by individuals alone and no wooing of girls individually. All things were done

---

87 L. Imsutoshi Jamir, *Communication in Action: The Pattern of Naga Cultural Shift*, 44.

88 Lovely Awomi James, *Tribal Theology, Reviewing the Naga Traditional Worldview* (New Delhi: Christian World Imprints, 2017), 34.

89 Imsopangla, "A Liberative of Inheritance: A Critique of the Ao Naga Customary Law of Inheritance," *Side by Side*, edited by Limatula Longkumer & Talijungla Longkumer (Kolkata: ESPACE, 2013), 48.

90 Yiepetso Wezah, *Tribal Ethical Values and Practices-a Search for a Better World* (Dimapur, Nagaland: Lhiweko-u Wezah, 2015), 29.

in groups and in the full presence of their entire community. Individual had no existence apart from the community.[91] R. R. Shimray comment about traditional Naga Community life thus: This organized conception of the village-state merits well in comparison to Plato's concept of city-states as organic bodies in which the rulers, the soldiers and the producers performed their own functions and thereby the failure of one class could bring disaster to other classes.[92]

From time immemorial Naga community living was a moralizing agent. Unlike Christian belief, which says that the salvation is the individual's faith in the Lord Jesus Christ: 'the just shall live by faith alone' (Rom.1:17) but for the Nagas, it was the community that was important. The sin of an individual could adversely affect the whole group. For instance, it was believed and experienced that when an individual violated the village taboo by sowing or planting seeds ahead of the village chief, the whole community suffered from famine. Also, if an individual violated the war taboo by sleeping with his wife, the night before the war, it was believed, would suffer loss of life. Hence, for the Nagas, the Christian people would have been: the just shall live by faith in community living alone. Since loss of life and failure of crops and famine, etc., were involved, the individual and community as a whole could not but observe the moral laws and instruction carefully. It is true that, the social values of their religious faith would have been as low as that of the barbarians and the observance of religious genna, The Nagas got the social values in their religion and, as a result, they see that the total life of a Naga was controlled by those norms, belief and values.[93]

The tribal's though educated and in touch with modernity, have not been entirely captivated by ideas like individualism and private ownership. When a person is waned from parental ties it is not individualization but individuation for a combat in defense of familial, kinship and societal ties. Shame and sin are experienced not much from the person's inner conscious but more from the judgment of the community. One's right or wrong conduct is evaluated on the basis of the community's verdict. Family is the primary community but each member of the family has one's age group companies to which each is registered by participation. These groups are not in rivalry with one another but for a graded socialization for nurturing the individuals with age appropriate information and experience. Each person's identity is formed in a group experience and they establish their self—esteem in such supportive companies. If humans are known as social being the tribals are the prototype of it. Tribal communitarian life is an organic togetherness unlike the professional groups of individualistic societies.[94] In the words of Thanzauva, "The destructive effect of modern individualism so widely

91 L. Imsutoshi Jamir, *Communication in Action: The Pattern of Naga Cultural Shift*, 46.

92 R. R. Shrimray, *Origin and Culture of Nagas*, 121.

93 L. Imsutoshi Jamir, *Communication in Action: The Pattern of Naga Cultural Shift*, 49.

94 Ezamo Murry, "Bible and Culture: A Model of Christian Acculturation of Tribal Culture," *Doing Tribal Christian Theology with Tribal Resources: Cultural Resources from North East*

establishing a true community."[95] The individual's identity is found in the village community and in the age group. The village is the guardian of the individual. To be banished from the village, therefore, is the greatest punishment and humiliation for any individual.[96]

2.3.7. Role and Status

Like any other patriarchal societies, Naga society is also a patriarchal culture where the father or the male member controls all members of the family, all properties, politics, and other economic resources, and makes all the major decisions in the family.[97] However, woman also had to struggle with much hardship relating to household affairs and child caring.[98] The excepted norm of the Naga society is that household work and nurturing children are exclusively women's activities.[99] But in the cases where work or activity concerns the men, the women play the major role from behind the scene. And where women's task is to be performed, it is the men who play the major role from behind. Co-existence and co-activities is observed in all walks of life, which involves both the male and the female. Different sexes are expected to maintain strict discipline though they gave a remarkable degree of freedom to move and be together.[100] Owing to a Naga woman's overall shouldering ability over the domestic affairs and chores, very often it is perceived as a reference point denoting her dominion position and role within the social context of the Nagas. Moreover, a Naga woman is often praised and honored on account of her work, ability in fulfilling her home-ward chores like cooking, weaving, fetching water, collecting firewood, cook and feed the house animals, brew rice-bear, pound paddy, washing, cleaning and mopping the floors, etc., as well as her share of field work. A woman's worth and value is measured by the amount of work that she performs. As the traditional understanding of the human race is concerned, each had to struggle with one's own responsibilities and tasks, strictly believing and following the culturally-defined set of roles and status.[101]

India, edited by Razouselie Lasetso, Eyingbeni Humtsoe (Jorhat, Assam: Eastern Theological College, 2009), 15.

95 K. Thanzauva, *Theology of Community: Tribal Theology in the Making* (Aizawl, Mizoram: Mizo Theological Conference, 1997), 10.

96 Ezamo Murry, "Bible and Culture: A Model of Christian Acculturation of Tribal Culture," 15.

97 Limatula Longkumer, *Women in Theological Education: Pedagogical Issues* (Bangalore: Board of Theological Education of the Senate of Serampore College, 2012), 151.

98 Joseph S. Thong, *Glimpses Of Naga Legacy And Culture,* edited by Phanenmo Kath (Kottayam, Kerala: Society for Naga Students' Welfare, Kerala, 2011), 84.

99 Limatula Longkumer, *Women in Theological Education: Pedagogical Issues* 152.

100 Joseph S. Thong, *Glimpses Of Naga Legacy And Culture,* 88.

101 Lovely Awomi James, *Tribal Theology,* 36.

2.3.8. Language

Peculiar characteristics of Naga culture which is not found in many other states in the country is the diversity of linguistic communities. In many cases, a single village alone possesses its own language which is not intelligible to others. Since written systems in these languages are only recently introduced and many of them are still yet to be introduced, the clear identity of standard language is not yet fully established in any of the languages. However, enormous vocabularies have been borrowed from outside sources. This is necessary because, with the acquisition of knowledge, many new elements have been borrowed and incorporated in their culture. But they cannot be translated into an appropriate term in their languages.[102]

One should confess the fact that very little is known about the Naga dialect. Also it is sad to note that the Nagas have no written script of their own. Tradition says that at one time they had their own written literature recorded on an animal skin, but it was through the carelessness of the scribe, that the skin was devoured by a dog. So, they lost their literature.[103] Though,.Nagas do not have their own written literature. It is obvious that Nagas have a very rich means in communicating what they feel and believe, who they are, etc., through poetry, songs and music, dress and ornaments and the like.[104]

The Nagas still use the Roman script introduced by the American Baptist missionaries. Missionaries transcribed Naga dialect to writing by introducing the Roman script.[105] Through the introduction of literature, many changes have occurred in the Naga culture. Along with the introduction of literature and the educational system Naga youth must realize their dialect/language, as an important element and formation to adhere one's own cultural identity. Today, one must revitalized and understand that losing a language is losing one's own identity.

2.3.9. Dresses and Ornaments

The Nagas are distinguished by an impressive bearing and splendid dress. Among their clothes, the most significant is the shawl. It is different for every tribe and, besides, there are varieties and sub-varieties in every group. A warrior's shawl or the shawl of a man who has performed the feast of merit is different from that of an ordinary villager.[106] In the past, it was possible to identify, simply looking at the shawl of the wearer, the tribe he belonged to and occasionally even the

102 B. Pakem, ed., *Nationality, Ethnicity and Cultural Identity in North-East India*, 334.

103 P. T. Philip, *The Growth of Baptist Church in Nagaland* (Guwahati, Assam: Christian Literature Centre, 1983), 10.

104 L. Imsutoshi Jamir, *Communication in Action: The Pattern of Naga Cultural Shift*, 56.

105 A. Wati longchar, *The Traditional Worldview and Modernity* (Jorhat, Assam: ETC, 1995), 137.

106 Hargovind Joshi, ed., *Nagaland Past and Present* (New Delhi: Akansha Publishing House, 2001), 153.

group of villages he comes from, his social status, whether he was a rich man or a commoner, and the number of gennas he had performed. But nowadays patterns have been introduced. People of one tribe do not hesitate to wear another tribe's shawl.[107] The most prominent ones are Aviki-iphi (Semas), Tsungkotepsu (Aos), Kaksi nei (Chang), and Lohe (Angamis). The most popular decoration for male dresses is ivory armlet, leggings, headdress, earrings, ornamented belts and embroidered cross-straps. Women wear shawl-skirts and knotted sleeves of shawls, necklaces,[108] and brass earrings.[109]

Tattooing is fairly common in the Naga tribes. Among the Konyaks, Changs and Phoms, both men and women are tattooed, among the Aos and Sangtams, only women are tattooed. The Konyaks usually tattoo their faces. In earlier days, they could do so only after they had taken a head, but this restriction does not apply any longer. A wonderful compromise was struck by some Konyaks who made a show of killing an effigy to get them the right to tattoo. The Phoms tattoo their women only on the legs, but an Ao woman could be tattooed anywhere from face down-ward to the legs. A girl, after she is tattooed, becomes a full-fledged member of the community. Henceforth, she is allowed to grow her hair, and she must also observe the food restrictions in the clan.[110]

The Nagas, though called by others as half naked in their custom and dress, were not immoral by nature. It was also not because they did not have clothes to wear, but because of their custom they were half-clad. In fact they had different clothes to wear on different occasions. Also there were special type of shawls and ornaments to be worn by those who performed feast of merit, warriors, leaders, etc., each clan had its own distinct dress. Also, not all the dresses and ornaments were exposed to common ordinary people. It was from the dresses and ornaments, the public could easily make out the special status of the person; from the dresses and ornaments people could easily make out the clan to which one belonged.[111]

In the traditional Naga society, weaving was practiced by almost every girl. They made shawls and skirts of different designs and styles. Today this practice is dying and more and more girls opt for western dresses and fashion.

2.3.10. Songs and Music

In the Naga community, folk songs were regarded as more authentic and authoritative medium than verbal communication, because it preserved and transmitted their culture, the good and bad memories and events of the by gone

107 Hargovind Joshi, ed., *Nagaland Past and Present*, 156.

108 A necklace of beads is generally worn round the neck. These beads may be made of some kind of stone or shells.

109 P. Dozo, *The Growth of the Baptist Church in Chekhesang Naga Tribe* (Kohima, Nagaland: NMM, 1978), 22.

110 Hargovind Joshi, ed., *Nagaland Past and Present*, 158.

111 L. Imsutoshi Jamir, *Communication in Action: The Pattern of Naga Cultural Shift*, 59.

days. Because of this reason, without a song and music, there is no right and authentic explanation of the Naga culture and of their historical details. Since they had no written culture, folk songs were much authoritative than the oral tradition. Thus, the past events were recollected and sung through songs and transmitted from one generation to another.[112] A common musical instrument played by the Nagas is Petu. It is a string instrument. Another popular string instrument is theku.[113]

The Naga culture and tradition is rich and varied. One of the fundamental characteristics of the Nagas is their ability to sing and to use music for everything and everywhere. It is not an exaggeration to say that the life of a Naga is a life of singing and dancing. They love singing when they come together for secular and religious festivals, for work, etc., they derive their inspiration for music from the vibrant nature in which they live, move and have their being.[114] Folk songs are song for people. The tribal go on singing a small poem consisting of four to eight verses for hours together with the help of folk music. Folk song often embodies something of people's character, and composers have long turned to it for ideas and inspiration.[115] Songs and music have become part of a people's heritage through oral tradition.

Unfortunately, Naga culture underwent a drastic change with the rest of the world and a new social consciousness. As a result, the Nagas are in danger today of losing their identity as people with a distinct culture.

2.3.11. Naga Traditional Structures of Learning

2.3.11.1. Morung or Male Dormitory

Morung[116] system is an organized structure for purpose of training male youths in the ways of men. Every village has this morung built and its serves as a men's club or male dormitory where youth (beginning from adolescence till one marries or settles himself for life) becomes an inmate, residing there for specific period of time in his life. Morung very importantly serves as a learning institution for all-round development, especially in the sphere of one's intellectual and

112 Sentimeren Jamir, "The Naga Folk Songs: Its Relevance in Church Worship," *Communication and Culture,* edited by L. imsutoshi Jamir and C. Alitemjen Longkumer (Dimapur, Nagaland: TDCC, 2007), 63.

113 Hargovind Joshi, ed., *Nagaland Past and Present*, 158.

114 Sentimeren Jamir, "The Naga Folk Songs: Its Relevance in Church Worship," *Communication and Culture*, 59.

115 Sentimeren Jamir, "The Naga Folk Songs: Its Relevance in Church Worship," *Communication and Culture,* 60.

116 The word 'Morung' is believed to have originated from Assamese. For the Nagas, a morung was the pivot around which the social, religious, educational and cultural activities of the young people revolved. The morung (bachelor's dormitory) and (ladies dormitory) are, therefore rightly called the Naga Schools.

physical skills, one's political and cultural development skills. Youth were thus trained under extreme disciplinary methods. It is also a place where the youth receive training in various vocations or skills like arts and woodcarvings, cottage industries as well as sportsmanship. The elders of the morung who are responsible for training the youth teach them various wars tactics as a way of preparing them for war.[117] Morung serves not just to impart its members for fighting the enemy and of guarding the village, but it also functions as an important institution for imparting ethics of social, religious, political and economic values to the members.[118] V. K. Anand observes "But how a Naga boy grows up to be a man and how he milled to become a useful and disciplined member of the community can be understood by examining their almost universally existing institutions of community dormitories."[119]

2.3.11.2. Ladies' Dormitory

While the morung serves center for boys, ladies' dormitory serves the same for young Naga girls or women. Unlike the common name for males' dormitory-morung, there is no common name given so far for the ladies dormitory. Each Naga tribe has its own name for it in one's own dialect. For the Sumi Nagas the name given for ladies' dormitory is *Illiki* which means females or females' house. For the Rengma Nagas the term is *Katseni* which is also similar in meaning. Once the girls reach puberty stage, they must leave their parents' home and come and sleep in the dormitories till they get married. Among some tribes, girls as early as seven years of age are made to start sleeping in the dormitories. Ladies' dorms play an important role as learning and training institution for Naga girls in the olden days. All skills like weaving, handicrafts, folk songs, folk tales and dance, all behaviors, manners, and values taught are purely based on the traditional understanding of the female.[120]

Naga society is facing a major and urgent problem of undisciplined youth who are caught at the crossroads between tradition and modernity. Cases of a boy/girl challenging an elder, a thing unheard of in the past, are quite common today. In many homes there is rebellion against parents, and respect for elders and parents which used to be a sacred duty is diminishing. The disintegration of the morung and ladies dormitory system resulted in weakening discipline and orderliness particularly among the youth and it weakened the spirit of social life.

---

117 Lovely Awomi James, *Tribal Theology*, 41.

118 As Cited by Yanbemo Lotha, *Making A Theology Of Naga Community*, (Dimapur, Nagaland: Abeni Lotha, 2005), 36.

119 V. K. Anand, *Nagaland in Transaction* (New Delhi: Associated Publishing House, 1967), 88.

120 Lovely Awomi James, *Tribal Theology*, 42.

2.3.12. Socialization

On Socialization K. Young writes,

> "Socialization means the process of inducing the individual into the social and cultural world; of making youth a participate member in society and its various groups and inducing them to accept the norms and values of that society....Socialization is definitely a matter of learning and not biological inheritance."

It is through the process of socialization that an individual is molded into a social being and fined their fulfillment within the society. It is a fact that youth becomes what they are by socialization. Morung organization is a process of working together for developing group responsibility guided by the welfare needs. It is through socialization that an individual learns the skills, beliefs and standards of judgment that are necessary for his/her effective participation in social groups and enable youth to perform social roles and develop the community feeling.[121] J. H. Hutton observes that youths were disciplined by means of clear instructions given by the elders. To train a boy/girl to become a disciplined person before shouldering the responsibilities of youth was one of the objectives of the society. Integrity, obedience and self-discipline were largely the concern of the Nagas in Naga society, achieved through the instruction of the elders.[122] However, today individualism has affected the Naga society because the regular system of socializing and training as it was practiced under the morung elders could not be sustained.[123]

2.3.13. Work Culture

By work the Naga mean the things or activities done to sustain life. They survive on food grains, fruits, etc. which are grown in the earth or field; plant and trees drawn their sustenance from the earth. The Nagas love to work hard, and want others to do so. Throughout the year, from early morning to dark they work incessantly. The most impression in their work culture was that one has in mind to do more than the other. Whenever they work together, one thinks of doing a bigger share and whenever they eat together, he/she has in mind to offer the best to the other. Work made them responsible members of the society. There was always a sense of duty and responsibility towards one's society. [124] They had imprinted in themselves a sincere work ethic. They were very energetic and always

121 As Cited by Joseph S. Thong, *Glimpses Of Naga Legacy And Culture*, 79.

122 J. H. Hutton, *The Angami Nagas* (London: Oxford University Press, 1969), 101.

123 Mar Pongener, *Morung Speaks: Cultural Values and Elements for the Enrichment of Naga Christian Community* (Jorhat, Assam: CTC and TDCC, 2011), 121.

124 Tasoni Moon, *Naga Work Culture: A Theological Reflection* (Dimapur, Nagaland: Published by the Author, 2004), 6.

ready to resume work. Thus, by nature the Nagas were hard working people. Working hard was an honor and brought a lot of respect.[125]

Early anthropological descriptions confirm Nagas as honest and hardworking people with a sincere work ethic. In the traditional village system of the Nagas, there were no people who did not work. The Nagas had a conviction that everybody should work. The spirit of willingness to work hard by accepting a range of responsibilities was promoted in the morung. All members were trained to work hard not only for themselves but for the welfare of the community. The youths were taught by the elder's that "to work is ethical and that idleness or laziness was unethical" thus they strongly supported work-based income. It was in the morung that youth developed a healthy work culture because they were taught that the success and failure of a person were determined by his or her work habits.[126]

Like most mountainous people all over the world, Nagas were very spirited in their outlook and have never been ashamed to earn their livelihood by the sweat of their brow. It is very rare to see a Naga sitting idle and indulging, in gossiping. Idleness was thought to be the cause of poverty. Even very old men and women are found working in the vegetable garden or preparing food for pigs. They want to die working.[127]

2.4. Factors Influencing the Loss of Naga Culture

Due to the impact of modernization, globalization, migration, media and technology, Naga youth have gradually begun to give up certain aspects of the traditional cultural values. Like all cultures, Naga culture has own components of culture like handicrafts, arts and woodcarvings, music and dance, folk tales, feast and festivals, traditional costumes, community life, dignity of labor, etc where Naga people were proud of their culture. However, today Naga youth have come across radical changes into a new standard of living and it does affect the society as a whole. The Naga society has been uprooted from an ordered life where social responsibilities were laid down in a very meticulous way both in morung and homes, with the roles of persons and groups clearly defined in keeping with their age and gender.

The essentially communal lifestyle, value system, family activities and cultural ethos, which were once the core of Naga society, steadily eroded as the current flowed strongly towards individualism with people focused on their own welfare and advancement. This change has made people, particularly youth irresponsible. Egalitarianism, for which the Nagas were famous in the olden days, is fast disappearing. The fellow feelings, born out of community living, have now

125 Tasoni Moon, *Naga Work Culture: A Theological Reflection*, 7.

126 Mar Pongener, *Morung Speaks: Cultural Values and Elements for the Enrichment of Naga Christian Community*, 123.

127 Tasoni Moon, *Naga Work Culture: A Theological Reflection* , 5.

given way to rapacious greed based on the principle that "might is right."[128] The following are some of the loss of aesthetic components of Naga culture.

2.4.1. Naga Handicrafts, Arts and Woodcarvings Taught at Morung and Homes

The various colorful Naga handicrafts represent the rich heritage of Naga culture. In the olden days, the traditional morung and ladies' dorms system and even at homes provided education which was beneficial and relevant for the Nagas and their society. The learning process was based on the daily practical life of a person. The teaching and learning of Naga handicrafts, arts and woodcarvings were compulsory subjects for the members in the morung and ladies dormitory handicrafts like making of Naga spears and Dao, the art of house building, weaving clothes, embroidery and designs, the art of house building, weaving mats and winnowing fans, making baskets and earthen pots were regular features of the training for the members.[129] Nagas also love carvings and they are gifted at creating them. Different forms of carvings like tiger, hornbill, elephant, human head, sun, moon and stars were made on panels of wood which were hung in front of their houses. Wood carvings were used by Nagas as primary vehicles for communicating the symbols and value systems of the Naga tribe and their culture. Behind the artistic beauty and the technical skill of the carver, there was a whole history and meaning attached to the woodcarvings.[130]

Today, with the disintegration of the morung and ladies' dorms system, forming into group and making traditional handicrafts and arts and crafts has been faded away from the Naga society. Another means of losing such practices are the replacement or adoption of western culture and ideologies, where youth determine the greatest technology along with the new gadgets that offered. Many view that traditional learning processes were out there, which includes the disintegration of handicrafts, arts and woodcarvings and other cultural artifacts. Doing so has created many incredible opportunities for youth to break of the traditional method of learning and work towards creating knowledge community.

---

128 M.M. Thomas, *Nagas Towards A.D. 2000 and Other Selected Addresses and Writings*, 6.

129 Mar Pongener, *Morung Speaks: Cultural Values and Elements for the Enrichment of Naga Christian Community*, 125.

130 Mar Pongener, *Morung Speaks: Cultural Values and Elements for the Enrichment of Naga Christian Community*, 126.

2.4.2. Folk Songs, Folk Tales, Dances, and Feasts and Festivals

Folk songs,[131] folk tales, dances, and feast and festivals[132] which contain Naga historical traditions like the origin of the Nagas, their ancestors, clans and villages were recounted by the elders in the morung. Unlike the modern educational system, the learning activities in the morung were not usually systematic but spontaneous as the members responded to them. The teaching and learning process was carried on in the form of transmitting the lessons orally from elders to the younger generation. There are several Naga songs, folktales told and retold by the elders to the youngsters not simply to make an unruly child to be quiet or obey but because they are full of meaning and encouragement. The Naga folksongs and folktales contain the whole meaning of Naga culture and its traditions. This was the reason why all the members in the morung were required to be attentive in learning folk songs and folktales which were beneficial both for the individual and the Naga society.[133]

Folk songs, folktales, and dances are the spontaneous creation of unsophisticated popular imagination, is not just the traditional source of entertainment to the people. But it embodies the ancient observation and customs, beliefs, especially the value systems and the moral laws of a community or a tribe that makes them distinct from others.[134] Dancing is natural to the Naga tribes. It is full of vigor and vitality. Strangely, it is the monopoly of men, except in zeliang tribe where women join menfolk in dancing. Naga dancing is always in a group. It is difficult to generalize, but roughly it could be said that the artistes first slowly enter the arena or stage, make a circle or any other geometrical formation, and gradually work up the tempo with the stamping of feet, interspersed with clapping and chanting of some formula. The spear, dao or the shield are swung to the rhythm of the dance. After the climax is reached, the tempo is brought down again and there is a satisfying finale. The beauty of the dances is heightened by the colorful costumes.[135]

---

131 The term "folk song" was invented by the nineteenth- century scholars to describe the music of peasantry, age old and anonymous. Folk songs have become part of the life a people's heritage through oral tradition. Sentimeren Jamir, "The Naga Folk Songs: Its Relevance in Church Worship," *Communication and Culture,* 61.

132 Traditional feast and festivals were always celebrated with religious and spiritual meanings for the tribals. Their feast and festivals are designed around the significances of the blessings of the natural world. Lovely Awomi James, "North East Christianity and Traditional Religio-Cultural Elements: Implications for Theology of Religions today." *Issues Confronting Church and Society Today,* edited by, Lovely Awomi James & Razouselie Lasetso (Jorhat: ILEMA-ETC & WSC-ETC, 2017), 71.

133 Mar Pongener, *Morung Speaks: Cultural Values and Elements for the Enrichment of Naga Christian Community*, 129.

134 Shashinungla Ao, "Oral Tradition and Historical Discourse," *Tribe Culture Art,* edited by Vanlalnghak Siby K. George (Guwahati, Assam: DVS Publishers, 2001), 15.

135 Hargovind Joshi, ed., *Nagaland Past and Present,* 158.

Nagas are lovers of festivities and celebration of any kind. Feasts and festivals were also accompanied a period of gaining new vigor for their seasonal agricultural tasks and an occasion for commemorating their culture; it was closely in tune with the celebration of the feasts and festivals. Sharing of wealth was a way of life in the Naga community and it was demonstrated by hosting feasts for the whole village.[136]

Today, owing to the present formal educational system, age of technology and social media, Christianization, and urbanization has ushered tremendous changes in the life of the Naga youth. It has opened many opportunities and also has made every aspect of life easier and comfortable however, it has also upheaval in many life aspects of the present youth. They are no longer interested in learning old traditional folk songs, folktales, dances, etc., particularly the youth wanted to adapt to a new culture, new lifestyle. There is no time for the youth to sit and learn stories, songs, sayings, etc., that has been handed down through generation. The impact of the forgotten history of the foreparents has ushered in so many changes in social, political, economic, and religious spheres of life.

2.4.3. Traditional Costumes

The value of traditional costumes and their meaning seems no longer relevant for the modern Nagas striving to make their lifestyle comparable with other modern societies. Many youth feel that being identified with the cultural ethos of their ancestors will rather make them misfits in modern society. To them, the traditional clothing is not adequate in today's world. As a result youth are reluctant to wear traditional costumes as the older people do, even during special occasions because they feel that these are not compatibility with modern society. Considering the necessity of compatibility with modern societies, Naga youth are more and more attracted by the western way of dressing and lifestyle. Western styles like jeans, tee shirts and miniskirts are now more popular in Naga society than traditional wear.[137]

The unique way of identifying Nagas is having own traditional unique attires, where one could easily tell to which tribe a man/ woman belonged to by the way he/she dressed. Today with the impact of modernization and westernization, educated Naga youth wanted to wear modern styles of dress, giving up forms of dress and ornamentation.[138] It has been happening from the time of the American Baptist Missionaries who were the pioneers of Christianity, education, and modernization in Nagaland, who discouraged the traditional costumes and

136 Mar Pongener, *Morung Speaks: Cultural Values and Elements for the Enrichment of Naga Christian community*, 130.

137 Mar Pongener, *Morung Speaks: Cultural Values and Elements for the Enrichment of Naga Christian Community*, 131.

138 Narola Imchen, *Women in the History of Christianity* (Jorhat: Tribal Development and Communication Centre, 2014), 179.

practices and its values to a great deal. This has led the foreparents to avoid so many oral traditions that have been handed down from their foreparents. In this crucial time, people gradually, adapted western dress, and western lifestyle. The treasured culture had only a little space for its survival.

2.4.4. Loss of Community Spirit

One of the most important characteristics of Naga society was the community life. An egalitarian spirit was a feature of the community life of the Naga where all members-rich and poor, old and young, strong and weak- were treated equally. The system of allocating equal work according to the peer group during community social work and the practice of giving equal punishment to the violators of rules irrespective of one's family status were some of the good examples of egalitarianism practiced and fostered in the Naga society. These activities made the youth value the importance of every individual in the community. Thus, the spirit of companionship in the caring, sharing, fellowship and goodwill shown to one another, maintained and practiced in Naga society became a model for the Naga community.[139]

The Nagas in the past had a very strong feeling of community. A feeling of isolation by the individual was not felt in any circumstance. And there was no place for individualistic tendencies. In most cases, they maintained the same status, there were no distinction between rich and poor nor were partiality practiced. Every individual felt an equal treatment in the community. In any situation, the welfare of the community was given first preference. The respect between elders and younger people were highly maintained. The poor and the needy in the community was taken care by the whole community. In fact, the values and ethos of the Naga in the past vividly shows a clear concept of communitarians.[140]

However, today, in the process of modernization, the essence of communitarian aspect prevailed in the lives of the Nagas[141] is being faded to a great extent. The rich principle of communitarians is being crept by the ideology of individualism. The respect and equality in the community is being replaced by the distinction between rich and poor and moreover, ethical principle of respect has fewer places in the community. As a result, the element of social segregation among the Naga tribes is endangering the lives of the Nagas; once the lives of the Nagas were clothed with the principle of communitarians.[142]

---

139 Mar Pongener, *Morung Speaks: Cultural Values and Elements for the Enrichment of Naga Christian Community*, 119.

140 K. Thanzauva, *Theology of Community: Tribal Theology in the Making*, 106.

141 Yanbemo Lotha, *Making A Theology of Naga Community*, 4.

142 Yanbemo Lotha, *Making A Theology of Naga Community*, 5.

2.4.5. Loss of Dignity of Labor

Diminishing dignity of labor among the youth is a serious concern today.[143] Naga youth in the past were a band of disciplined warriors and hard working people. Those traditional values had a role to play in making the community life meaningfully applied for the betterment of the society and for making the modernization process more meaningful. Nagas can never stop the process of modernization now, but they can stop the evil forces of this transformation. Problems were fewer in the past, because everybody had a sense of duty and a commitment towards his/her community. Individuals lived for the sake of the community. It was always "community first and then only the individual." The dream of making the community first was made a reality through the application of ethical and moral principle that was expressed in that community in a number of beliefs and practices.[144]

Many Naga youth are ashamed to do any manual work. They think that their status will be questioned if people see them doing manual work. They often suffer because of their pride. This is a wrong type of pride. They should be ashamed if they are not useful or able to contribute anything to the society. On the other hand, they should be proud of themselves if they can do anything which is constructive by using their hands, legs, minds, brain, and so on. This type of pride can be considered as "real pride." Many Naga youth loiter around doing nothing. It does not mean that they do not have any work to do. They are lazy and have no personal motivation to work. They have no goal or vision in life. Most Naga youth are only after government job. They attached value to a job if only it is under the government. If the government does not provide any job, many remain jobless. They categorize themselves as educated but unemployed, majority of the educated Naga youth failed to venture into other opportunities for work apart from government jobs. Being educated but not engaging in any work may lead to hopelessness. It is possible that one may have a degree, but not educated. If one's degree does not allow a person to take pride to engage in some kind of work to survive, something is wrong. If one's education makes him or her feel ashamed to work, that person may have the degree but not necessarily educated.[145]

2.5. Conclusion

This chapter surveyed Naga culture with a brief historical background. In fact there are cultural features of the Nagas which were highly organized and well

143 Razouselie Lasetso, "Introduction : Shaping a Relevant Theology for the Indigenous People of North East India," *Tribal Christian Theology*, edited by Razouselie Lasetso, Yangkahao Vashum (Jorhat, Assam: Eastern Theological College, 2007), 3.

144 Takatemjen, *Studies on Theology and Naga Culture* (Jorhat, Assam: Published by the Author, 1997), 49.

145 Coppe Mero, "Current Social Issues among the Naga Youth," *Doing Youth Ministry in a Naga Context*, edited by Soren Oestergaard & Adelo Mero (Dimapur: NBYF, 2004), 114.

established, which explain the ancient Naga traditions that were imprinted in the social, religious and political structures. These cultural features controlled every individual in his/her total life existence be it social, religious, political and economic life. One must realize that Nagas had concrete ideas, theories and beliefs rooted in their history. Nagas should clearly see through various cultural features like equality of all people and respect towards fellow humans, strong customary laws that govern every individual; joy in community living; hospitality and truthfulness blend with honesty and hardworking; strong morality blend with free life. Also, in spite of not having written language, Nagas could communicate and preserved their tradition, history, norms and values, and their practices and beliefs through songs, dances and poetry. More than that, their dresses and ornaments speak who they are. It also speaks about one status, clan, tribe, and history. Therefore, the Naga youth should made an attempt to understand and return to at least some of distinct features of the Naga culture, which have gone unappreciated and devalued.

Chapter 3

Impact of Migration on Fidelity to Naga Culture

3. Introduction

Today, concern over the disappearance of the cultural features is one of the most complicated and challenging issues facing by the Nagas. Nagas has been created out of the adjustments in the lives and the minds of the people. This is the consequence of the influence to which the Nagas have been exposed to Metropolitan cities and mixed culture came into existence. Serious consideration is now being given to restore Naga cultural elements virtually non-existent in the recent past. Therefore, this chapter dealt with impact of migration on fidelity to Naga culture, its multidimensional influence in the concept of culture. It also employed interdisciplinary studies on anthropology, psychology, sociology, influence of modernization, globalization, Christianization, social media, education, and factors of migration and its effect on the youth in the present scenario.

3.1. Youth

'Youth' in this research generally covers the group of men and women in the age group ranging from 20-30 years. Because this range of age group usually migrate to other parts of India in the context of Nagaland. This group is the biggest reservoir of human resource because of its energy, the potentialities and the tremendous hope it can offer towards a brighter future if its energies are channelized properly.[146] Youth is considered to be a powerful force in society. In

146 Nazarine V. Marbaniang, "Youth Participation in Socio-Political Awareness in the North-East," *Society and Culture in North-East India: A Christian Perspective*, edited by Saral K. Chatterji

Naga society, youth is the most active and dynamic group. The presence of many youth in a society is a clear sign of progress of a nation. Today, the youths are influenced by many factors like migration, globalization, urbanization, etc., that fidelity to Naga culture seems eroding away among the migrant youths. Not only loosing the culture, but these youths faces social, cultural and psychological crises.

Psychologist G. Stanley in his research on Youth suggests a more social orientation, a concern with youth as a socially constituted group and an interest in the ways in which they are positioned and defined within society. This approach is commonly associated with social constructionist, a set of ideas and theories that explore the ways in which concepts are made and shaped by society. A social constructionist approach to youth examines beliefs, ideas and images of youth is the product of cultural knowledge that changes over time and place.[147]

S. Cohen in his book "Folk Devils and Moral Panics" marked the emergence of a new and highly influential approach to Youth: the sub cultural. The concept of 'subculture' is important in understanding the social lives of youth. In simple terms a subculture can be seen as a group within a group. The social group frequently referred to as 'youth' has thrown up many subgroups over the years which come to be regarded as teddy boys, skinheads, punks and Goths. There is a rich vein of research that uses the concept of subculture to illustrate the many ways in which youth can be observed and studied. It is through the concept of subculture that the activities of many youths have become visible.[148] Participants in subculture often see themselves, and are seen by others, as different or oppositional in some way. Youth subcultures frequently seek to define themselves as against the culture that exists around them and particularly against the values they associates with the parental home. It could be argued that there is a tendency in traditional studies of subcultures to emphasis the unconventional, deviant and nonconformist aspects of sub cultural groups. However, within the context of nonconformity, participation in subcultures also demands considerable amount of conformity. Sub cultural groups are commonly marked by their distinctive appearance, a particular style, mode of dress, and adornment that make the participants look different, sometimes even spectacular and shocking. In the context of sub cultural groups style takes on a particular meanings as 'the means by which cultural identity and social location are negotiated and expressed.'[149] This is also true in the context of Nagaland.

(Delhi: ISPCK, 1996), 36.

147 As Cited by G. S. Hall, *Adolescence: its Psychology, and its Relations to Physiology, Anthropology, Sociology, Sex, Crime, Religion and Education* (2vols) (New York: Appleton, 1904), 74.

148 S. Cohen, *Folk Devils and Moral panics* (London: Paladin, 1972), 16.

149 Sullivan O, Etal, *Key Concepts in Communications and Cultural Studies* (London: Rout ledge, 1994), 305.

3.1.1. Present Naga Youth

The dwindling of Naga traditional culture and values within a century is the cause of human-made phenomena called 'cultural shift' in which societies change their cultural patterns such as patterns of thought, language, behavior, customs, and values as a result of encountering different influences, both superior and inferior.[150]

The cultural identity of the Naga youth today has become very vague and confusing. For Nagas, in the past, for example, looking traditional was a part of celebration during festivals and festivals were a part of their life. But this has become a mere history today. Youth do not take their festivals as a part of their life any more. There no more charm and enthusiasm in them. This obviously is due to the coming of Christianity and modernity. They take Christmas as more important than their traditional festivals. The system of boys and girls sleeping in a dormitory no more existed.[151] The easiest way to identify a Naga tribe is their tribe shawls. Every tribe has its own shawl. To have their identity of shawl is a pride for every tribe. The colors of their clothes are however, greatly changed. They modified them so that they become more sophisticated. The tribe consciousness among Nagas can be found through the identification of their color distinction. Very occasionally, Nagas use to organize cultural shows. The motive for it is to keep their culture alive. But even if they organize such a programme, the main items include only traditional dances. Every tribe has their own way of dancing with a combination of traditional dresses. They also have their own traditional musical instruments, drawings, wood carving, shaping stones, etc., they also have folk tale which can be arranged in dialogue and act them on the stage. But these are not taken due importance. Sometimes they pay due importance to their folk songs which are very long and boring for audience of this modern age. They could be modified like their shawls, but they don't do it. Due to the influence of western culture, youth do not pay any more interest in them. This too, affects the studies of literature by Naga students. Since they are so much inclined to studying western literature, which are unseen worlds for them, but an imagination, students take the view as if literature is only for fiction. The estimation about "literature as reality" is not born in their mind. It would be nothing surprising if their cultural identity is extinguished one day unless someone volunteers for its rescue.[152]

In the traditional Naga society, when a person reached old age he/she was considered as a 'know all', everyone in the community respected him/her. Wati Longchar, stated that to respect elders and parents is an ethical principle which every good citizen should follow. But today the trend is, when a person becomes

150 Inato Yekheto Shikhu, *A Rediscovery and Rebuilding of Naga Cultural Values*, 170.

151 B. Pakem, ed., *Nationality, Ethnicity and Cultural Identity in North-East India*, 331.

152 B. Pakem, ed., *Nationality, Ethnicity and Cultural Identity in North-East India*, 333.

very old, he or she is seen as useless, old fashioned and is placed out of sight.[153] It is evident that our present culture regards only youthfulness. Everybody admires primarily one's own beauty and energy. People think that happiness lies in being youthful. Deep down, most adults covet such characteristics which leave youth largely free to explore life, to take chances, and simply to have fun without the incumbrances of adult obligations. To some extent, parents want their teenage children to grow up fast not because they value so highly maturity, but because they want, eventually, to lighten their own load. Today the signs and symbols of the youth culture pervade the whole of society.[154]

Due to modernity and the influence of social media, youth are brain washed by western ideologies and consumeristic life-style of the western society. Beautiful tribal cultures are look down upon as inferior, backward, and regarded as something which needs to be discarded. Many youths become the victims of this influence and have enslaved into the consumerist fashion world.[155]

3.1.2. The Counter-Culture Youth

The counter-culture youth represents the popular youth culture and form the largest group of youth in the Naga society. They can be described as seekers who look for acceptance. They are found everywhere, from the remotest village to the urbanized towns in Nagaland and elsewhere. They share the same cultural traits with the hangover youth and live under much peer pressures. In the process of adjustment many of this counter-culture youth fall into the hangover group. Most of the counter-culture youth attend college and university. They are to a certain degree sure of what they want in life and therefore knew that they have to invest their life wisely for the sake of their future. They are also found in work places doing very well. They are educated, knowledgeable, dependable at the same, innovative and energetic. They have a wide array of exposures and are free from tight parental control and are able to make choices of their own without interference. Since this group represents the popular youth culture portrayed by the mass media, they think and conduct their lives differently from the older generation. They have to be seen from the perspective of the present day youth culture. They are found actively involved in the church and social functions. The youths know that they are the future of the church and the society and therefore are indispensable. They are more verbal in communication and constructive in their participation but have a high tendency to withdraw when their views are not respected and understood. They have a high sense of respect and responsibility towards family, church and society. They are curious and adventurous and these lead them to experiment with drugs, alcohol and sex. Often these actions are out

153 As Cited by L. Imsutoshi Jamir, *Communication in Action: The Pattern of Naga Cultural Shift*, 73.

154 L. Imsutoshi Jamir, *Communication in Action: The Pattern of Naga Cultural Shift*, 74.

155 Limatula Longkumer, *Christian Education for Adults in Tribal Context*, 39.

of peer pressures and frustration. Many get hooked up to these practices and are lost to the whirlwind of modern culture.[156]

3.1.3. Naga Youth in a Changing Scenario

Advancement in science and technology which made possible modern communication system and mass media, schools and universities, cities and towns, etc., have brought about a total revolution in modern society. Indeed, they are powerful instruments to shape people's culture, namely, their thinking, their attitudes and their behavior, their pattern of living and so on. Along with the rest of the human race, Naga society is also caught up in a world of revolution which is so dynamic and powerful that it has become almost out of human control. Naga society has been awakened from its century's old slumber. There is a tremendous shift in its culture; shift from its traditional culture to the so called modern and popular culture.[157] It is rather unfortunate that, even today there is a considerable section of people in India to whom the Naga society means nothing else than a society of head hunters, of rebellious and naked people, living in dense jungles, wielding spears. But it is not so. Like any other advanced society Naga community is also experiencing the wind of change in their behavior, thinking, life style and dress etc. biased minds may not believe it, but the present Naga society lives in the same condition and fashion as that of the present westerners or people in the other parts of India. They dress, act, eat, sleep, think and behave like any other advanced people.[158] The Nagas had gone through a period of rapid change such as humanity has never before experienced a traumatic transition in their history.[159]

Especially the contemporary Naga generation which is experiencing the era of information technology is by far the most removed and alienated from the traditional norms and values. They are not what their foreparents used to be in the past three decades. Those good old days and that peaceful environment has become a myth. The simplicity of life, the simplicity of thought and activities has taken a new shape of complexity and corruption. The division of society on the basis of the 'haves' and 'have-nots', it has become a crystal in the Naga society which was once founded on equality and respect. Community leaving has become an impossible dream in the age of consumerism.[160]

3.1.4. Transition Period

There comes a time in the life of groups as well as in the life of individuals when the old has not been completely demolished and the new has not yet taken shape. This phenomenon needs take place in all dynamic societies. The whole of

156 Zelhou Keyho, "Church and Naga Youth," 128.

157 L. Imsutoshi Jamir, *Communication in Action: The Pattern of Naga Cultural Shift*, 62.

158 L. Imsutoshi Jamir, *Communication in Action: The Pattern of Naga Cultural Shift*, 63.

159 J. H. Hutton, *The Angami Nagas*, 9.

160 L. Imsutoshi Jamir, *Communication in Action: The Pattern of Naga Cultural Shift*, 64.

Nagaland has been caught in the wind of change and age-old cultures; customs and traditions are fast changing in every society and group. Social values and social institutions are also changing rapidly.The cultural minorities therefore have often developed a sense of inferiority in recognizing the power and influence of people coming from more advanced cultures. On the contrary, it has a deep sense of pride in their own culture and way of life that they often look with disdain on the cultures of the lowlanders. That is why there is a tendency among their people to resist change and assimilation and to attempt to preserve their own identity even in extreme forms. Therefore, it is only when the majority has assured adequate safeguards in the constitution for the minorities that the latter may allow emotional integration to take place and identity themselves completely with the groups.[161] This is a period when the groups and the ethnic communities need a sense of balance and a new realization of incentives and values.

Periods of rapid change may bring about crises in the life of individuals, groups or nations. If one has a sense of balance and confidence, changes may lead to prosperity; but if balance is lost, changes may lead to disaster. That is why there is great need for a correct orientation in the life of communities. With a sense of self-direction and faith in their destiny, the cultural minorities can preserve their own cultural integrity and identity, and even integration with the nation. This integration is not acculturation or assimilation, but a sense of having come within the mosaic of the national pattern without losing one's own culture.[162]

3.2. Factors of Migration

Migration[163] issue is a complex one and to understand it, no single study can give sufficient information hence it demands wider range of interdisciplinary studies and research. It involves economics, politics, geography, demography, sociology, psychology, law, history, anthropology, environmental studies and theological as well. In a context of survival of the poor and globalization, migration becomes an option and it is not that people "want to" but "have to." The changes in the present world scenario precipitated by new wave of globalization compel people to migrate more than ever before.[164]

Migration is not just a recent development but it has been a very part of human history and intrinsic in human nature. Migration is an engine of human

161 M. M. Thomas, R. W. Taylor, ed., *Tribal Awakening*, 91.

162 M. M. Thomas, R. W. Taylor, ed., *Tribal Awakening*, 92.

163 Migration has been derived from the Latin word Migrare which implies a change of one's residence or change of one's habitation. Literally it means the shifting or moving of an individual, family, or a group of individuals from one socio-cultural area or place of locale to another, more or less permanently. S. C. Joshi, *Migration to a Metropolis* (Jaipur: RBSA Publishers, 1994), 3.

164 Gemma Tulud Gruz, "Between Identity and Security: Theological Implications of Migration in the Context of Globalization," *Theological Studies* 69/2 (2008), 356.

history.[165] Migration in itself is not at all anti-human rather it is a sign of going up to higher rung in the ladder of human existence.[166] According to the United Nations the term "migrant" refers to the people living outside their country for a year or more regardless of their reason or legal status, but excluded from this are economically disadvantaged people who are defined by the International Organization for migration as "undocumented" or "irregular migrants."[167] Whatever phrases are label to these people who are on the move for economic salvation as refugee, migrant, forced migrant, immigrant, undocumented, internally displaced person and alien have a kind of downgrading them and certainly has political, legal and social construction. These definitions rather give a complex set of values than identifying these people who are constantly on the move leaving migrants vulnerable to control, manipulation and exploitation.[168]

The pace of migration has accelerated with the growth of the cities. In this sense, the scale of migration is essentially related to the process of urbanization. Sociologists talk about the 'push-pull' factor that contributes to large-scale migration from rural and semi-urban areas to the cities and the mega cities. The rural push is created by chronic unemployment, higher education, fragmentation of landholding due to the increase in population, conditions of drought and other vagaries of nature, lack of industries, and the like. The 'urban pull' operates at the same time due to the lure of the cities. It is created by the projection of the city in popular imagination as the source of employment for the skilled and the unskilled, the growth of manufacturing industries in and around the cities, unprecedented growth of the tertiary sector, and so on.[169]

Today, people migrate due to different reasons. Scholars have put forward different theories but the very essence of migration is the same. On the context of contemporary globalization people migrate due to large economic divide between rich and poor. In this case migrant are not looking for a decent and sweet life, in fact, they leave reluctantly, out of necessity.[170] There is also "skilled transients" in the contemporary social integration where a large number of a country's highly skilled and educated population migrates to other countries that offer superior

165 Gemma Tulud Gruz, "Between Identity and Security: Theological Implications of Migration in the Context of Globalization," 357.

166 Imsenperong, "Theological Reflection on Migration," *Mapping The Context: An Interdisciplinary Exploration*, edited by Imsenperong, Menjiwapong Jamir, Walotemjen (Kohima, Nagaland: Published by the Authors, 2011), 64.

167 http://www.Iom.Int/jahia/jahia/cache/offence/pit/1674?entryID=932 (Accesses on September 13, 2011).

168 Roger Zetter, "Labeling Refugees: The forming of Transformation of a Bureaucratic Identity," *Journal of Refugee Studies* 4 (1991), 40.

169 M. T. Joseph, "Migration and Identity Formation: A Case Study of Dalit Assertation in Aurangabad, Maharashtra," *Migration and Mission in India*, edited by L. Stanislaus SVD and Jose Joseph SVD (Delhi: Ishvani Kendra / ISPCK, 2007), 95.

170 Imsenperong, "Theological Reflection on Migration," 65.

economic and social opportunities. While a diverse range of motivation lie behind skilled migrants- often associated with "brain drain", intentions to move, it is possible to draw some of the common factors such as wages disparity, employment opportunity, professional development, networks and socio-economic and political condition in countries of origin.[171]

S. Dorothy, in his research "Information on Migration Differentials," found that Territorial distribution continuously undergoes changes because of migration. Migration in search of education or occupations and better prospects or migration forced by deteriorating economic conditions and employment opportunities is an action primarily of the youth population. "Perhaps the most universal finding about the characteristics of migration is the fact that migrants tend to be young." Youth continues to be the main migration group, and also the principle contributor to urbanization. Migration is a phenomenon resulting from many socio-economic factors and in many countries the incidence of migration is noted to be especially high in the early working age among males and around the age of marriage among women.[172] Migration from rural to urban areas for education and unemployment, and search for white-collar jobs contribute to higher rate of unemployment in urban compared to rural India. This is also true in the context of Nagaland that many are migrating to urban areas for education and in search of jobs.

3.2.1. Impact of Globalization on Migrant Youth

Globalization is a complex multi-dimensional phenomenon that involves economic, political, social, cultural, technological, and environmental aspects. The whole world has become smaller. Political and economic development tends to have global implications. Migrations and population shifts in the wake of wars and natural catastrophes as well as new job opportunities in technologically developed countries have become a common phenomenon.[173] In the modern epoch of globalization, cultural contact between different communities will increase tremendously.[174] Globalization as a historical process is beyond ordinary individuals to change. The history of colonialism leading to worldwide migrations, improved modes of travel and trade, international media and technological expansion, the militarization of the world, are all parts of the historical process called globalization. Throughout history, communities and governments everywhere have seldom been satisfied staying within their immediate

171 Imsenperong, "Theological Reflection on Migration," 67.

172 As Cited by S. Saraswathi, *Youth in India* (New Delhi: Indian Council of Social Science Research, 1988), 29.

173 S. M. Michael, *Christianity and Cultures: Anthropological Insights for Christian Mission in India*, 28.

174 S. M. Michael, *Christianity and Cultures: Anthropological Insights for Christian Mission in India*, 35.

surroundings and have ventured out to other lands and climes for all kinds of reasons; from conquest, economic gain and proselytization to exploration and the advancement of knowledge. That is to say, globalization has been unstoppable and its effects have not been entirely pernicious.[175]

Globalization is more an internal attitude than a historical and external phenomenon. It is a way of being in the world; it sees the world as a cultural and intellectual global village. It takes a holistic view of things, it is sensitive to the interconnections among parts, and it responds favorably to the common good. That is, in the acceptance of the world as the common stage for all human beings, at the same time having ties to specific places and cultures. The function of human knowledge and understanding, and common good in world whose past has handed to a global village with global problems, along with the moral and technological tools to solve them.[176]

In the context of Nagaland, many youths than ever are on the move, the increasing flow and sharing of information, connections, or links of people around the world has impacted so much upon the migrant youth. This leads to increase of the greatest shift of culture among migrant Naga youth. Hence, the present migrant Naga youth with the contact of globalization soon get estranged from the Naga traditional activities and cultural values.

3.2.2. Family Life on the Migrant Youth

The status of youth in society and their physical and mental well-being are conditioned to some extent by their place, role, and status within the family set up. The inevitable process of migration, pressures of modernization and urbanization, and increasing influence of politicization, economic conditions and mass media, are slowly but definitely showing some changes from their traditional patterns. As the number of youth migrants in search of employment and education is showing an upward trend in certain metropolitan centers like Bangaluru, Mumbai, Kolkata, Delhi and Chennai, migration among youth have been variously described as 'inter-generational conflict' where the life-style, tastes and ambitions of the youth in general tend to collide with family norms.

It is quite likely that for the bulk of the rural youth who had 'migrated' from the villages to the university or the colleges with new aspirations and professional goals, the values and the life-patterns represented by their parents, had very little worth emulating. Once they had shifted to the cities, they were completely overwhelmed by the pattern of life, the news norms prevalent on the campuses,

175 Paul Pimomo, "From Naga Village to the Global Village: The Common Good and Human Rights," *Nagas Today Indigenous Discourse*, edited by Zuchamo Yanthan, et al., (Delhi: Published by Naga Students' Union, 2010), 261.

176 Paul Pimomo, "From Naga Village to the Global Village: The Common Good and Human Rights," *Nagas Today Indigenous Discourse*, 262.

and were dazzled by the new values.[177] In the rural context, also urbanization and differential impact of education and development have given rise to such conflicts. Family structure, concepts of obligations, decision-making patterns and inter-relationship between the youth and the old in various types of households are undergoing modifications. The linkage between them may be established by further probe into each area which may help in developing an integrated approach to the task of building the personality of youth.[178]

3.2.3. Social Impacts on the Migrant Youth

It has increased the struggle of the youth for identity and self-hood. This struggle is all the more crucial for the youngsters in the country. One cannot predict the social security and social status of youth of unemployment, and poverty by the influence of globalization.[179] Because of the social fragmentation and the moral erosion, some of the youth are involving in illegal activities, eg., liquor, smoking, drug addiction, etc., in cities and professional colleges and higher education institutions nowadays, the above vices are very common. This free value set-up swallows the youth and it affects the social and family fabric, and eventually destroy the church and society.[180] This is to be taken as an urgent concern of the church in Naga society today.

The other social impact of migration on youth is increasing greed, selfishness, and indiscipline on individual and corporate level. The result is fast erosion of traditional values, a constraint on the individual conscience, and the corporate responsibility. The consequences of the process of migration are fragmentation of the society and moral erosion of individuals, and these put great social impacts on youth today.[181]

3.2.4. Cultural Impacts on the Migrant Youth

It can be said that cultures fundamentally mediate power relations.[182] The fast diffusion of western-based customs and values has caused the destruction of traditional culture at a high rate not seen before. The growing homogenization in culture, consumption patterns, and values, imposed by globalization process is undermining or destroying cultural and biological diversities world over. This process never respects the blessing of diversity as a wealth of civilization, rather accelerates the chauvinistic elements that attempt to adulterate minority cultures

177 Sudhir Kakar, ed., *Identity And Adulthood* (Delhi: Oxford University Press, n.d), 63.

178 S. Saraswathi, *Youth in India*, 236.

179 Vinod Victor, "Contemporary Challenges of Youth Ministry," *NCC Review* 119/9 (October, 1999), 815.

180 Y. Moses, "Youth in India Today," *NCC Review* 119/10 (November, 1997), 686.

181 Nebu Mathson, *Impact of Globalization on the Indian Youth: A Review of the Response of NCCI*, 68.

182 S. Lazar, "Impact of Globalization on Culture," *NCC Review* 119/1 (January, 1999), 45.

and identities.[183] In homogenization, the local society and individual lose their identity and their problems remain unsolved. Youth in the world are generally sold out to media-induced consumer culture.[184] This can be seen very clearly in the life style of youth. The holistic understanding of reality was brushed aside in favor of fragmented understanding. Western culture emphasizes the importance of private interest. In place of personal dependence, it introduced personal indifference. These features of western culture has influenced youth and are slowly destroying community feeling. It turned youth into atomic individuals isolated from community, and forced them into self-indulgence to overcome boredom, fear and anxiety arising from their isolation from the community.[185]

Today more and younger people are "brand" conscious. Anyone not ascribing to the emerging foreign exhibitors is not considered as civilized or cultured. This phenomenon has also negated all forms of local cultural expressions. The folk songs and dances, which were considered as community-based activities, are now considered as backward and irrelevant. Instead they have pop, rap, and jazz of the exuberant West that teaches only a show biz. Another influence of western culture on youth is in attire. Now-a-days youth are imitating the western cultural dress and habits. The western culture is highly color-conscious. Young boys adopt the tall, muscular, and clean-shaven male method. The young girls are also trying to imitate the western culture in dress and style that in effect shows the mean goal of commercializing womanhood.[186]

3.2.5. Psycho-social Impacts on the Migrant Youth

The transition from one context to another for the migrant often encompasses changes in every aspect of daily life from the language one speaks to the ways in which groups and individuals interact. Once the migrant resettle in a host country new belief systems, values and more challenge their adjustment and at the same time create a psycho-social conflict and crisis.[187] There are two important factors in the adaptation to a new culture that either increase or decrease susceptibility to poor mental health. First, conflict in the development of identity among the adolescents has consistently been related to poor psychological adjustment. Second, even though the adaptive process to a new culture can make provision

183 Kishan Deheragoda, "Impact of Globalization on the Third World Cultures," *Dialogue* (NS) 24/ (1997), 12

184 Kishan Deheragoda, "Impact of Globalization on the Third World Cultures," 4.

185 S. Lazar, "Impact of Globalization on Culture," 49.

186 Nebu Mathson, *Impact of Globalization on the Indian Youth: A Review of the Response of NCCI*, 70.

187 Jaya Earnest, *Adolescent and Young Refugee Perspective on Psychosocial Wellbeing* (Melbourne: Common Ground Publishing, 2006), 80.

for good outcomes, it can also increase psychological vulnerability through the creation of inter-generational stress.[188]

Psychologist Durganand Sinha, analysis the results of three empirical studies on intergenerational differences, where he finds the youth of today characterized by a widespread ambiguity in values and the instability, and uncertainty in the choice of role-models. The historical background of rapid social change and the migration of youth from rural areas to the cities, makes him feel that this role diffusion and value ambiguity has exacerbated the identity confusion of youth and is putting a strain on society's institutions which depend upon youth for their renewal.[189]

Erik Erikson's account of migrant youth development is distinctive in that, he considers youth within the context of their society, paying attention to work, prevailing ideologies and cultural milieu. Youth will have most affirmatively exciting time of it which finds itself in the wave of a technological, economic or ideological trend seemingly promising all that youthful vitality could ask for. In general, it is the inability to settle on an occupational identity which most disturbs youth, to keep themselves together they temporarily over identity with the heroes of cliques and crowds to the point of an apparently complete loss of individuality.[190] Psychosocial issues are psychological well-being, social integration, or the reduction of discrimination and prejudice emphasis the role of variable that can facilitate structural level changes, as influencing social policies and programmes, efforts to translate theories and research into effective interventions to build active and effective partnership with community members.[191]

The psychological dynamics of this process are extremely complex even in the context of Naga migrant youth. The process of migration requires them to accommodate environment changes and obviously the environment is organized to induce such changes.

3.2.6. Everyday Life Impacts on Migrant Youth

Everyday life especially in metropolises is about the practices of the routine. It is about lifestyle, consumption, and social interaction/relations. Experience is the cornerstone of everyday life. Experience is everyday life- how they experience traffic, clothing, food, and social relations on public transport, the sense of community or entertainment constitutes their everyday culture. Cultural studies foregrounds experience, but see it as the means to analyze the relations that construct reality, in order to make this shift from experience to reality.[192]

---

188 Jaya Earnest, *Adolescent and Young Refugee Perspective on Psychosocial Wellbeing*, 81.

189 As Cited by Sudhir Kakar, ed., *Identity And Adulthood*, xii.

190 Erik Erikson, *Identity, Youth And Crises* (New York: Norton & Co, 1968), 128.

191 https:/www my.vanderbilt.edu/perkins/files/2011/09/perkins-etal-2011.psychosocial-studies-of-migration (Accesses, Dec. 29,2017).

192 Pramod K. Nayar, *An introduction to Cultural Studies* (New Delhi: Viva Books, 2009), 28.

Experience is express through language: how they express what they experience, how they speak with others and how they tell their stories. When they listen to others they decode their meanings, they mediate their experience through the language and cultural codes. Language and representation are therefore integral to the experience and construction of reality. If experience and everyday life are central to culture change, then it is important to see how these experiences of the everyday become language, images and representations.

Everyday life impacts on migrant youth proceeds through everyday living experiences: the food they eat the fashions they adopt, the entertainment they prefer or the festivals they celebrate. Thus, migrant people believe leading their everyday lives produce culture. Culture is not some distinct realm produced elsewhere to be consumed by the people. It is the consequences of experiences and responses. It is in the everyday that culture is made.[193]

3.3. Understanding Culture

The word "Culture" is derived from the Latin word "Cool-ere" which literally means, "to inhabit", "to cultivate", or "to honor" referring to the whole aspect of human activity. Thus to understand it wholly, culture is the way in which people humanize nature. Humans look at the world around them and make it a meaningful place to live in. This meaning is imposed upon the structures of nature in relation to human life. The meaning comes from the particular way they look at God, humans and the universe. They organize their community and their life in accordance with the meaning they give to the world. Their worldview gives them an orientation and a value system that guides their choices in life. Meaning and values system find expression in myths and symbols, in literature and art, in rituals and attitudes that structure social relationships, in festivals and other cultural products that celebrate life and relationships. Thus with its complexity, it is understood that culture is not an entity in itself, but also in relation to the existence of nature, community and society.[194] No culture can remain totally static and unchanging, because humans have the capacity to cumulate knowledge and alter their external surroundings and internal thought processes. They are also highly prone to be influenced by external forces and ideas. The more opportunity a society gets to know another society, the more it undergoes transformation. Once an individual or institution in a society accepts something new, it gets diffused depending upon other conditions. It has been pointed out that all elements of culture are interrelated; even a minor change in one element of one cultural system can have a profound impact on the other cultural system. Although, one may agree with the view of some scholars to guard against seeing culture only in terms of a hoary and unsullied past, it must also be accounted that what one particular society or community has today is dominantly the residue of

193 Pramod K. Nayar, *An introduction to Cultural Studies*, 29.

194 Inato Yekheto Shikhu, *A Rediscovery and Rebuilding of Naga Cultural Values*, 25.

the past. They judge and determine things based on their cultural understanding whether the issues are modern, post-modern, or traditional. When people speak of their own culture, there is generally a tendency to make it a sustained song of praise about its enduring values, overlooking often that, as in all other human cultures, there are imperfections and inadequacies, arising sometimes as a result of the nature of the continuance of habits and traditions suited to an earlier age.

Experts in the field of cultural study has given the terms in various aspects, K. M. Panikkar defines culture, as the complex of ideas, conceptions, developed qualities, and organized relationships and courtesies that exist generally in a society and a civilized society. The difference between a cultured society and a civilized society is that, while the latter is one which is organized under conditions ministering to the welfare of the community, the former, the cultured society, is one which emphasizes the ideals, conduct, relationships, aesthetic and other values which are cherished in the society. So, the problem of culture can be discussed from the point of view of the whole people only on the assumption that there are, broadly speaking, a community of thought, a similarity of conduct and behavior, a common general approach to fundamental problems, which arise from shared traditions and ideals. It is this common outlook which is described as the culture of a country or a people.[195]

Bronislaw Malinowski defines, culture is an integral composed of partly autonomous, partly coordinated institutions. It is integrated on a series of principles such as the community of blood through procreation; the contiguity in space related to cooperation; the specialization in activities; and last but not least, the use of power in political organization. Each culture owes its completeness and self-sufficiency to the fact that it satisfies the whole range of basic, instrumental and integrative needs.[196]

3.3.1. Culture is Understood as a Human Universal

"Culture" has "nature," therefore, as its contrast term. What is not culture is natural, in the sense of being merely "physio-biological" or "biological" are quite closely associated to form this contrast with culture. Animals are biologically determined in their behaviors. Human beings because they lack biologically based blueprints for behavior, are formless and aimless, hardly human at all, without culture:

> The behavior patterns of...animals are...to a much greater extent, given them their physical structure...For man (sic), what are innately given are extremely general response capacities...Undirected by culture...man's behavior would be virtually ungovernable, a mere

195 K. M. Panikkar, *The Features of Indian Culture* (Chowpatty: Bombay-7: Bharatiya Vidya Bhavan, 1967), 2.

196 Bronislaw Malinowski, *A Scientific Theory of Culture* (Chapel Hill: University of North Carolina Press, 1994), 40.

> chaos of pointless acts and exploding emotions, his experiences virtually shapeless. Culture...is not just an ornament of human existence but...an essential condition for it.[197]

All people have culture but they do not have the same one. What culture amounts to varies widely with time and place? "The fact of 'culture' is common to all; the particular pattern of culture differs among all."[198] Culture therefore comes in the plural; the anthropologist speaks of cultures. The search for commonalities in culture has had its ups and downs in anthropology, but the recognition of marked differences in human behavior is the prior founding intuition of the discipline generally. Anthropology's object is to come to terms with significant differences in human behavior worldwide. It justifies its existence as a discipline by a distinctive account of such differences-they are cultural, and not products, say, of biology or climate. Indeed, the primary indicator of culture for the anthropologists is diversity. Forms of human behavior are usually discussed in terms of culture precisely when it is clear that such forms may be absent elsewhere. That human beings eat is not attributable to culture; all people do so as a function of somatic needs. That some humans never eat domesticated pigs and cows can be attributed to culture just because it is known that others do.[199]

3.3.1.1. Culture Varies with Social Group and Conceived as Their Entire Way of Life

The differences that break culture into a plurality of forms follow differences between such groups. If cultures differ from one another, that is because they are the cultures of different societies. "A Culture: the specific pattern of behaviors which distinguishes any society from all others."[200]

Everything about the group, distinguishes it from others, be it social habits, institutions, rituals, artifacts, categorical schemes, beliefs and values. Thus, "culture is essentially a construct that describes the total body of beliefs, behaviors, knowledge, sanctions, values and goals that mark the way of life of the people.... In the final analysis it comprises the things that people have, the things they do, and what they think."[201] If it is the culture of a group, a culture is evidently what every member of the group more or less shares. "They may...identify 'culture' with the extent to which the conventionalized behavior of members of the society

197 Kathryn Tanner, *Theories of Culture* (Minneapolis: Fortress Press, 1997), 26.

198 John Bennett and Melvin Tumin, *Social Life* (New York: Alfred A. Knopf, 1948), 209, cited in Alfred L. Kroeber and Klyde Kluckhohn, *Culture: A Critical Review of Concepts and Definitions* (Cambridge, Mass: Papers of the Peabody Museum of America Archaeology and Ethnology, Harvard University, 1952), 51.

199 John Bennett and Melvin Tumin, *Social Life*, 209.

200 Melvin Herskovitz, *Man and His Works* (New York: Alfred A. Knopf, 1948), 625, cited by Kroeber and Kluckhohn, *Culture*, 44.

201 Kathryn Tanner, *Theories of Culture*, 27.

is for all the same."[202] Culture does not function to regulate or repress it. Indeed, there is nothing to human life with any definite form or shape of its own that might exist outside culture so as to be so regulated or repressed. Culture makes human life from the first; it is in that sense a constitutive medium and not some secondary influence on it. Human beings get from culture all the shape, form, and definiteness their actions manifest. Culture is therefore not talked about as redirecting or constraining already-established behaviors, with clearly defined goals and underlying interests-not talked about as redirecting or constraining, say, the rapacious and willful inclinations of the profligate and unrefined. If culture works on anything, it works on bare animal or bodily based capacities with an extensive and indefinite range of possible outcomes. Those capacities, of themselves and without the guidance of culture, might lead in any number of different directions and take any number of different forms.[203]

3.3.1.2. Cultures are Conventions in the Sense that they are Human Constructions

"Everything…created by human, in the process of living, comes within the concept of culture."[204] Human beings may be nothing without culture but they are responsible for what culture amounts to in any particular place and time, i.e., for the particular shapes cultures take, and for their maintenance. An anthropologist in the field observes a culture only insofar as it is already formed and up and running in the lives of human beings, but he or she nevertheless presumes its emergence as the cumulative effect of past human interactions that have become habitual or routine over time, and he or she has direct observational knowledge in any case of the ongoing educative efforts necessary to transmit it to future generations. A culture is viewed by the anthropologist, in short, as "the accumulated transmissible results of past behaviors in association,"[205] culture in this way becomes another name for traditional inheritance, for the customary behaviors that result from and are handed down by way of human historical processes. "Culture means…traditional behavior which has been developed by the human race and is successfully learn by each generation."[206] Society decisively shapes the character of its members: The character of one's culture is contingent but one's conformity to it is not. Individuals may influence the furthering or hampering its continuation over time. Their capacity to do so is implied by the conventional character of culture. But this agency on the part of individuals is

202 Robert Redfield, *The Folk Culture of the Yucatan* (Chicago: University of Chicago Press, 1941), 133.

203 Kathryn Tanner, *Theories of Culture*, 28.

204 Edward Reuter and R. E. Park , ed., *Race and Culture* (New York: McGraw-Hill, 1939), 191.

205 L. J. Carr, "Situational Psychology," *American Journal of Sociology* 51 (1945), 137.

206 Margaret Mead, *Cooperation and Competition among Primitive Peoples* (NewYork: McGraw-Hill, 1937), 17.

always subsequent to, and predicated upon, their prior formation by the culture into which they were born. They first became the people they are by being formed by the culture of their society, by internalizing as children, in the process of being socialized, and already existing culture, a culture of which they simply found themselves apart and could have done "passive potters" of a culture: "they are born into different...ways of life, and these they must follow because they have no other choice."[207] The moment a baby is born, the customs and habits of the society into which he/she is born is imparted to him/her and becomes part of that society and culture, which condition the thinking, and acting of a community or people. Culture finds conceptual expression in ethics, philosophy and law. It also embodied in economic, social, political, and cultural institutions and structures.[208]

The above discussion is concerned with how culture manifests itself in the migration process, for culture are shared beliefs, customs, values, attitude, etc., which identify a central role in understanding migration. Therefore, it is to understand migration as cultural events, it has linked beneath the surface for time and space. As such migration and cultural contact draws from subject matters covering the entire social sciences, anthropology, psychology, sociology, and other related fields of the study.

3.3.2. Cultural Anthropology

Anthropology[209] is the study of human in his/her relation to the society. According to Eugene Nida, "Anthropology is essentially the science of learned human behavior." Nida's further words: "the science of human culture."[210] Kroeber, has defined anthropology as "the science of groups of human, and their behavior and productions."[211] It is the study of human culture, or the study of the works of humans, meaning all the things they do and make. It includes pre-historic cultures, known as archaeology; the analytical study of human societies is called ethnology, social anthropology, or socio-cultural anthropology. Anthropology is total or holistic study of human. This science is total study of human because it studies human as a whole. The study of human as a whole includes their biological, cultural, social, economic, political, religious, aesthetic, artistic, linguistic, historical, medical and developmental beings.[212]

---

207 John Dollard and Allison Davis, *Children of Bondage* (Washington, D.C.: American Council on Education, 1940), 4.

208 S. Kappen, *Towards a Holistic Cultural Paradigm* (Tiruvalla: Christava Sahitya Samithy, 2003), 79.

209 Anthropology is the "The Science of Man and his Work" as defined by M. J. Herskovits. S. D. Ponraj, *An Introduction to Missionary Anthropology*, rev.ed. (Chennai: Mission Educational Books, 2010), 35.

210 Eugene A. Nida, *Customs and Customs* (New York: Harper and Brothers, 1954), 15.

211 A. L. Kroeber, *Anthropology*, rev. ed. (New York: Harcourt, Brace and company, 1948), 1.

212 Gaya Pandey, *Developmental Anthropology* (Delhi: Concept Publishing Company, 2008), 1.

Cultural Anthropology is socially learned traits- traits are learned by an individual through communication and interaction with other individuals. Technically, cultural anthropology has three major subdivisions- archaeology, linguistics, and ethnology. Archaeology attempts to reconstruct and describe the socially learned traits of prehistoric and historic populations. In the absence of written records, archaeology relies heavily on the excavation and interpretation of material remains or artifacts. Linguistic is concerned with language as a socially learned trait. Ethnology, by investigating the socially learned traits of historic and contemporary populations, attempts to describe the world's diverse cultural system and, through the cross-cultural comparison of these systems, to arrive at valid generalizations about human nature and the human condition.[213]

According to anthropologists, one commonly understood meaning of culture is that it is a learned behavior as opposed to the instinctual behavior of animals. Although in human history, people as individuals and as groups have been coping with their individual and social needs. Through trial and error method, they have been learning their life lessons. These, include how to produce, distribute and consume material goods; how to relate to one another as social beings leading to family, kinship and other social organizations; how to organize society politically so that every member of a group may feel safe and secure; and how to give meaning to one's life[214] experience through religion, philosophy, world-view, etc. All this learned and accumulated wisdom of humanity is known as culture. Thus, culture becomes a kind of a plan or a design by which older members of a society educate the younger members to meet their life needs. The experience of different groups of people at different places and times bring forth innumerable cultural ways. In the words of Clyde Kluckhohn "culture refers to the distinctive way of life of a group of people, their complete design of living."[215]

Cultural anthropology presumes that every socio-cultural environment depends on the way human beings give each cultural context meaning and are in turn changed in response to that socio-cultural environment. Shweder defines cultural anthropology as "the study of the ways subject and object, self and other, psyche and culture, person and context, figure and ground, practitioner and practice live together, require each other, and dynamically, dialectically and jointly make each other up."[216] The study of anthropology and its findings can be applied to identify and solve a wide range of human problems, both

213 S. M. Michael, *Christianity and Cultures: Anthropological Insights for Christian Mission in India* (Delhi: ISPCK, 2015), ix.

214 S. M. Michael, *Christianity and Cultures: Anthropological Insights for Christian Mission in India*, 1.

215 As quoted by S. M. Michael, *Christianity and Cultures: Anthropological Insights for Christian Mission in India*, 2.

216 As quoted by Paul B. Pedersen, *Culture-Centered Counselling Interventions* (London: Sage Publications, 1997), 8.

secular and spiritual.[217] By living and doing fieldwork in a particular society over a long period of time, anthropologists try to discover what is the cultural system of a community. Cultures are built on guidelines and rules. By doing fieldwork the anthropologists discover these guidelines and rules. Two basic field research techniques are employed by anthologists to gather this type of cultural data- participant observation and interviewing. Using these techniques, the anthropologists carefully keeps written records (field notes) about what people do (actions), what people say (speech/words), and what people make (artifacts) so that a systematic analysis of the cultural system can be made at a later time. Without carefully written field notes, the anthropologists cannot study cultural behavior of human beings.[218] The only distinguishing characteristic between the animal and human world is that humans possess culture.

Anthropology is the study of human beings; a question of great interest to anthropologists is the origin of humanity. Many- but by no means all- anthropologists see human beings as a product of an evolutionary process. Charles Darwin's specific scheme of evolution has long since been replaced by newer schemes, all the schemes hold to the following basic principles:

1. Living things change from generation to generation, producing descendants with new characteristics.
2. The process has continued for such a long period of time that it has produced all the species of life now present or extinct.
3. That all living things, plants, animals, and humans are related to each other and have a common origin.[219]

Human beings have been migrating from one place to place and they have been building cultures through inventions, discovery and diffusion. An anthropological view of humanity is holistic in nature, i.e., anthropologists seek generalizations about humans and their behavior from all dimensions, economic, social, political and religious.[220] Thus, the key concept in the study of anthropology is migration. People migrating from one place to another have a prominent place in the discipline of anthropology, which includes the study of the interaction between beliefs and behaviors, corporate groups, and social relationships, resulted in an emphasis in migration studies on matters of adaption and cultural change.

---

217 S. D. Ponraj, *An Introduction to Missionary Anthropology*, rev.ed., 42.

218 S. M. Michael, *Christianity and Cultures: Anthropological Insights for Christian Mission in India*, 1.

219 As Cited by Stephen A. Grunlan & Marvin K. Mayers, *Cultural Anthropology: A Christian Perspective*, 2nd ed. (Grand Rapids, Michigan: Zondervan Publishing House, 1988), 37.

220 S. M. Michael, *Christianity and Cultures: Anthropological Insights for Christian Mission in India*, 149.

3.3.3. Psychology and Culture

Psychology is the science of human behavior. This science, more than any other social science, focuses on the individual. Psychology shares one major field of interest with sociology, namely social psychology. Social psychology is the science of the behavior of the individual in society. It studies the way in which personality and behavior are influenced by the social context.[221] Psychology studies the human as a behaving individual.[222] In recent years considerable attention has been paid on the cultural perspectives in Psychology. It has been found that multidimensional variations of behavior are prompted by cultural differences because culture is the experience of nature which is revealed in the modes of living and thinking, literature, religion, customs and all other possible roots of life which could be inculcated by a person. Cultures, in the form of shared organization of human creations like symbols and ideas, are often revealed to as narratives and to understand them.[223] Culture is the full set of specific knowledge, attitude, behavior and a product that characterizes an identifiable group of people. It appears that variations in culture cause variation in behavior.[224]

The initial premise of cultural historical school is that human psychological processes emerge through culturally mediated historically developed, practical activity. Human mind and the associated psychological processes emerge simultaneously with a new form of behavior in which humans modified the material objects as means of regulating interactions with the world and one another.[225] It is being realized that psychological processes are rooted in historically variable and culturally mediated practical activities. Construction of multiple socio-historically grounded realities and apprehending reality from an observer-independent perspective by people is virtually impossible. Cultural psychological studies underscore the constitutive role of the context of activities.[226] The culture embedded of thought and action is being emphasized. This change signifies the possibilities of developing a situated and shared conception of reality. It goes beyond the positivist position and proposes that the knowledge claims in the human domain are relative to the setting in which they are grounded.[227]

---

221 C. N. Shankar Rao, *Sociology: Principles of Sociology with an Introduction to Social Thought* (New Delhi: S. Chand & Company, 2009), 8.

222 C. N. Shankar Rao, *Sociology: Principles of Sociology with an Introduction to Social Thought*, 17.

223 Aradhana Shukla, "Culture and Our Understanding," *Culture Cognition and Behaviour*, edited by Aradhana Shukla (New Delhi: Concept Publishing Company, 2009), 15.

224 Aradhana Shukla, "Culture and Our Understanding,"16.

225 Minati Panda and Ajit K. Mohanty, "Socio-Cultural Construction of Mind and Language," *Culture Cognition and Behaviour*, edited by Aradhana Shukla (New Delhi: Concept Publishing Company, 2009), 191.

226 Girishwar Misra and Ajit K. Mohanty, *Perspectives on Indigenous Psychology*, edited by Girishwar Misra and Ajit K. Mohanty (New Delhi: Concept Publishing Company, 2002), 16.

227 Girishwar Misra and Ajit K. Mohanty, *Perspectives on Indigenous Psychology*, 17.

Psychologically, the doctrine holds that "the resemblances between institutions of different cultures are to be accounted for by the similar capacities of all human". This psychic unity results both in cultural similarities and in rather impressive similarities in the thought processes of the people of various cultures. The reason for the differences between cultures does not seem to lie in differences in people's fundamental reasoning processes but in differences in "the premises on which such reasoning rests and the basic categories that influence the judgment of different peoples."[228] Kluckhohn states, that behind the differing cultural approaches to reasoning and thinking, there is a series of basic psychological needs. Among these are (1) the need for meaning in life and (2) the need for people to maintain their individual psyches. People seek understanding of life and freedom from the threat of psychological crippling. The psychologist, Maslow attempts to distinguish various levels of psychological needs that are basic to humankind. He sees these needs as biologically based or "instinctual." They are: *the safety needs*- the need people have for security, stability, dependency, protection, freedom from fear, from anxiety and chaos, need for structure, order, law, limits, strength in the protector, and so on. *Love and belonging needs*- people need to feel wanted and loved by other people. *Esteem needs*- the desire for strength, achievement, adequacy, mastery and competence, reputation or prestige, status, fame and glory, dominance, recognition, attention, importance, dignity of appreciation. *Spiritual characteristics*- men and women were made God, the Christian contends, and they will not find the true meaning of life until they get into a relationship with God. *Socio-culturally*- the high rate degree of human commonality in biological, psychological, and spiritual realms is expressed in the development and maintenance of human society and culture.[229] This results in widespread and striking similarities in the basics of the socio-cultural systems in terms of which human beings operate.

Likewise, psychological determines on the motivational and decisional approaches to migration behavior at the most basic level, the biological, psychological, and spiritual needs give rise to a series of universal cultural functions- functions performed by every culture. Biologically, the need for such necessities like food, shelter, air, etc., requires that each culture provide for the continuous obtaining of these biological necessities. Psychological level, psychological integration, some degree of freedom, and whatever other basic psychological needs human beings have. Spiritually, all cultures provide explanations of and response to beings and/or powers beyond the biological and psychological.

---

228 Charles H. Kraft, *Christianity in Culture* (New York: Orbis Books, 1979), 85.

229 As Cited by Charles H. Kraft, *Christianity in Culture*, 86.

3.3.4. Sociology and Culture

Sociology is the study of social life and behavior, especially in relation to social systems, how they work, how they change, the consequence they produce and their complex relation to people's lives. Sociology has been called the study of society, of human societies and their cultures, of human behaviors, of social interactions and relationships, of human in groups, of groups of people, of human's social life, of the social bond, of social institutions, of social actions, of social structure and social systems, and in various other ways.[230] Auguste Comte, who invented the word sociology, did not specify in detail the sub-fields of sociology, but he did propose to divide the sociology into two major groupings: 1. Social Statics: study of social structure, functions, social system, social relationships, etc., 2. Social Dynamics: Study of social change, development, transformation and revolutions, etc. He argued that sociology should contribute to the welfare of the humanity by using science to understand and control human behavior.[231]

3.3.4.1. Social Change and Cultural Change

The difference between social change and cultural change has a great sociological importance. 'Social change' means only such alterations as occur in social organization, that is , structure and functions of society. Social change, in this sense, is only a part of what is essentially a broader category called "cultural change." The term 'cultural change' according to Kingsley Davis, "embraces all changes occurring in any branch of culture including art, science, technology, philosophy, etc., as well as changes in the forms and rules of social organization."[232] As he says, culture change is broader than social change, and social change is only a part of it. All social changes are cultural changes, but all cultural changes need not necessarily be the social changes also. Cultural changes can be called social changes only when they affect human relations and the social organization and cause some variation in them. Cultural change is thus much broader than the social change. No part of culture is totally unrelated to the social order, but it remains true that changes sometimes occur in these branches without noticeably affecting the social system. Sociologically, therefore, change in culture only to the extent that it arises from or has an effect on social organization.[233]

Contemporary change is probably everywhere and its consequences may also be everywhere. Besides, increasing the expectations of life, it has brought many social problems in its train to humanity. In the modern world social change has taken on some special qualities and magnitudes. The modes of life and social

---

230 H. K. Rawat, *Sociology: Basic Concepts* (New Delhi: Rawat Publications, 2007), 4.

231 As Cited by H. K. Rawat, *Sociology: Basic Concepts*, 12.

232 As Cited by C. N. Shankar Rao, *Sociology: Principles of Sociology with an Introduction to Social Thought*, 485.

233 C. N. Shankar Rao, *Sociology: Principles of Sociology with an Introduction to Social Thought*, 486.

institutions characteristic of the modern world are radically different from those even the recent past. During the period of only two or three centuries human social life has been wrenched away from the types of social order in which people lived for thousands of years.[234]

All cultures change, although they do so in different ways and at different rates. Culture is normally regarded as conservative, especially in its non-material aspects. For example, people are reluctant to give up old values, customs and beliefs in favor of new ones. Changes in one area of culture affect in some way or the other, some other parts of culture. This is so because culture is strongly integrated. Further, on change may lead to another. Some of the basic changes, for example, the ways in which a society earns its living or conducts its economic activity and exploits the environment, can affect almost all the other cultural elements.[235] Variety is endless in human life. Changes in culture may also add to it. Culture is neither uniform nor static. It is dynamic. In complex societies culture is changing all the times. In every passing period it presents new facets and elements. Hence, its influence on the developing personality cannot be uniform.[236]

Culture tends to give direction and momentum to social change and to set limits beyond which social change may not go. Social change is a distinct thing from cultural or civilization change. Cultural change includes change in ideology, administrative system, technology, etc., cultural change indicates changes in the accepted mode of life, habit patterns, and the life-style. These changes may include such things as the invention of the automobile, TV, changing concepts of property and morality, new forms of music, art, or dance or the trends of sex quality. Cultural change refers to all changes occurring in any branch of culture including art, science, technology, philosophy, etc., as well as changes in the forms and rules of social organizations. In a nutshell, it may be said that social relationships among people in groups, whereas cultural change refers to change in material and non-material cultural elements both.[237]

3.3.4.2. Stability and Change in Culture

Culture is a living system. A culture will often have to adapt to changes occurring in the world. Interventions, discoveries, conquests, and contacts with other cultures often bring new challenges which necessitate adaptation to new situations. Hence, cultures will often be in the process of change. Today, almost all cultures are affected by modern global trends and the enormous technological innovations. The ability of cultures to adapt to change differs. Some cultures tend to stress the need for stability in order to preserve their cultural identity in the

234 H. K. Rawat, *Sociology: Basic Concepts*, 72.

235 C. N. Shankar Rao, *Sociology: Principles of Sociology with an Introduction to Social Thought*, 201.

236 C. N. Shankar Rao, *Sociology: Principles of Sociology with an Introduction to Social Thought*, 2.

237 H. K. Rawat, *Sociology: Basic Concepts*, 272.

fast changing world of today. Others adjust their institutions fast to fit into the process of change.[238]

3.4. Modernization and Urbanization

Modernization[239] is a process which indicates the adaptation of the modern ways of life and values. It refers to an attempt on the part of the people, particularly those who are custom-bound, to adapt themselves to the present time, conditions, needs, styles, and ways in general. It indicates a change in people's food habits, dress habits, speaking styles, tastes, choices, preferences, ideas, values, recreational activities, and so on. People, in the process of getting themselves modernized give more importance to science and technology. The scientific and technological inventions have modernized societies in various countries. They have brought about remarkable changes in the whole system of social relationship and installed new ideologies in the place of traditional ones.[240] Modern Culture has led to the countless evils that plague human society today: restless consumerism, individuality taken to excess, breakdown of families, alcoholism and drug-abuse, urban violence and political terrorism, ethnic conflicts, increased number of psychologically abnormal cases, shockingly uneven distribution of income, corruption in high places, exam, over-use of energy and natural resources, unemployment, injustice to women, to indigenous people, to minorities and weaker nations; and a vast variety of ideological, psychological, social and organizational contradictions.[241]

It also indicates an enormous increase in the size of population in urban centres. "Urbanization[242] covers the movement of people permanently or temporarily from village to city; it refers to the effect upon village manners of

238 S. M. Michael, *Christianity and Cultures: Anthropological Insights for Christian Mission in India*, 17.

239 Modernism has its root in 17th century Enlightenment philosophy. The Enlightenment was a period of remarkable intellectual development and activities within the field of philosophy. A number of traditional ideas and beliefs were overthrown and replaced by modern ones. Overall, the Enlightenment was characterized by rationalism, skepticism about traditional doctrines, and support for the empirical method in science. The proponents of the Enlightenment were critical of traditional authorities and discarded the idea of biblical revelation as superstitious. They had supreme confidence in human as a rational being and believed in a rational, scientific approach to religious, social, political, and economic issues. They promoted a secular view of the world and a general sense of progress and perfectibility. With supreme faith in rational human, they sought to discover and act upon universally valid principles governing humanity, nature and society. S. M. Michael, *Christianity and Cultures: Anthropological Insights for Christian Mission in India*, 26.

240 C. N. Shankar Rao, *Sociology: Principles of Sociology with an Introduction to Social Thought*, 503.

241 T. Menamparampil, "The Phenomenon of Culture," *Understanding Tribal for Effective Education*, edited by Joseph Anikuzhikattil, George Palackapillil, Joseph Puthenpurakal (New Delhi: Commission for Education and Culture, CBCI Centre, 2003), 233.

242 'Urbanization' refers to the growth of cities.

city habits…"[243] Importance of cities is today widely recognized. But cities are more often studied with 'moralistic' rather than 'scientific' approach. Some have highlighted the significance of city, past and present, and its dominant role in the building civilization. They have argued that cities have led in the creation of art, advancement of science and the spread of knowledge. They have also stated that without huge cities the modern complex and industrial civilization could not have developed. …"[244] The lure of 'the urban' has been a potent force triggering large-scale migration to the cities of India. Many theorists have traditionally conceptualized urbanization and urban culture in terms of the growth of 'civilization.'[245]

Urbanization created concentrated economic and political power in the hands of a few in urban sectors that made decisions that affected people in far-flung rural areas. As a result, people in villages lost the traditional practice of independence and the ability to decide for themselves. Today, Nagas perceive living in the urban or urbanized environment as having made progress. For the past two decades, Nagaland has had the highest rate of urbanization in the whole India. In contrast, living in a village is considered a sign of stagnation or being primal. As the Naga society becomes more and more bureaucratized, and as power and wealth are concentrated in urban centres, educated Naga youths, in search of progress, are lured away from villages. The growth of urban settlements, has come not only reshaped the actual landscape of the Nagas but it also had profound effects on the psychology, values and mindset of the people.[246] The process of rapid urbanization in most parts of the world has led to the emergence of a new type of 'Universal Civilization.' There is little chance, however, that other cultures are going to die out. All available evidence points in another direction. While in absolute terms, the number of people who travel or study abroad or enter into international commerce is steadily on the increase with Globalization, they merely make a pragmatic use of the facilities of 'Modern Culture' and return to their own cultural nests.

With the influence of modernization and urbanization, Naga youth have started adopting new modes and standards of living. In fact, the Naga society is alienated much from their tradition and is inclined towards the change. Youth seeks comfortable life in the urban environment with disappointment, at the same time; they do not like to go back to village's hard life. So, many youths get involve with bad habits for their survival. Some even often face themselves with marriage and parenthood unprepared personally as well as economically. Thus,

---

243 C. N. Shankar Rao, *Sociology: Principles of Sociology with an Introduction to Social Thought*, 40.

244 C. N. Shankar Rao, *Sociology: Principles of Sociology with an Introduction to Social Thought*, 41.

245 M. T. Joseph, "Migration and Identity Formation: A Case study of Dalit Assertation in Aurangabad, Maharashtra," 96.

246 Tezenlo Thong, *Progress and its impact on the Nagas A Clash of Worldviews* (England: Ashgate Publishing Limited, 2014), 149.

this leave them with double burden of marriage and economic strain which lead to further frustration in life.[247]

3.5. Christianization

For Nagas, conversion to Christianity called for a cultural reformation. Even though, the primary objective of the missionaries was to preach the gospel and win souls, in practice, conversion to Christianity also meant conversion to modernity and western morality. Particularly American Protestant Puritanism, Mary Clark writes:

> Every form of demon worship, open or suspected, was attacked- Sunday-breaking, rice-beer drinking, licentiousness, and all social vices....Instead of congregating promiscuously at different houses to sleep at night, singing objectionable songs, telling doubtful stories, and engaging in lewd conversation, these young reformers separated themselves and build a dormitory for their own accommodation, in which purity and holiness should reign. Here at morning and evening time the voice of prayer and songs of praise are heard.[248] (1907:138-139)

Christianity was an important force in westernizing the Nagas. In fact, it was in itself a form of westernization, because what was thought to be Christianity has an enormous baggage of western culture. The missionaries brought money with them and introduced monetary culture that paved the way for the inception of the western culture of materialism and consumerism among the contemporary Nagas. They not only set up schools and trained students on western values, but they also provided cash-based employment, promoting a culture that increasingly became dependent on money.[249] On the other hand, the concern of the Christian missionaries was to bring about cultural change and to prepare the Nagas for the inevitable modernization. Christianity certainly functioned as the conduit for conversion to modernity, but modernity was not the primary motive for the Nagas' conversion to Christianity. Some converted to Christianity because of a personal belief in the truth of the gospel; others found Christianity more rational, and some others found answers to their personal spiritual quest, and still others, because they were taken up by the life of the missionaries and other Naga Christians.[250]

---

247 Limatula Longkumer, *Christian Education for Adults in Tribal Context*, 39.

248 As Cited by Abraham Lotha, "Nagas' Conversion to Christianity and Modernity in Colonial India," *Nagas Today Indigenous Discourse*, edited by Zuchamo Yanthan, et al., (Delhi: Published by Naga Students' Union, 2010), 79.

249 Tezenlo Thong, *Progress and its impact on the Nagas A Clash of Worldviews*, 154.

250 Abraham Lotha, "Nagas' Conversion to Christianity and Modernity in Colonial India," *Nagas Today Indigenous Discourse*, 84.

The American Baptist Mission which was flourished under the patronage of the colonial administration has made an abiding impact on the cultural life of the Nagas. They deserve the acclaim and merit for pacifying and stamping out feral practices, putting down bloodthirsty and reprehensible customs and abolishing many evil practices and beliefs based on superstitions, such as headhunting, inter-tribal vendetta, slavery, coveting of land and women. They also replaced the vengeful and villainous customs of the Nagas with the spirit of forgiveness and reconciliation through their teaching and preaching. Consequently, a new society emerged out of it and slowly evolved into Christian culture. The Christian doctrines such as the body of Christ, unity in Christ, and fellowship gave the Nagas a new sense of belonging, closeness, and unity that scarcely ever existed. Thus, it unshed the Naga into a new era of peace, freedom, security, progress and stability.[251] Significant detrimental impacts of encountering Western Christianity was the gradual diminishing of the social institution called Morung, their beautiful ornaments of great artistic and human value like cowries, ivory, scarlet hair, and hornbills were all burnt as they were ornaments used for worshipping the spirits. The art of dancing and colorful social ceremonies were all given up. The result is that all beautiful art and culture of the Nagas almost fully disappeared. Christianity and their culture seemed pole opposites to them, but the missionaries made few attempts to bring the two into harmony and build which was valuable in tribal life.[252]

From the Nagas' perspective, through conversion to Christianity and modernity, missionaries and colonialism may have brought about changes in the cosmologies and world-view of the Nagas. Today, most Nagas remain Christians; there are no movements to revert to the traditional Naga religion. Rather, the emphasis is more and more towards enculturation and theologizing in the Naga context.

3.6. Social Media

Social media is the collective of online communication channels dedicated to community based input, interaction content-sharing and collaboration like facebook, whatsapp, twitter, google, wikipedia, etc.[253] In essence, the media are tools or technologies that facilitate dissemination of information and entertainment to a vast number of consumers. Media are in fact tools of large-

251 Inato Yekheto Shikhu, *A Rediscovery and Rebuilding of Naga Cultural Values*, 77.

252 Inato Yekheto Shikhu, *A Rediscovery and Rebuilding of Naga Cultural Values*, 78.

253 Social media is becoming an integral part of life online as social websides and application proliferate. In business, social media is used to market products, promotes brands, connect to current customers and foster new business, http://www.google.co.in.definition+of+the+term+social+media (Accesses, Dec. 29, 2017).

scale manufacture and distribution of information and related messages.[254] It requires some stretching of the established meaning of the term to include recent developments in information technology such as cellular phones, computers and its related facilities such as electronic mail and internet as mass media. It suggests that the modern media are experienced not only by individuals and groups in terms of their own cultures but as part of the 'mass' and as 'mass culture.' The term 'mass' also suggest that people's interaction with media is homogeneous, inactive and unquestioning. They are so termed-'mass media' because their reach extends to vast heterogeneous masses of the population living in a wide and extensive area of a country or of the world. They are not only technological device used for mass communication but they can look at as industries, as cultural or entertainment industries.[255]

Media culture has merged in which images, sounds and spectacles help produce the fabric of everyday life, dominating leisure time, shaping political views and social behavior, and providing the materials out of which people build their very identities. It also provides the materials out of which many people construct their sense of class, ethnicity and race, nationality, sexuality. It also helps shape the prevalent view of the world and deepest values. It defines what is good or bad, truth or lie, good or evil. This social media stories and images provide the symbols; myths and resources, which help constitute a common culture for the majority of individuals in many parts of the world. Therefore, for those immersed from cradle to grave in a media and consumer society, it is important to learn how to understand, interpret and critic its meanings and messages.[256] Cultural studies also explore the processes through which a culture produces meaning, where the meaning is the effect of communication and representation and negotiated through power relations. Communication and representations are two-way processes: the message is sent from an addresser to an addressee through a medium. Therefore, it is not enough to speak of the discourses that construct meaning, objects and events. It is not enough to speak of the ways in which advertisements, media, propaganda and other cultural forms represent women, men, family or the nation. Cultural studies are interested in the ways in which audiences receive the message, how they respond to it, and the effects the message generates. When people (audience) use and identify with particular symbols and artifacts, they express their cultural identities.[257]

I. Asenla says that the age of technology and modern communication has ushered a tremendous change in Naga society. It has opened many opportunities and has also made every aspect of their life easier and comfortable. But it has also

254 L. Imsutoshi Jamir, *Sites in Tribal Cultural Studies* (Mokokchung: TDCC Publications, 2015), 92.

255 L.Imsutoshi Jamir, *Sites in Tribal Cultural Studies*, 94.

256 L.Imsutoshi Jamir, *Sites in Tribal Cultural Studies*, 96.

257 Pramod K. Nayar, *An Introduction to Cultural Studies*, 45.

brought many upheavals in the economic, social, political, cultural and religious spheres of their lives. The communication media has reached every nook and corner of the world and has affected the lives of the young and the old, men and women, the rich and the poor, the educated and the uneducated alike. Moreover, the modern communication means, such as the radio, TV, computer etc., has completely sidelined the traditional media, which were once the only means of communication for the people. Traditional media are the media used locally in a community. They are also called folk media, which has been handed down from generation to generation. Some of the well-known folk media are folk songs, folk tales, folk dance, folk theater, proverbs, riddles, legends, ballads, fables, charms, fairs, festivals, religious superstition, custom and tradition.[258]

Cultural values presented by social media are more accessible, attractive, powerful and seductive than the traditional cultural values. Often than not, the latter is diminished to the extent of portraying it as valueless and irrelevant. Several scholars have accused the social media for misleading individuals, misrepresenting reality, commercializing feelings and distorting people's way of life, thinking, language, mannerism and in general corrupting the whole communitarian life of the tribal. It is understood in terms of a verifying process of social knowledge and behavioral norms as well as its overall style of life.[259] The influence of social media also increases migration. Through radio and television urban ideas, values, and lifestyles are projected. When urban people control the media, most of what is telecast reflects the urban mindset yet, backward areas of the country are exposed to new ideas and information. Cinemas, newspapers and growing literacy influences urbanization. Given an opportunity, many people, especially the youth, choose to move toward the cities.[260]

3.7. The Process of Enculturation

Enculturation is in essence a process of conscious or unconscious conditioning, or as kind of indoctrination. The process of enculturation is so thorough and subtle that even one's emotional reactions and muscular movements reflect one's cultural conditioning.[261] Cultural anthropologists points out that the enculturation process is the prime factor which governs an individual's ability to face the ongoing challenges of life in the midst of cultural change. During early life, a person is

258 I. Asenla Jamir, "Naga Traditional Media and its Usefulness," *Communication and Naga Culture*, edited by L. Imsutoshi Jamir, C. Alitemjen Longkumer (Dimapur: TDCC, 2007), 100.

259 L. Imsutoshi Jamir, *Sites in Tribal Cultural Studies*, 90.

260 Atul V. Aghamkar, "Tribal migration to the Cities," *Tribes in Transition: Indian Christians Reflect on the Original Inhabitants of the Land*, edited by, F. Hrangkhuma and Paul Hiebert (Bangalore: SAIACS Press, 2004), 50.

261 S. M. Michael, *Christianity and Cultures: Anthropological Insights for Christian Mission in India*, 9.

to a large extent passive in assimilating the traditions of the group and tends to be molded into the kind of person the group finds desirable. In later years, however, enculturation demands a reconditioning to the new situations in life which the early enculturation was not sufficient to meet. By its very nature culture is dynamic. New ideas and modes of life are introduced within culture, and the individual must reorient his or her life through acceptance or rejection of these changes. In this process of selective assimilation of cultural forms from within and without, the early enculturation play an important role. The enculturation of the individual in the early years of his/her life is the prime mechanism making for cultural stability, while the process, as it is operative on more mature folk, is highly important in inducing change.[262]

Enculturation, as this complex process is called, prepares the individual, from infancy through adulthood, to orient himself/herself to his/her group, adjust itself to its demands and expectations, and acquire skill in interpersonal relationships. The assimilation by a human organism of the customs and traditions of his/her group has shown and demonstrated that one's feelings towards other people are affected more profoundly by the degree to which one think they share their attitudes and values than by any other social categorization, including their race or ethnic grouping.[263] Enculturation internalizes his/her culture and becomes thoroughly acculturated. One internalizes the dreams and expectations, the rules and requirements not just for the larger society seen as a whole, but also for every specific demand within the whole. Society does whatever is necessary to aid any one of its members in learning proper and appropriate behavior for any given social setting and in meeting the demands of any challenge.[264]

Thus, even in the case among the migrant Naga youth that the enculturation in the given culture is very important for its people to play a creative role in the midst of constant change. Only to the extent, that the enculturation has been in cultured in a given milieu will make people be faithful to their traditions as well as play a creative role in the midst of changes.

3.8. Education

Education is the process by which people acquire knowledge, skills, habits, values, or attitudes. It is a process whereby the powers of human nature become developed by good habits.[265] The current system of education among Nagas lacks cultural

262 S. M. Michael, *Christianity and Cultures: Anthropological Insights for Christian Mission in India*, 182.

263 Anita Sharma and Dalip Malhotra, *Personality and Social norms* (New Delhi: Concept Publishing Company, 2007), 24.

264 Stephen A. Grunlan & Marvin K. Mayers, *Cultural Anthropology: A Christian Perspective*, 2nd ed., 72.

265 Tuisem A. Shishak, "Nagas and Education: Back to Basic," *Nagas Today Indigenous Discourse*, edited by Zuchamo Yanthan, et al., (Delhi: Published by Naga Students' Union, 2010), 214.

relevance to the needs of the learner or society and does not take into account the applicability of what is being taught and learned and has miserably failed in meeting the needs of the society. It insists on implanting a particular body of knowledge and a specific view of the world that often does not correspond to the life experiences that people have or might be expected to encounter. The school curriculum contains very little or no Naga culture and history. Students compete to learn and take examinations on European history, Renaissance, western industrialization, American democratic system, Keynesian economics and English literature. This social and cultural irrelevance means that the students often lack the motivation to study. They have difficulty in relating to what they learn to their frame of reference and in making it a part of their knowledge or themselves. Therefore, there is an urgent need to examine the basic organization of education structures and systems and the philosophical foundation on which they rest.[266]

Today, many youths choose to go for higher education outside Nagaland. The youth who attended high school and college outside Naga territory began to come home with the influence of outside lifestyles and practices. The Nagas have for the most part swallowed other culture without chewing it. This process of uncritical enculturation has continued, and today the Naga youth, mostly educated are half-western and half-Naga.[267] The spread of education also has its share in changing its cultural civilization. Not only did it improve tools for survival, but opened the gate from darkness to the new world, the world of technology. Now the literacy percentage of Nagaland has risen up to 42% which is higher than many of the other states in the country. Many have become scientists, doctors, engineers, etc.; employment problem for educated class has become a major burden for the government now.[268]

As Dominic says,

> "There appears to be some contradiction. Youth having a positive value for education, but on the other a negative attitude towards it. Yet a thoughtful consideration would reveal the underlying truth that though they value and appreciate education, they have a negative, dissatisfied attitude towards education in the present form."[269]

Aesthetics as a value seems to have fallen in the esteem of youth. But social values, the concern for the upliftment of fellow humans seems to be highly prized by youth.[270] Education should be aimed at the moral and intellectual

266 Tezenlo Thong, *Progress and its Impact on the Nagas A Clash of Worldviews*, 143.

267 Tuisem A. Shishak, "Nagas and Education: Back to Basic," *Nagas Today Indigenous Discourse*, 221.

268 B. Pakem, ed., *Nationality, Ethnicity and Cultural Identity in North-East India*, 328.

269 Dominic Jala, "Youth and the Challenges of the Twenty-First," 92.

270 Joe Arimpoor, *Indian Youth in Perspective: A Research Study*, 101.

development. When people are educated the living standard will change, however, today, education, instead of becoming a means of liberation, has turned out to be a means of exploitation and domination. The creation of different classes effectively works in their places and conscientize youth regarding the impact of globalization.[271]

3.8.1. Education and Social Change

The function of the educational institution is to train the intellect, transmit what is permanently worthwhile in the cultural heritage, and adjust the youth to society as it is. It regards it only as an institution of learning and is against turning it into an agency of reform. It thinks that such a course, instead of 'arousing and developing in the child a certain number of physical, intellectual and moral states which are demanded of him/her by both the political society as a whole and the special milieu for which he/she is specially destined'[272] will prepare him/her for a milieu that may never be realized. Such a viewpoint can be sociologically acceptable with reference to more or less static societies where change takes a very long time to occur.[273]

3.8.2. Education as an Agent of Social Change

This view regards that education can engage itself in much more positive action and can rebuild society by inculcating in the young a programme of social reform. It regards those who assume change as universal and inevitable as wrong.

As Bremeld says,

> They ...overlook the supra-individual nature of many forces and institutions such as socio-economic classes, mass-media, pressure groups and other centre's of power in society. (They) understate the persistence and recurrence of cultural patterns and therefore over emphasize the novelty of history, opportunities of unplanned change and the inevitability of progress.[274]

They do not see, therefore, that broad social change must be planned rationally and executed firmly so that reactionary pressures can be eliminated and specific goals may be achieved. This view, however, is sociologically not acceptable for several reasons: a. the future of any society remains very uncertain

271 Nebu Mathson, *Impact of Globalization on the Indian Youth: A Review of the Response of NCCI*, 92.

272 Emile Durkheim, *Education and Sociology*, translated by, D. Fox. Sherwood (Glencoe: The free press, 1956), 71.

273 B. V. Shah, "Education and Social Change Among Tribals In India," *Tribal Communities and Social Change*, edited by Pariyaram M. Chacko (New Delhi: Sage Publications, 2005), 115.

274 Theodore Bremeld, *Philosophies of Education in Cultural Perspectives* (Newyork: Dryden, 1955), 183.

and it is impossible to chart it in detail; any realized reform is always a product of compromise and mutual adjustment of various forces in society; b. deeply entrenched cultural patterns mould the way in which people conceive and implement change.[275]

3.8.3. Education as a Cooperative Force in Social Change

The contemporary world is a world of changing societies. Changes that occur in them 'are frequent, occur in sequential chains and affect a wider range of individual experience and functional aspects of societies.'[276] In such societies therefore, an educational system that performs the function of conservation only soon becomes either dysfunctional or undergoes a change in its function as well as structure to suit the new needs. However, it is not called upon as a prime mover of social change, but only as a cooperative force. It can a. deliberately cultivate among youth the necessary intellectual and emotional dispositions and attitudes for dealing with change in general. b. imparts to them the necessary technical and social skills, and c. teach them to react to change intelligently when it occurs. It can do this by keeping abreast of social changes and modifying in each generation the heritage it may teach in its schools. Warner says, 'As long as we have our present social structure, education must be adapted to it or we will produce a generation or more of maladjusted children and unhappy youth.'[277] Ottaway argues that education can produce changes in culture and society only under orders from those in power: 'Education is a force which supports and develops the changes in social aims already decided by those in power, but it does not initiate the changes.'[278] Dewey endorses this; he envisages three choices for the education in face of social change; they 'may drift' according to him or may observe 'the newer forces that are producing change in the old order', estimate 'their direction' and 'see what can be done to make schools their ally', or may become 'intelligently conservative.'[279]

Thus, in complex nation societies of today, education can neither be regarded as a conserver nor as an agent of change. It can only be regarded as a cooperative force in social change decided by forces more pervasive in society.[280] One aspect of the impact of education on the Naga society is that when they have become educated, they love town life only, and are loath to go back to their villages or even to work for the welfare of their own fellow-people. The modern education system has been deprived of all cultural values. In the traditional Naga society, education

---

275 B. V. Shah, "Education and Social Change Among Tribals In India," 116.

276 Wilbert E. Moore, *Social Change* (New Delhi: Prentice-Hall of India Limited, 1965), 2..

277 W. L. Warner, etal., *Who Shall Be Educated* (Newyork: Harper, 1944), 143.

278 A. K. C. Ottaway, *Education and Society-An Introduction to the Sociology of Education* (London: Routledge and Kegan Paul, 1953), 56.

279 John Dewey, *Education and Social Change*, Social Frontier, 2 (May 1973), 235.

280 B. V. Shah, "Education and Social Change Among Tribals In India," 117.

was non-formal and was based on societal needs. Today persons who turn out to be graduates think very high of themselves and do not bother to think about the welfare of the society, neither tradition nor culture to which they belong. Today's education is not based on society-building rather modern system of education have made the Naga youth to neglect their own rich cultural values.

3.9. Effects and Challenges on Culture

The impact of modernization and urbanization, social media, Christianization, etc., in Nagaland is being mediated through a number of contemporary historical events such as the arrival of the missionaries and conversion to Christianity, beginning with the later part of the eighteenth century; the introduction of ordered administration by the British; English education; Second world war; the Naga armed struggle for political independence and the establishment of statehood within the Indian union, the penetration of money-economy, the growing urbanization and so on. And with the coming of modernization the jungle civilization is no more. The result effect of modernization is not pleasant because it brings "process of disorganization and dislocation." It has given rise to anomie, which is "a looseness of individuals, a hopelessness of persons, a fellness from the potentiality of I-Thou person's which makes a real hell of modern life-which is much more hellish than was possible within traditional structures…."[281] A sudden surge of modernity and modern facilities and in many instances the IT invasion has left the Naga's to think inferior of their own ways of successful living. Naga society was generally egalitarian in nature. But today individualism and class differences between rich and poor have become very obvious.[282] Globalized and market oriented economic activities act not only to widen the gap between the rich and poor, but also weaken the sovereignty of nation. Its operation is backed by the information technology and military power, and has led to the decline of the weaker cultures, discrimination against minorities such as aborigines or tribal's and the exploitation of women and children.[283] Some of the challenges are as follows:

3.9.1. Social Challenges

The expression of sin in terms of greed for power and wealth experienced by the peoples has had a tremendous effect on the community, especially the poor and marginalized. Ethical problems such as corruption, abuse of power, and prostitution; poverty realities such as indentured child labor and population

281 Takatemjen, *Studies on Theology and Naga Culture*, 46.

282 Razouselie Lasetso, "Introduction: Shaping a Relevant Theology for the Indigenous People of North East India," 54.

283 Wati Longchar, "Revisiting Tribal Theology In Changing Context Today," *Tribal Christian Theology*, edited by Razouselie Lasetso, Yangkahao Vashum (Jorhat, Assam: Eastern Theological College, 2007), 50.

explosion; communal problems such as ethnic conflicts, racial tensions and breakdown of family structures and continued marginalization of women, children, and person with disabilities continue to rise.[284]

3.9.2. Individualism/Collectivism

In a Naga context each individual is accountable to the community. The community is extremely important and one cannot survive without the community. Hence the needs of the society are strongly heightened in the reading process. The groups intentionally as well as instinctively, thrash out ways and means of solving societal problems and not just personal problems and throughout the discussions the issues conferred are community based.[285]

3.9.3. Reinterpretation of Traditional Values

Naga society changed a great deal within a short span of time. The outlook of their past ancestors has now been destroyed. The once honest, truthful, hardworking and God-fearing people have been tied up in a system that has led to a complete change over that none can be proud of. R. E. Lotha rightly comments: "Such looses of cultures and values have brought forth many counterproductive social evils such as violence, disunity, extortion, rape, disharmony, insecurity and restlessness."[286] The need of the hour is to introspect the past, dig out the treasures of the old cultural values. Those values could provide an answer to all their chronic misunderstanding and social disunity.[287]

3.10. Conclusion

As Nagas open up themselves to embrace the modern cultures, they are also confronted with more and more issues and questions at the same time. The culture of modernism is such that the very idea of 'culture' is venerated as the 'final' arbiter of human experience. Naga youth are left lacking in a complex set of rules, norms, beliefs, habits, and values. The ongoing influence of migrating to urban areas being exerted by modern medias, technology and other trends of globalization. Consequently, the greater the loss of culture and diminishing identity the Nagas suffer, and unless the Naga youth make a concerted and determined effort to reclaim what is left of their culture, they will soon be left

284 Wati Longchar, "Revisiting Tribal Theology In Changing Context Today," 50.

285 Akhrieno Savi, "Intercultural Bible Reading-A Case Study," *Tribal Christian Theology*, edited by Razouselie Lasetso, Yangkahao Vashum (Jorhat, Assam: Eastern Theological College, 2007), 65.

286 As Cited by Tasoni Moon, "The Mao Naga Traditional Values of Peace and Reconciliation in the Context of Conflicts and Violence in Naga Society Today," *Tribal Christian Theology*, edited by Razouselie Lasetso, Yangkahao Vashum (Jorhat, Assam: Eastern Theological College, 2007), 183.

287 Tasoni Moon, "The Mao Naga Traditional Values of Peace and Reconciliation in the Context of Conflicts and Violence in Naga Society Today," 183.

with no cultural roots or identity from the past. Understood thus, the following chapter leads to identify important variables of cultural fidelity on both the Naga youth living in and outside Nagaland to examine how far such values, beliefs and practices have maintained and imparted on current Naga youth.

Chapter 4

Analysis, Interpretation, and Findings

4. Introduction

This chapter deals with the analysis, interpretation, and findings of empirical data. The methodology followed in this study is outlined in detail in the first chapter. The present study on the fidelity to Naga Culture among migrant Naga youth is undertaken in the context of extensive migration. Migrants usually have a tendency to organize themselves into a group with a view to retain or preserve their socio-cultural characteristics. In other words, they intend to retain or reproduce the structure and culture of their native origin at the place of migration. The retention of structural and cultural identity to some extent solves the problem of adjustment in the new surroundings.[288] The healthy coexistence of both, of one enhancing the other is vital. The present generation is integrating traditional culture with modernity, they must also understand that there is huge responsibility for them to transmit what they received from their parents and grandparents in order not to make their culture extinct. Many youth still have not come to the realization that to be someone in a society one has to be rooted in one's own culture.

In the light of the above, the author designed the study with the aim to compare fidelity to Naga culture among Naga youth living in and outside Nagaland, since, the youth who are living in Nagaland are likely to carry with them ineradicable traces of the Naga tradition. Like their parents they experience considerable difficulty in adopting new methods of work and new behavior patterns. At the same time, they are generally much influenced by advancement

288 Joseph Guglar, *On the Theory of Rural-Urban Migration: The Case of Sub-Saharan Africa* (Cambridge: University Press, 1969), 149.

of modernization and information technology. Hence, the author would like to identify the problems in relation to the place of stay in order to find out how much the variables significantly determine the 'Fidelity to Naga culture among the Migrant Naga Youth.' The data collected through a structured questionnaire schedule is analyzed and interpreted in this chapter.

4.1. Plan of Analysis

A brief description on the plan of analysis had mainly the following parts. The following areas were considered; (a) Details of socio-demographic such as age group, gender, profession, place of stay, and their family monthly income. (b) Places of stay: Kolkata, Bengaluru, Delhi, Hyderabad, Pune, Chennai, Kochi, and Nagaland. (c) Variables on Cultural Fidelity, Dignity of Labor, Education and Language, Family System, Generation Gap between Parents and Naga Youth, Present Naga Youth Style, Equality and Respect, Dresses and Ornaments, Music and Dance, Behavior and Attitude , Hospitality, Communitarian Spirit, Folklore and Art crafts, Information Technology, and Church and Naga Youth.

4.2. Statistical Analysis

Data were analyzed using suitable computer software. All the scores are unified, i.e., positive and negative questions were given corresponding weightage and the entire data is transformed into percentages. Then the percentages were converted to five point scale with equal divisions and the data were subjected to statistical scrutiny. The analyzed data are expressed in its frequency and percentage as well as mean and standard deviation. To elucidate the associations and comparisons between different parameters, Chi square (c^2) test was used as nonparametric test. Student's t test was used to compare mean values between two groups. Analysis of variance (One Way ANOVA) was performed as parametric test to compare different variables. For all statistical evaluations, a two-tailed probability of value, < 0.05 was considered significant.

4.2.1. Socio-Demographic Details

This section gives personal details such as, gender, profession, place of stay, family monthly income, and age group in relation to total cultural fidelity.

In the sample that was studied 46.7% were Male and the remaining 53.3% were Female. The researcher identifies that the migration tends to increase the ratio of female members.

The figure shows that among the Naga youths, students constituted 81.3%, employed youth were 18.7 percent. The study reveals more respondents are from the students than the employed. As the researcher include only the students and the employed in the study, the employed members are less as compared to students' population. This chart shows that majority of the migrant youths outside Nagaland are students.

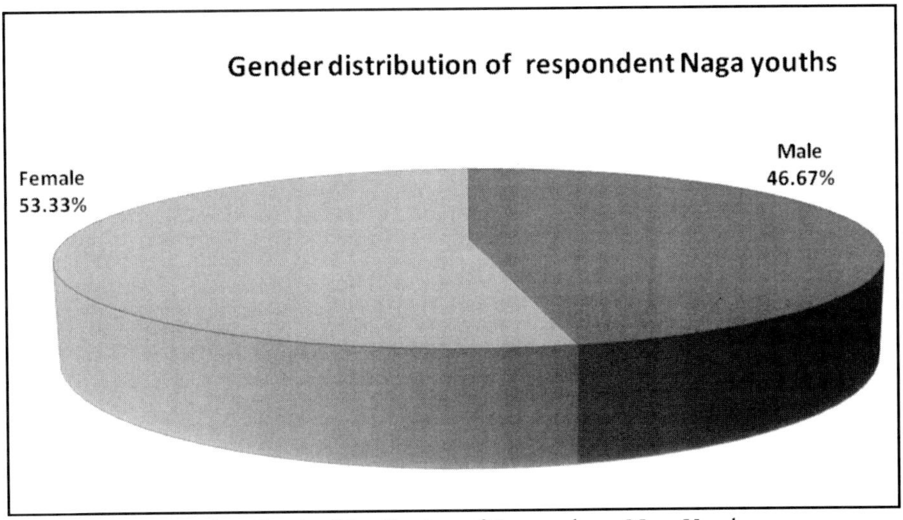

Fig.4.0. Gender Distribution of Respondents Naga Youth

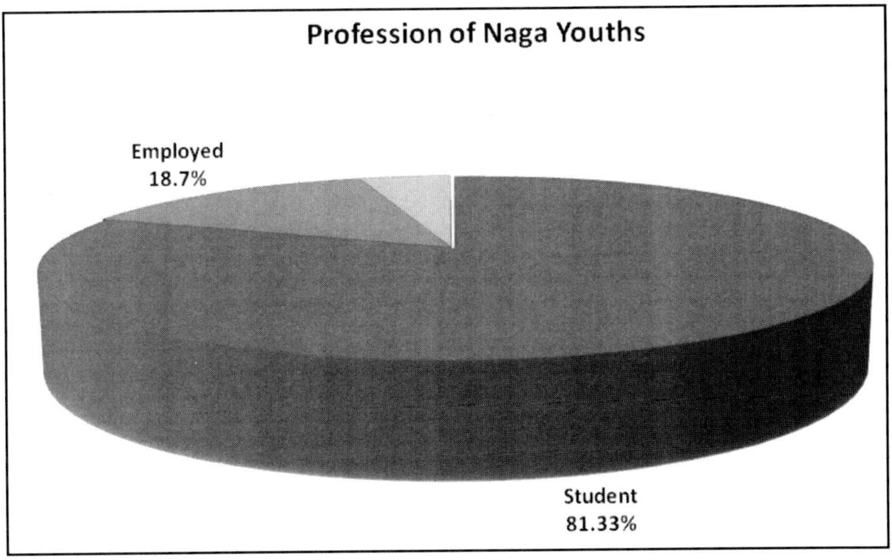

Fig 4.1. Distribution of Youth in Different Professions

With regard to the place of stay, majority of the Naga youth were from Nagaland itself, i.e., about 50%. Among the migrant youth, 14.3% were from Hyderabad, 8.3% from Bengaluru, 8% from Delhi, 6% from Kolkota, 5.7% from Pune, and 4.7% from Chennai. There were only 3.3% from Kochi. The total population, included in the study were among 300 Naga youths with regard to the place of stay. This study is important to determine the fidelity to Naga culture from the perspective of stay or location.

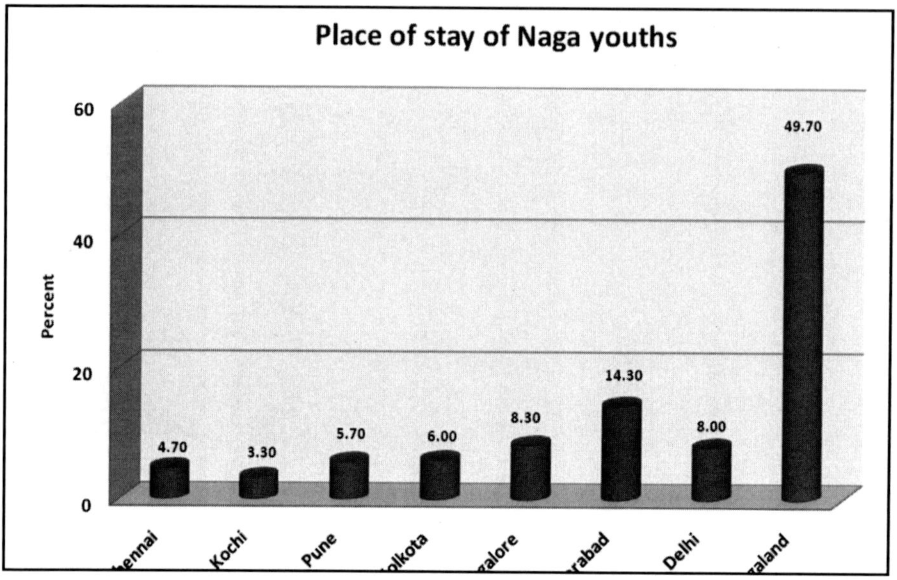

Fig. 4.2. Distribution of Place of Stay

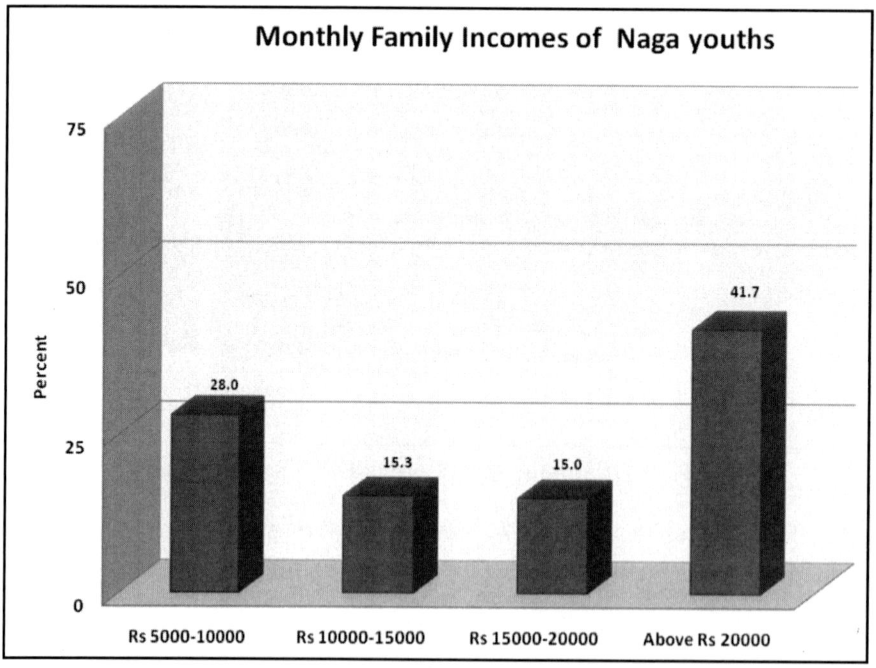

Fig. 4.3. Distribution of Family Monthly Income

The monthly family income of the Naga youths showed variation. The greater number belonged to the group of above Rs 20000, the percentage being 41.7. Around 15% of the families each had incomes in the groups 10000-15000 and 15000-20000. This figure shows that majority of the respondents' family have economic stability, as a result family could sent their children for education and employment outside Nagaland.

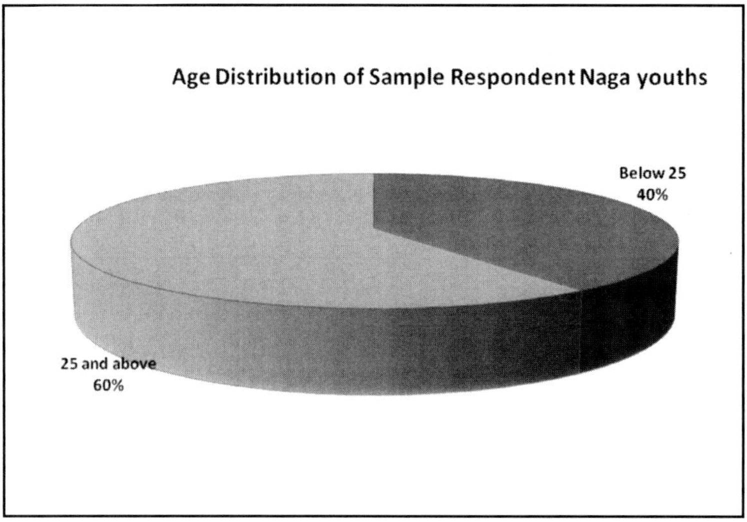

Fig. 4.4. Age Distribution of Respondent Naga Youth

Considering the age category according to the figure above, 40% were below the age of 25 years and 60% were above 25 years. Out of the total population, 120 fall under the age category 20-25 years, 180 under the age category 26-30 years. Respondents were more of the age 25 years and above.

4.2.2. Distribution of Total Cultural Fidelity Score of Total Naga Youth

In this section, the analyzed data are expressed in its frequency and percentage as well as mean and standard deviation.

Table 4.0. Distribution of Dignity of Labor score of total Naga youth population

Dignity of Labor	Frequency	Percent
Agree	92	30.7
Don't Know	143	47.7
Disagree	65	21.7
Total	300	100

Dignity of labor of Naga youth was assessed using the questionnaire and the results were consolidated to five point scale starting from strongly agree to strongly disagree through agree, don't know and disagree. Four to five a question regarding their attitude towards dignity of labor irrespective of their job was evaluated. Distribution of response is given in table 4.0. Majority of the respondents responded as don't know (47.7) followed by agree (30.7). It can be inferred from their response of don't know to the dignity of labor, the Naga youth consider no dignity to any of the job or all jobs with same dignity especially they don't have any particular opinion about dignity for labor. But (30.7) of Naga youth consider their job or labor with due respect and dignity whereas (21.7) of Naga youth disagree to the fact that their labor has any dignity.

Table 4.1. Distribution of Education and Language score of total Naga youth population

Education and Language	Frequency	Percent
Strongly Agree	3	1.0
Agree	108	36.0
Don't Know	141	47.0
Disagree	48	16.0
Total	300	100

Education and language of Naga youth was assessed using positive and negative questions. Their attitude and deeds about education and language was evident from the present study result which is depicted in table 4.1. Majority of the Naga youth responded either positively or neutral towards education and language. (47.0) of subjects responded don't know which was followed by agree (36.7) responses. More positive attitude towards education and language may be due to high literacy of the subjects as majority profession (81) of the study population were students pursuing their college education. Even though Naga population had a positive attitude, (47) gave neutral response and (16) of study population who disagree to all types of education and language aspect. This may be due to the ignorance of the value of education and language, and shows that the present condition of the Naga youth misses educational system, such as speaking in their own mother tongue and ethics of social, religious, political, and economic value imparted in the past. The present education system is purely academic in nature. Youth are now so much busy learning from the ready-made books and in the process of learning; they are alienated from the traditional values.

Table 4.2. Distribution of Family System score of total Naga youth population

Family System	Frequency	Percent
Strongly Agree	5	1.7
Agree	145	48.3
Don't Know	127	42.3
Disagree	22	7.3
Strongly Disagree	1	0.3
Total	300	100

Family relationship among Naga family was assessed by using suitable questions and the sum percentage of all the scores were categorized into five through strongly agree to strongly disagree. Majority of the respondents responded agree (48.3) followed by don't know (42.3). The study depicted in table 4.2 shows that Naga youth have a close association within family members. Only (7.3) of the respondents disagree to all kinds of Family system. Despite of some disagreements, major respondents are agreed to healthy family relationship where parent and youth sit together and impart wisdom and knowledge that has been handed down through generations.

Table 4.3. Distribution of Generation Gap score of total Naga youth population

Generation Gap	Frequency	Percent
Strongly Agree	3	1.0
Agree	81	27.0
Don't Know	79	26.3
Disagree	112	37.3
Strongly Disagree	25	8.3
Total	300	100

Generation gap was assessed by using positive and negative questions and the sum percentage of all the scores were categorized into five through strongly agree to strongly disagree. Majority of the respondents responded disagree (37.3) followed by agree (27.0). Respondents of the study population opined to disagree with regard to Generation gap. Their attitude about generation gap was evident from the present study result which is depicted in table 4.3. Majority of the Naga youth responded either positively or neutral towards generation gap (26.3) of subjects responded don't know. This means there is a generation gap between

Naga youth and parent. Today, there is a fear among the youth that their cultural values, traditions, and heritages may wane due to the generation gap between parent and youth.

Table 4.4. Distribution of Present Naga Youth Style score of total Naga youth population

Naga Youth	Frequency	Percent
Strongly Agree	1	0.3
Agree	75	25.0
Don't Know	79	26.3
Disagree	101	33.7
Strongly Disagree	44	14.7
Total	300	100

Naga youth was assessed by using suitable questions on the present living style, and the sum percentage of all the scores were categorized into five through strongly agree to strongly disagree. Majority of the respondents responded disagree (33.7) followed by don't know (26.3) of the population responded. Only (25.0) agree to the questions relating to the present Naga youth living style. This result revealed that the Naga youth had lost the will power to reassert their Naga Identity. The moral values and the living standards have changed to a great deal which reveals Naga youth have become more individualistic and as a result affecting the society as a whole.

Table 4.5. Distribution of Equality and Respect score of total Naga youth population

Equality and Respect	Frequency	Percent
Strongly Agree	2	0.7
Agree	101	33.7
Don't Know	171	57.0
Disagree	23	7.7
Strongly Disagree	3	1.0
Total	300	100

Equality and respect was assessed by including 4 suitable questions in questionnaire and the sum percentage of all the scores were categorized into five through strongly agree to strongly disagree. Majority of the respondents responded don't know (57.0) followed by agree (33.7). Number of population (7.7) expressed to disagree. It is due to the respondents' lack of practice and associations with regard to Cultural values. On the other hand, respondents who agree still withhold the loyalty and respect toward elders as well as obedience to cultural truth.

Table 4.6. Distribution of Dress and Ornaments score of total Naga youth population

Dress and Ornaments	Frequency	Percent
Strongly Agree	2	0.7
Agree	86	28.7
Don't Know	144	48.0
Disagree	63	21.0
Strongly Disagree	5	1.7
Total	300	100

Dress and ornaments was assessed by using positive and negative questions and the sum percentage of all the scores were categorized into five through strongly agree to strongly disagree. Majority of the respondents responded don't know (48.0) followed by agree (28.7). (21.0) respondents responded to disagree. This response was due to their non-preference to wear Naga traditional dresses and ornaments. Today Naga youth is neither a real Naga nor a modern one, because they are sandwiched between tradition and western culture. Dress code is purely westernized.

Table 4.7. Distribution of Music and Dance score of total Naga youth population

Music and Dance	Frequency	Percent
Strongly Agree	3	1.0
Agree	97	32.3
Don't Know	151	50.3
Disagree	47	15.7
Strongly Disagree	2	0.7
Total	300	100

Music and Dance was assessed using the questionnaire and the results were consolidated to five point scale starting from strongly agree to strongly disagree. Majority of the respondents responded don't know (50.3%) followed by agree

(32.3%). Majority of the study population viewed to don't know with regard to Music and Dance. The study shown in table 4.7 revealed that Naga youth have attempted to finesse and modify themselves to appeal to the taste of the present modern Music and Dance than the traditional ones.

Table 4.8. Distribution of Behavior and Attitude score of total Naga youth population

Behavior and Attitude	Frequency	Percent
Strongly Agree	4	1.3
Agree	144	48.0
Don't Know	143	47.7
Disagree	8	2.7
Strongly Disagree	1	0.3
Total	300	100

Behavior and Attitude was assessed using the questionnaire and the results were consolidated to five point scale starting from strongly agree to strongly disagree. Majority of the respondents responded agree (48.0) followed by don't know (47.7). The major study population responded to agree with regard to Behavior and Attitudes, whereas (2.7) disagree. The result depicted in table 4.8 revealed that there is a decline in respect, regard and care for someone elder, which have heard of being practiced in the past as the part of the Naga culture.

Table 4.9. Distribution of Hospitality score of total Naga youth population

Hospitality	Frequency	Percent
Strongly Agree	19	6.3
Agree	204	68.0
Don't Know	69	23.0
Disagree	8	2.7
Total	300	100

Hospitality was assessed using the questionnaire and the results were consolidated to five point scale starting from strongly agree to strongly disagree. Majority of the respondents responded agree (68.0) followed by don't know

(23.0). Many of the respondents expressed to don't know. According to the result shown in table 4.9 depicted that the Naga youth still maintain and uphold the spirit of hospitality.

Table 4.10. Distribution of Community Spirit score of total Naga youth population

Community Spirit	Frequency	Percent
Strongly Agree	6	2.0
Agree	105	35.0
Don't Know	155	51.7
Disagree	31	10.3
Strongly Disagree	3	1.0
Total	300	100

Community spirit was assessed by using suitable questions and the sum percentage of all the scores were categorized into five through strongly agree to strongly disagree. Majority of the respondents responded don't know (51.7) followed by agree (35.0). Major study population responded to don't know. This response was due to the lack of the community spirit among the Naga youth. Urbanization and the scattering of people is one of the reasons. More and more people are now living in mixed urban and semi urban communities under different laws and therefore it is only expected that traditional communitarian system will go through a shift.

Table 4.11. Distribution of Folklore and Art score of total Naga youth population

Folklore and Art	Frequency	Percent
Strongly Agree	1	0.3
Agree	84	28.0
Don't Know	86	28.7
Disagree	117	39.0
Strongly Disagree	12	4.0
Total	300	100

Folklore and Art was assessed by using suitable questions and the sum percentage of all the scores were categorized into five through strongly agree to strongly disagree. Majority of the respondents responded disagree (39.0) followed by don't know (28.7) and agree (28.0). Major study population responded to disagree. The result shown in table 4.11 revealed that many Naga youth still have not come to the realization that to be someone in a society one has to be rooted in one's own culture. Naga youth are found to have almost forgotten their cultural songs, folklores, and the most valuable oral tradition.

Table 4.12. Distribution of Information and Technology score of total Naga youth population

Information Technology	Frequency	Percent
Strongly Agree	1	0.3
Agree	104	34.7
Don't Know	80	26.7
Disagree	100	33.3
Strongly Disagree	15	5.0
Total	300	100

Information technology was assessed using the questionnaire and the results were consolidated to five point scale starting from strongly agree to strongly disagree. Majority of the respondents responded agree (34.7) followed by disagree (33.3). Majority of the respondents responded to agree with regard to Information and Technology. The table shown in 4.12 depicts that with globalization and technological advancement, youth' interests, hobbies, professional choices, nature of relationships are also undergoing a sea change. The information technology in fact considered as the highest of influential achievement. Unfortunately, through constant exposure to information technology, youth begin to accept the values that are contradictory to Naga cultural values and tradition.

Table 4.13. Distribution of Church and Youth score of total Naga youth population

Church and Youth	Frequency	Percent
Strongly Agree	41	13.7
Agree	210	70.0
Don't Know	47	15.7
Disagree	2	0.7
Total	300	100

Church and Youth was assessed using the questionnaire and the results were consolidated to five point scale starting from strongly agree to disagree. Majority of the respondents responded agree (70.0) followed by don't know (15.7). Only (0.7) of the study population responded to disagree with regard to the questions on Church and Naga youth. This result shows that Naga youth wants the Church to address to the needs of the present youth and to provide a platform where they can search for truth, at the same time to develop new skills and become more creative in reviving Naga cultural values.

Table 4.14. Distribution of Total Cultural Fidelity score of total Naga youth population

Total Cultural Fidelity	Frequency	Percent
Agree	73	24.3
Don't Know	196	65.3
Disagree	31	10.3
Total	300	100

Total Cultural fidelity was assessed using the questionnaire and the results were consolidated to five point scale starting from strongly agree to strongly disagree through agree, don't know and disagree. Majority of the respondents responded don't know (65.3) followed by agree (24.3). Majority of the study population responded to don't know on cultural fidelity. Yet another group of study population agrees on the cultural fidelity. The table shown in 4.14 depicts the sign of the overall disintegration of the traditional Naga culture.

4.2.3. Associations and Comparisons Between Different Parameters

To find out the factors that influence the total cultural fidelity of Naga youth, each demographic parameter were evaluated for its significant association. In this section, the statistical technique used is expressed in Chi square (c^2) test. The results and interpretation are presented in the following Tables.

Relationship among variables namely, Cultural Fidelity, sub scales of Dignity of Labor, Education and Language, Family system, Generation Gap between Parents and Naga Youth, Present Naga Youth Style, Equality and Respect, Dresses and Ornaments, Music and Dance, Behavior and Attitude, Hospitality, Communitarian Spirit, Folklore and Art crafts, Information Technology, and Church and Naga Youth.

Table 5.0. Association between total cultural fidelity score and age of Naga population

Age	Total Cultural Fidelity Score			Total
	Agree	Don't Know	Disagree	
< 25 yrs	26	78	15	119
	35.60%	39.80%	48.40%	39.70%
>= 25 yrs	47	118	16	181
	64.40%	60.20%	51.60%	60.30%
Total	73	196	31	300
Chi Square: 1.487; P > 0.05				

Total cultural fidelity score of the total population showed no significant (P>0.05) association with age of the population table 5.0. As the majority (60.3%) of the total population fell in >= 25 years of age group, major population with >= 25 years age group agreed (64.4%) to total cultural fidelity score. It was observed that the high age group Naga youth progressively agreed to their cultural fidelity with maximum (64.4%) score in agree, followed by 'don't know and disagree with (60.2%) and (51.6% respectively. Where as the low age group responded negatively with minimum in agree group followed by don't know and maximum in disagree group, which show that lower age group disagree to cultural fidelity of Naga. This shows that lower age group who falls under 25 years and below have almost lost the will power to work and hesitate to do all sorts of manual work, where as high age group agree or believe, more over want to follow the traditional work culture, which resulted high cultural fidelity score.

Table 5.1. Association between total cultural fidelity score and gender of Naga population

Gender	Total Cultural Fidelity Score			Total
	Agree	Don't Know	Disagree	
Male	38 52.10%	89 45.40%	13 41.90%	140 46.70%
Female	35 47.90%	107 54.60%	18 58.10%	160 53.30%
Total	73	196	31	300
Chi Square: 1.255; P > 0.05				

In the present study, the total cultural fidelity score of the total population showed no significant (P>0.05) association with gender table 5.1. As the majority (53.3%) of the total population were female, female population disagreed (58.1%) to the cultural fidelity of Nagas. It was observed that the male Naga youth progressively agreed to their cultural fidelity with maximum (52.1 %) score in agree, followed by don't know and disagree with (45.5%) and (41.9%) respectively. Where as the female youth responded negatively to fidelity score with minimum in agree group followed by don't know and maximum in disagree group, which show that female group disagree to cultural fidelity of Naga where as male members agree or believe, more over want to follow the traditional culture of their own, which resulted high cultural fidelity score. This shows that female members are highly influenced by the wave of social change and modernity.

Table 5.2. Association between total cultural fidelity score and profession of Naga population

Profession	Total Cultural Fidelity Score			Total
	Agree	Don't Know	Disagree	
Student	64	156	24	244
	87.70%	79.60%	77.40%	81.30%
Employed	9	40	7	56
	12.30%	20.40%	22.60%	18.70%
Total	73	196	31	300
Chi Square: 2.636; P > 0.05				

Majority of the study population were student, Major respondents of the study population were student agreed (87.70%) followed by 'don't know' and 'disagree' (79.60%) and (77.40%) to total cultural fidelity. No statistically significant relationship was found between profession and cultural fidelity score (P > 0.05). where as employed group maximum score in disagree (22.60%) followed by don't know (20.40%), agree (12.30%) which shows that student Naga youth are more interested and want to learn more traditional Naga culture.

Table 5.3. Association between total cultural fidelity score and place of stay of Naga population

Place of Stay	Total Cultural Fidelity Score			Total
	Agree	Don't Know	Disagree	
Chennai	6	7	1	14
	8.20%	3.60%	3.20%	4.70%
Kochi	5	5		10
	6.80%	2.60%		3.30%
Pune	8	8	1	17
	11.00%	4.10%	3.20%	5.70%
Kolkata	8	9	1	18
	11.00%	4.60%	3.20%	6.00%

Bengaluru	11	13	1	25
	15.10%	6.60%	3.20%	8.30%
Hyderabad	11	26	6	43
	15.10%	13.30%	19.40%	14.30%
Delhi	10	13	1	24
	13.70%	6.60%	3.20%	8.00%
Nagaland	14	115	20	149
	19.20%	58.70%	64.50%	49.70%
Total	73	196	31	300
Chi Square: 44.455; P < 0.001				

Total cultural fidelity score of the total population showed an association with place of stay. Majority of the study population in Nagaland disagreed (64.50%). There was very highly significant association between place of stay and cultural fidelity score (P < 0.001). Where as other cities agree maximum in Chennai (8.20%), Kochi (6.80%), Pune (11.00%), Kolkata (11.0%), Delhi (13.70%), except Hyderabad (19.40%) and Nagaland (64.50%) maximum score to total cultural fidelity. Which show that Naga youth residing at Chennai, Kochi, Pune, Kolkata, Delhi are more interested to know, learn, and true to Naga culture, which depicts that despite of locale of migration they still want to withhold the significance and the values of Naga tradition, and the Naga youth residing at Hyderabad and Nagaland disagree to cultural fidelity of Naga which shows that they have less sense to recognize the unique Naga cultural values and ethos.

Table 5.4. Association between total cultural fidelity score and Family monthly income of Naga population

Monthly Income	Total Cultural Fidelity Score			Total
	Agree	Don't Know	Disagree	
5000 - 10000	22 30.10%	54 27.60%	8 25.80%	84 28.00%
10000 - 15000	9 12.30%	31 15.80%	6 19.40%	46 15.30%
15000 - 20000	12 16.40%	28 14.30%	5 16.10%	45 15.00%
>= Rs. 20000	30 41.10%	83 42.30%	12 38.70%	125 41.70%
Total	73	196	31	300
Chi Square: 1.259; P > 0.05				

Total Cultural Fidelity score of the total population showed no association with Monthly Income of the population. Major population under 20000 expressed don't know (42.30%) followed by agreed (41.10%) to total cultural fidelity score. No significant association was noticed between monthly income and cultural fidelity score (P > 0.05). Where as maximum score comes under the population who receive 5000-10000 agreed (30.10%) followed by disagreed (25.80%) to cultural fidelity score. This shows that who comes under 20000 and above are more concern and true to traditional Naga culture. It indicates that higher family monthly income members have come to the realization of the need and aware of unique Naga cultural values and ethos.

Table 6.0. Association between Dignity of Labor and Age

Age	Dignity of Labor			Total
	Agree	Don't Know	Disagree	
< 25 yrs	32 34.80%	61 42.70%	26 40.00%	119 39.70%
>= 25 yrs	60 65.20%	82 57.30%	39 60.00%	181 60.30%
Total	92	143	65	300
Chi Square 1.454; P > 0.05				

Dignity of Labor score of the total population showed no association with Age of the population. Major population under >= 25 years age group agreed (65.20%) to Dignity of Labor. Majority of the population were >=25 years of age. No significant association was noticed between age and Dignity of Labor (P > 0.05) It was observed that the high age group Naga youth progressively agreed to their cultural fidelity with maximum (65.20%) score in agree, followed by and disagree don't know with 60.00% and 57.30% respectively. Where as the low age group responded negatively to fidelity score with minimum in agree group followed by maximum in don't know and disagree group, which show that lower age group disagree to Dignity of Labor. It is evident from the above table that majority youth who falls under the age group of 25 years and below feels ashamed to do manual work, and cannot do all personal and household work by them. Where as the high age group consider their job or labor with due respect and dignity which resulted high Dignity of Labor score.

Table 6.1. Association between Dignity of Labor and Gender

Gender	Dignity of Labor			Total
	Agree	Don't Know	Disagree	
Male	41	74	25	140
	44.60%	51.70%	38.50%	46.70%
Female	51	69	40	160
	55.40%	48.30%	61.50%	53.30%
Total	92	143	65	300
Chi Square 3.405; P > 0.05				

Dignity of Labor score of the total population showed no association with Gender of the population (P > 0.05). Gender difference in opinion towards all life activities is an expected fact. As the majority (53.30%) of the total population were female, female population disagreed (61.50%) to dignity of labor. It was observed that the male Naga youth responded negatively to the dignity of labor score (44.60 %) score in agree, followed by maximum score don't know and disagree with (51.70%) and (38.50%) respectively. Where as the female youth progressively agreed to dignity of labor score with minimum in don't know (48.30%) group followed by agree (55.40%) and maximum in disagree group (61.50%), which show that male group disagree to dignity of labor. This depict that female members are proud to be called themselves as hardworking person and can do all kinds of manual work where as male members were of less opinion to dignity of labor.

Table 6.2. Association between Dignity of Labor and Profession

Profession	Dignity of Labor			Total
	Agree	Don't Know	Disagree	
Student	79	111	54	244
	85.90%	77.60%	83.10%	81.30%
Employed	13	32	11	56
	14.10%	22.40%	16.90%	18.70%
Total	92	143	65	300
Chi Square 2.474; P > 0.05				

Majority of the study population were students, Majority of the study population were students agreed (85.90%) followed by 'disagree' and 'don't know' (83.10%), (77.60%) respectively to Dignity of Labor. Where as employed population score maximum in don't know (22.40%), disagree (16.90%), and agree (14.10%) No statistically significant relationship was found between Profession and Dignity of Labor (P > 0.05). This table 6.2 depicts that the student Naga youth have higher dignity score. They give more importance and value to the dignity of labor with compared to the employed Naga youth.

Table 6.3. Association between Dignity of Labor and Place of Stay

Place of Stay	Dignity of Labor			Total
	Agree	Don't Know	Disagree	
Chennai	6	8		14
	6.50%	5.60%		4.70%
Kochi	7	2	1	10
	7.60%	1.40%	1.50%	3.30%
Pune	4	8	5	17
	4.30%	5.60%	7.70%	5.70%
Kolkata	9	5	4	18
	9.80%	3.50%	6.20%	6.00%
Bengaluru	12	7	6	25
	13.00%	4.90%	9.20%	8.30%
Hyderabad	18	17	8	43
	19.60%	11.90%	12.30%	14.30%
Delhi	9	11	4	24
	9.80%	7.70%	6.20%	8.00%
Nagaland	27	85	37	149
	29.30%	59.40%	56.90%	49.70%
Total	92	143	65	300
Chi Square 34.526; P < 0.001				

Dignity of Labor score of the total population showed a very highly significant relationship between Place of Stay and Dignity of Labor (P < 0.001). Maximum score in agree are the Naga youth who are residing outside Nagaland. They are Chennai (6.50%), Kochi (7.60%), Kolkata (9.80%), Bengaluru (13.00%), Hyderabad (19.60%), and Delhi (9.80%). Where as Naga youth staying in Nagaland and Pune score maximum to disagree (56.90%), (7.70%) respectively to Dignity of Labor. This table 6.3 showed highest dignity of labor score responded by the Naga youth living outside Nagaland. The result revealed that, there was very highly significant association between Place of Stay and Dignity of Labor. Despite of the migration to different places, Naga youth have acknowledged the importance of manual work. Even though they are educated they do not hesitate to do all sorts of laborious work and considered traditional work culture as due dignity.

Table 6.4. Association between Dignity of Labor and Monthly Income

Monthly Income	Dignity of Labor			Total
	Agree	Don't Know	Disagree	
5000 - 10000	27	35	22	84
	29.30%	24.50%	33.80%	28.00%
10000 - 15000	16	23	7	46
	17.40%	16.10%	10.80%	15.30%
15000 - 20000	12	20	13	45
	13.00%	14.00%	20.00%	15.00%
>= Rs. 20000	37	65	23	125
	40.20%	45.50%	35.40%	41.70%
Total	92	143	65	300
Chi Square 5.248; P > 0.05				

Dignity of Labor score of the total population showed no association with Monthly Income of the Population Major population under 20000 expressed don't know (45.50%) followed by disagree (35.40%) to Dignity of Labor score. However, maximum score in agree also responded by the population group under 20000 (40.20%). No significant relationship was found between Monthly Income and Dignity of Labor (P > 0.05). The table 6.4 depicted that the Naga youth who comes under 20000 and above monthly income are more concern and value the Naga dignity of work.

Table 7.0. Association between Education and Language Score and Age

Age	Education and Language				Total
	Strongly Agree	Agree	Don't Know	Disagree	
< 25 yrs	2	32	56	29	119
	66.70%	29.60%	39.70%	60.40%	39.70%
>= 25 yrs	1	76	85	19	181
	33.30%	70.40%	60.30%	39.60%	60.30%
Total	3	108	141	48	300
Chi Square 14.096; P < 0.01					

Education and Language score of the total population showed highly significant relationship with age of the population. Major population under >=25 years Age group agreed (70.40%) to Education and Language. Majority of the population were >=25 years of age. There was highly significant relationship between Age and Education and Language (P < 0.01). It was observed that the low age group Naga youth progressively agreed to their Education and Language with maximum (66.70%) score in agree, followed by and disagree don't know with (60.40%) and (39.70%) respectively. Where as the high age group responded negatively with minimum in agree group followed by maximum in don't know and disagree group, which show that lower age group strongly agree (66.70%) to Education and Language. This table reveals that lower age group which fall under 25 years and below are eager to learn more of cultural norms and values, instructions and practices, and learning and speaking in their own mother tongue.

Table 7.1. Association between Education and Language score and Gender

Gender	Education and Language				Total
	Strongly Agree	Agree	Don't Know	Disagree	
Male	2	48	64	26	140
	66.70%	44.40%	45.40%	54.20%	46.70%
Female	1	60	77	22	160
	33.30%	55.60%	54.60%	45.80%	53.30%
Total	3	108	141	48	300
Chi Square 1.874; P > 0.05					

Education and Language score of the total population showed no association with Gender of the population (P > 0.05). Major populations were Male strongly agreed (66.70%) to Education and Language. Majority of the population were female. Gender difference in opinion towards all life activities is an expected fact. Major population of male strongly agreed to Education and Language. It was observed that the male Naga youth responded positively to their Education and Language (44.40 %) score in agree, followed by maximum score don't know and disagree with (45.40%) and (54.20%) respectively. Where as the female youth progressively agreed to Education and Language score with minimum in strongly agree (33.30%) group followed by disagree agree (45.80%) and maximum in agree group (55.60%), which show that female group are reluctant to learn social, political, economic, and religious values. where as Naga male agree to know more of cultural norms and values, and have high respect of Naga tradition with regard to Education and Language.

Table 7.2. Association between Education and Language score and Profession

Profession	Education and Language				Total
	Strongly Agree	Agree	Don't Know	Disagree	
Student	3	87	112	42	244
	100.00%	80.60%	79.40%	87.50%	81.30%
Employed		21	29	6	56
		19.40%	20.60%	12.50%	18.70%
Total	3	108	141	48	300
Chi Square 2.269; P > 0.05					

Majority of the study population were students, Major respondents of the study population were students strongly agreed (100.00%), followed by 'disagree' and 'don't know' (87.50%) and (79.40%) respectively to Education and Language. No statistically significant relationship was found between Profession and Education and Language P > 0.05. Where as employed Naga youth score minimum to disagree, agree and don't know. The table 7.2 depicts that the student population have high value and regard to Education and Language. Student respondents wanted to be acquainted themselves with more cultural values, instructions, and practices.

Table 7.3. Association between Education and Language score and Place of Stay

Place of Stay	Education and Language				Total
	Strongly Agree	Agree	Don't Know	Disagree	
Chennai		7	6	1	14
		6.50%	4.30%	2.10%	4.70%
Kochi		3	5	2	10
		2.80%	3.50%	4.20%	3.30%
Pune		7	7	3	17
		6.50%	5.00%	6.30%	5.70%
Kolkata		5	9	4	18
		4.60%	6.40%	8.30%	6.00%
Bengaluru		11	11	3	25
		10.20%	7.80%	6.30%	8.30%
Hyderabad	2	16	19	6	43
	66.70%	14.80%	13.50%	12.50%	14.30%

Delhi		12	7	5	24
		11.10%	5.00%	10.40%	8.00%
Nagaland	1	47	77	24	149
	33.30%	43.50%	54.60%	50.00%	49.70%
Total	3	108	141	48	300
Chi Square 15.521; P > 0.05					

Education and Language score of the total population showed no significant relationship between Place of Stay and Education and Language. Majority of the study population was in Nagaland. However, Naga youth living in Hyderabad score maximum to strongly agreed (66.70%) followed by those living in Nagaland (33.30%). And the Naga youth living at Chennai (6.50%), Pune (6.50%), Benguluru (10.20%), Hyderabad (14.80%), and Nagaland (43.50%) in agree. Where as Naga youth living at Kochi (4.20%), and Kolkata (8.30%) scored disagree to Education and Language. This table 7.3 depicts that, there was no significant association between Place of Stay and Education and Language P > 0.05 which means Naga youth living outside Nagaland are giving much importance to Education and Language. Though they are living outside Nagaland, they still want to learn more of social, political, economic, and religious values which contribute to cultural fidelity.

Table 7.4. Association between Education and Language score and Monthly Income

Monthly Income	Education and Language				Total
	Strongly Agree	Agree	Don't Know	Disagree	
5000 - 10000	1	27	45	11	84
	33.30%	25.00%	31.90%	22.90%	28.00%
10000 - 15000	2	21	18	5	46
	66.70%	19.40%	12.80%	10.40%	15.30%
15000 - 20000		12	24	9	45
		11.10%	17.00%	18.80%	15.00%
>= Rs. 20000		48	54	23	125
		44.40%	38.30%	47.90%	41.70%
Total	3	108	141	48	300
Chi Square 13.958; P > 0.05					

Education and Language score of the total population showed no association with monthly income of the population. Major population under 10000-15000 expressed strongly agreed (66.70%) followed by respondents who comes under

5000-10000 (33.30%) to Education and Language. No significant relationship was found between Monthly Income and Education and Language P > 0.05. This table 7.4 shows that the Naga youth who come under monthly income 20000 and above pay high respect to Naga cultural practices with regard to Education and Language.

Table 8.0. Association between Family System and Age

Age	Family System					Total
	Strongly Agree	Agree	Don't Know	Disagree	Strongly Disagree	
< 25 yrs	2 40.00%	53 36.60%	54 42.50%	10 45.50%		119 39.70%
>= 25 yrs	3 60.00%	92 63.40%	73 57.50%	12 54.50%	1 100.00%	181 60.30%
Total	5	145	127	22	1	300
Chi Square 1.985; P > 0.05						

Family System score of the total population showed insignificant relationship with Age of the population. Major population under >=25 years age group strongly disagreed (100.00%) to Family System. Majority of the population were >=25 years of age. There was no significant relationship between Age and Family System P > 0.05. Study populations under 25 years of age have low score to Family system, maximum to disagree, don't know, and agree. This shows that the Naga youth have fidelity to culture with regard to family system. It depicts that Naga youth still maintain family relationships, sense of belongingness in the family, sharing and communicating between parent and youth.

Table 8.1. Association between Family System and Gender

Gender	Family System					Total
	Strongly Agree	Agree	Don't Know	Disagree	Strongly Disagree	
Male	1 20.00%	63 43.40%	65 51.20%	11 50.00%		140 46.70%
Female	4 80.00%	82 56.60%	62 48.80%	11 50.00%	1 100.00%	160 53.30%
Total	5	145	127	22	1	300
Chi Square 4.045; P > 0.05						

Family System score of the total population showed no association with Gender of the population. Major population were female strongly disagreed (100.00%) followed by agree score (80.00%) to Family System. Majority of the population were female. No significant relationship was noticed between

Gender and Family System P > 0.05. Study population of male score minimum to strongly agrcc (20.00%), agree (43.405), disagree (50.00%), and don't know (51.20%). This table 8.1 shows that females are much more true to the concern on Naga family system compared to male respondents. Female members develop ways to communicate with each other, and build trust and respect among family members. Male members are of less opinion in building and maintaining healthy family relationship.

Table 8.2. Association between Family System and Profession

Profession	Family System					Total
	Strongly Agree	Agree	Don't Know	Disagree	Strongly Disagree	
Student	4 80.00%	120 82.80%	101 79.50%	18 81.80%	1 100.00%	244 81.30%
Employed	1 20.00%	25 17.20%	26 20.50%	4 18.20%		56 18.70%
Total	5	145	127	22	1	300
Chi Square 0.706; P > 0.05						

Majority of the study population were students, Major respondents of the study population were students strongly disagreed (100.00%) followed by agree (82.80%) to Family System. No statistically significant relationship was found between Profession and Family System P > 0.05. Naga employed youth score minimum agree (17.29%), and disagree (18.20). This table 8.2 depicts that student Naga have more concern or true to Naga family system. It reveals that Student Naga has learned about loving, caring, and sharing among family members.

Table 8.3. Association between Family System and Place of Stay

Place of Stay	Family System					Total
	Strongly Agree	Agree	Don't Know	Disagree	Strongly Disagree	
Chennai	1 20.00%	7 4.80%	6 4.70%			14 4.70%
Kochi		6 4.10%	4 3.10%			10 3.30%
Pune	2 40.00%	11 7.60%	3 2.40%	1 4.50%		17 5.70%

Kolkata		15 10.30%	2 1.60%		1 100.00%	18 6.00%
Bengaluru		16 11.00%	9 7.10%			25 8.30%
Hyderabad		21 14.50%	20 15.70%	2 9.10%		43 14.30%
Delhi		9 6.20%	14 11.00%	1 4.50%		24 8.00%
Nagaland	2 40.00%	60 41.40%	69 54.30%	18 81.80%		149 49.70%
Total	5	145	127	22	1	300
Chi Square 59.654; P < 0.001						

Family System score of the total population showed a very highly significant relationship between Place of Stay and Family System. Majority of the study population in Kolkata expressed strongly disagreed (100.00%). Where as Naga youth living at Pune (40.00%) and Nagaland (40.00%) score maximum to strongly agree. There was very highly significant association between Place of Stay and Family System P < 0.001. It was observed that Naga youth irrespective of their locale of migration have high value and concern on Naga Family system. This shows that Naga youths are maintaining a close relationship with parents irrespective of the locale of migration. This results in unity, sharing, mutual caring, understanding, and support.

Table 8.4. Association between Family System and Monthly Income

Monthly Income	Family System					Total
	Strongly Agree	Agree	Don't Know	Disagree	Strongly Disagree	
5000 - 10000		44 30.30%	37 29.10%	3 13.60%		84 28.00%
10000 - 15000		25 17.20%	19 15.00%	2 9.10%		46 15.30%
15000 - 20000	1 20.00%	22 15.20%	15 11.80%	6 27.30%	1 100.00%	45 15.00%
>= Rs. 20000	4 80.00%	54 37.20%	56 44.10%	11 50.00%		125 41.70%
Total	5	145	127	22	1	300
Chi Square 16.861; P > 0.05						

Family System score of the total population showed no association with Monthly Income of the population. Major population under 10000-15000 expressed strongly disagreed (100.00%) to Family System. No significant relationship was found between Monthly Income and Family System P > 0.05. Naga youth who are getting family monthly income under 20000 and above (80.00%) followed by agree (30.30%) under 5000-10000 and 10000-15000 (17.20%) to agree. This table 8.4 depicts that Naga youth who come under 20000 and above monthly income has higher sense of maintaining traditional Naga family system. They maintain good communication spirit and develop strong healthy relationship among family members.

Table 9.0. Association between Generation Gap and Age

Age	Generation Gap					Total
	Strongly Agree	Agree	Don't Know	Disagree	Strongly Disagree	
< 25 yrs		30 37.00%	33 41.80%	39 34.80%	17 68.00%	119 39.70%
>= 25 yrs	3 100.00%	51 63.00%	46 58.20%	73 65.20%	8 32.00%	181 60.30%
Total	3	81	79	112	25	300
Chi Square 11.837; P < 0.05						

Generation Gap score of the total population showed significant relationship with age of the population. Major population under >=5 years age group strongly agreed (100.00%) followed by agree (63.00%) to Generation Gap. Where as under age group 25 (37.00%) score minimum to agree followed by disagree (34.80%). Majority of the population were >=25 years of age. There was a significant relationship between Age and Generation Gap P < 0.05. This shows that the Naga youth could identify the generation gap between parent and youth. It is evident that there is a wide gap between parent and youth, where many youths considered their parents as old fashioned.

Table 9.1. Association between Generation Gap and Gender

Gender	Generation Gap					Total
	Strongly Agree	Agree	Don't Know	Disagree	Strongly Disagree	
Male	1 33.30%	37 45.70%	42 53.20%	46 41.10%	14 56.00%	140 46.70%
Female	2 66.70%	44 54.30%	37 46.80%	66 58.90%	11 44.00%	160 53.30%
Total	3	81	79	112	25	300
Chi Square 3.870; P > 0.05						

Generation Gap score of the total population showed no association with Gender of the population. Major population were female strongly agreed (66.70%) followed by male (33.30%) to Generation Gap. Where as female disagree (58.90%) and don't know (46.80%) and agree (45.70%) and the male strongly disagree (56.00%) followed by don't know (53.20%). Majority of the population were female. No significant relationship was noticed between gender and Generation Gap P > 0.05. This table 9.1 depicts that the female respondents are aware of the generation gap between parent and youth. Different people may have different attitudes. People of different gender may exhibit different attitudes. Lack of understanding and generation gap between parent and youth were found significant among the female respondents.

Table 9.2. Association between Generation Gap and Profession

Profession	Generation Gap					Total
	Strongly Agree	Agree	Don't Know	Disagree	Strongly Disagree	
Student	1	73	65	82	23	244
	33.30%	90.10%	82.30%	73.20%	92.00%	81.30%
Employed	2	8	14	30	2	56
	66.70%	9.90%	17.70%	26.80%	8.00%	18.70%
Total	3	81	79	112	25	300
Chi Square 15.458; P < 0.001						

Majority of the study population were students, Major respondents of the study population were students strongly disagreed (92.00%) followed by don't know (82.30%), agree (90.10%) to Generation Gap. Where as employed Naga youth score highest to strongly agree (66.70%) followed by disagree (26.80%) and don't know (17.70%). There is very highly statistically significant relationship was found between Profession and Generation Gap. It was observed that the employed Naga youth consider the existence of the generation gap between parent and youth and the parents do not even know many of the modern technologies and equipment youth use.

Table 9.3. Association between Generation Gap and Place of Stay

Place of Stay	Generation Gap					Total
	Strongly Agree	Agree	Don't Know	Disagree	Strongly Disagree	
Chennai		7	2	4	1	14
		8.60%	2.50%	3.60%	4.00%	4.70%
Kochi	1	3	4	2		10
	33.30%	3.70%	5.10%	1.80%		3.30%
Pune		9	2	4	2	17
		11.10%	2.50%	3.60%	8.00%	5.70%
Kolkata		7	4	6	1	18
		8.60%	5.10%	5.40%	4.00%	6.00%
Bengaluru		14	3	7	1	25
		17.30%	3.80%	6.30%	4.00%	8.30%
Hyderabad	1	14	14	12	2	43
	33.30%	17.30%	17.70%	10.70%	8.00%	14.30%
Delhi		8	8	6	2	24
		9.90%	10.10%	5.40%	8.00%	8.00%
Nagaland	1	19	42	71	16	149
	33.30%	23.50%	53.20%	63.40%	64.00%	49.70%
Total	3	81	79	112	25	300
Chi Square 56.414; P < 0.001						

Generation Gap score of the total population showed a very highly significant relationship between Place of Stay and Generation Gap P < 0.001. Majority of the study population in Nagaland expressed strongly disagreed (64.00%). Where as Naga youth residing in Kochi, Hyderabad and Nagaland score the same (33.30%) to strongly agree followed by Chennai (8.605), Pune (11.10%), Kolkata (8.60%), Benguluru (17.30%), and Delhi (9.90%) agree to generation gap between parent and youth. This shows that the Naga youth irrespective of their locale of migration have concern on generation gap. This is evident that generation gap is nothing but certain psychological and emotional gap between parents and youth. Generation gap creates misunderstanding and lack of communication between parents and youth.

Table 9.4. Association between Generation Gap and Monthly Income

Monthly Income	Generation Gap					Total
	Strongly Agree	Agree	Don't Know	Disagree	Strongly Disagree	
5000 - 10000		29	19	28	8	84
		35.80%	24.10%	25.00%	32.00%	28.00%
10000 - 15000	1	12	13	16	4	46
	33.30%	14.80%	16.50%	14.30%	16.00%	15.30%
15000 - 20000	1	8	10	24	2	45
	33.30%	9.90%	12.70%	21.40%	8.00%	15.00%
>= Rs. 20000	1	32	37	44	11	125
	33.30%	39.50%	46.80%	39.30%	44.00%	41.70%
Total	3	81	79	112	25	300
Chi Square 11.458; P > 0.05						

Generation Gap score of the total population showed no association with Monthly Income of the Population. Major population under 20000 expressed strongly disagreed (44.00%) to Generation Gap. Where as Naga youth who comes under the monthly income of 10000-15000, 15000-20000, and 20000 score the same to strongly agree (33.305) followed by 20000 and above (39.50) to agree. No significant relationship was found between monthly income and Generation Gap P > 0.05. This depicts that Naga youth who come under the category of the monthly income 20000 and above have admitted that there is a generation gap between parent and youth. This table 9.4 depicts that many parents do the mistake of evaluating youth by comparing their age with that of parents when he/ she was in the same age. Therefore, this shows Naga parents and youth needs deep attachment, where they will learn to respect and obey one another.

Table 10.0. Association between Naga Youth Style and Age

Age	Naga Youth					Total
	Strongly Agree	Agree	Don't Know	Disagree	Strongly Disagree	
< 25 yrs		31	26	42	20	119
		41.30%	32.90%	41.60%	45.50%	39.70%
>= 25 yrs	1	44	53	59	24	181
	100.00%	58.70%	67.10%	58.40%	54.50%	60.30%
Total	1	75	79	101	44	300
Chi Square: 3.022; P > 0.05						

Naga Youth Style score of the total population showed no significant in association with the Age of Population as shown in table 10.0 P > 0.05. As the majority (60.30%) of the total population fell in >= 25 years of age group strongly agree to Naga youth style, major population with >= 25 years age group agreed (100.00%) to Naga youth style. It was observed that the high age group Naga youth progressively agreed to their Naga youth style with maximum (58.70%) score in agree, followed by don't know and disagree with (67.10%) and (58.40%) respectively. Where as the low age group responded negatively with minimum in agree group followed by don't know and maximum in disagree group, which show that lower age group disagree to Naga youth style, where as higher age group 25 years and above agree or believe, more over want to follow the traditional culture of their own, also agrees on youth values and morals are not distinct from those of their parents, which results high cultural fidelity scores. This shows youth who falls under the age group 25 years and below are differ from those of their parent's culture. It clearly depicts Naga youth style differs from the culture of older generation.

Table 10.1. Association between Naga Youth Style and Gender

Gender	Naga Youth					Total
	Strongly Agree	Agree	Don't Know	Disagree	Strongly Disagree	
Male		36	39	53	12	140
		48.00%	49.40%	52.50%	27.30%	46.70%
Female	1	39	40	48	32	160
	100.00%	52.00%	50.60%	47.50%	72.70%	53.30%
Total	1	75	79	101	44	300
Chi Square: 9.179; P < 0.05						

In the present study, the Naga youth style score of the total population showed a significant (P<0.05) association with Gender table 10.1. As the majority (53.30%) of the total population were female, major female population strongly agree (100.00%) to the present living Naga style. It was observed that the female Naga youth progressively agreed to their Naga youth style with maximum (52.00 %) score in agree, followed by don't know and disagree with (50.60%) and (47.50%) respectively. Where as the male youth responded negatively with minimum in agree' group followed by don't know and maximum in disagree group, which show that male group do not agree to traditional values, norms, behavior, and present Naga youth style vary widely where as female Naga agree or believe, more over want to follow the traditional culture of their own, having interest, opinion, behavior of culture, which results high cultural fidelity score.

Table 10.2. Association between Naga Youth Style and Profession

Profession	Naga Youth					Total
	Strongly Agree	Agree	Don't Know	Disagree	Strongly Disagree	
Student		66	66	79	33	244
		88.00%	83.50%	78.20%	75.00%	81.30%
Employed	1	9	13	22	11	56
	100.00%	12.00%	16.50%	21.80%	25.00%	18.70%
Total	1	75	79	101	44	300
Chi Square: 8.615; P > 0.05						

Majority of the study population were students, Major respondents of the study population were employed strongly agreed (100.00%) to Naga youth style. Followed by strongly disagree and disagree score (25.00%) and (21.80%). Where as student score maximum in agree (88.00%) followed by don't know and disagree score. There was no statistically significant relationship was found between Profession and Naga Youth Style $P > 0.05$. This showed that the employed have a positive outlook to the present Naga youth living style. This group has developed shared experience and meanings of Naga culture.

Table 10.3. Association between Naga Youth Style and Place of Stay

Place of Stay	Naga Youth					Total
	Strongly Agree	Agree	Don't Know	Disagree	Strongly Disagree	
Chennai		5	4	4	1	14
		6.70%	5.10%	4.00%	2.30%	4.70%
Kochi	1	5	2	2		10
	100.00%	6.70%	2.50%	2.00%		3.30%
Pune		7	3	3	4	17
		9.30%	3.80%	3.00%	9.10%	5.70%
Kolkata		7	6	4	1	18
		9.30%	7.60%	4.00%	2.30%	6.00%
Bengaluru		9	7	7	2	25
		12.00%	8.90%	6.90%	4.50%	8.30%
Hyderabad		13	15	8	7	43
		17.30%	19.00%	7.90%	15.90%	14.30%
Delhi		9	7	5	3	24
		12.00%	8.90%	5.00%	6.80%	8.00%

Nagaland		20	35	68	26	149
		26.70%	44.30%	67.30%	59.10%	49.70%
Total	1	75	79	101	44	300
Chi Square: 68.177; P < 0.001						

Naga Youth score of the total population showed a very highly significant relationship between Place of Stay and Naga Youth. Majority of the study population were in Nagaland expressed strongly disagreed (59.10%) followed by disagree, don't know, and agree. Where as Naga youth living at Kochi score strongly agree to the present living style of Naga youth (100.00%) followed by agree score those living at Chennai, Pune, Kolkata, Bengaluru, and Delhi. Naga youth living at Hyderabad score maximum to don't know. It was observed there was very highly significant association between Place of Stay and Naga Youth Style $P < 0.001$. The table 10.3 showed that the youth living at Kochi have highest observation on the present living style of Naga youth. This depicts that Naga youth living outside Nagaland had strong influence on present youth living style and were influential in fashion and lifestyle.

Table 10.4. Association between Naga Youth Style and Monthly Income

Monthly Income	Naga Youth					Total
	Strongly Agree	Agree	Don't Know	Disagree	Strongly Disagree	
5000 - 10000		20	25	29	10	84
		26.70%	31.60%	28.70%	22.70%	28.00%
10000 - 15000		10	15	16	5	46
		13.30%	19.00%	15.80%	11.40%	15.30%
15000 - 20000		14	5	21	5	45
		18.70%	6.30%	20.80%	11.40%	15.00%
>= Rs. 20000	1	31	34	35	24	125
	100.00%	41.30%	43.00%	34.70%	54.50%	41.70%
Total	1	75	79	101	44	300
Chi Square : 13.891; P > 0.05						

Naga Youth Score of the total population showed no association with Monthly Income of the population. Major population under 20000 expressed strongly agreed (100.00%) to Naga youth followed by strongly disagree and don't know. Where as respondents comes under the category of monthly income 5000-10000 and 10000-15000 score highest to don't know (31.60%) and (19.00%) respectively No significant relationship was found between Monthly Income and Naga Youth $P > 0.05$. This table 10.4 showed that the respondents who come under the monthly of 20000 and above are agreeing to the present living style of the Naga youth. This shows that higher family monthly income have influenced their youth culture to create a new freedom that allowed them to move in ways one was unable to before.

Table 11.0. Association between Equality and Respect Score and Age

Age	Equality and Respect					Total
	Strongly Agree	Agree	Don't Know	Disagree	Strongly Disagree	
< 25 yrs		39	67	11	2	119
		38.60%	39.20%	47.80%	66.70%	39.70%
>= 25 yrs	2	62	104	12	1	181
	100.00%	61.40%	60.80%	52.20%	33.30%	60.30%
Total	2	101	171	23	3	300
Chi Square: 2.932; P > 0.05						

Equality and Respect Score of the total population showed insignificant relationship with age of the population. As the majority (60.30%) of the total population fell in >=25 years of age group strongly agree to Equality and Respect, major respondents of population with >=25 years age group agreed (100.00%) to Equality and Respect. It was observed that the high age group Naga youth progressively agreed to their Equality and Respect with maximum (61.40%) score in agree, followed by don't know and disagree with (60.80%) and (52.20%) respectively. Where as the low age group responded negative score progressively to Equality and Respect with minimum in agree group followed by don't know and maximum in disagree group, which show that lower age group disagree to Equality and Respect, where as high age group Naga considered their loyalty and respect towards their elders as well as obedience to the social norms and practices. They agreed to strong sense of equality and respect, which results high Equality and Respect score's than the lower age group.

Table 11.1. Association between Equality and Respect Score and Gender

Gender	Equality and Respect					Total
	Strongly Agree	Agree	Don't Know	Disagree	Strongly Disagree	
Male		53	81	6		140
		52.50%	47.40%	26.10%		46.70%
Female	2	48	90	17	3	160
	100.00%	47.50%	52.60%	73.90%	100.00%	53.30%
Total	2	101	171	23	3	300
Chi Square: 9.692; P < 0.05						

Equality and Respect score of the total population showed an association with Gender of the population. Major population were female strongly disagreed (100.00%) followed strongly disagree agreed (100.00%) to Equality and Respect. Majority of the population were female. A significant relationship was noticed between Gender and Equality and Respect (P > 0.05). Gender difference in opinion towards all life activities is an expected fact. It was observed that the female Naga youth responded positive to the Equality and Respect score (47.50 %) score in agree, followed by maximum score don't know and disagree with (52.60%) and (73.90%) respectively. Where as the male youth progressively agreed to Equality and respect score with minimum in strongly disagree (26.10%) group followed by don't know (47.40%) and maximum in agree group (52.50%), which show that female group agree to Equality and Respect. Where as Naga male disagree to Equality and Respect and have low respect of Naga values with regard to Equality and Respect.

Table 11.2. Association between Equality and Respect Score and Profession

Profession	Equality and Respect					Total
	Strongly Agree	Agree	Don't Know	Disagree	Strongly Disagree	
Student	2	89	133	17	3	244
	100.00%	88.10%	77.80%	73.90%	100.00%	81.30%
Employed		12	38	6		56
		11.90%	22.20%	26.10%		18.70%
Total	2	101	171	23	3	300
Chi Square: 6.496; P > 0.05						

Majority of the study population were students, Major respondents of the study population were students strongly agreed (100.00%) followed strongly disagreed (100.00%) to Equality and Respect. Where as employed score minimum in agree, don't know and disagree. There was no statistically significant relationship was found between Profession and Equality and Respect P > 0.05. The study depicts that the student Naga youth have more honor and Respect to the traditional practices and values with regard to Equality and respect. This shows they still maintain the sense of honesty, equality, humility, and respect for others.

Table 11.3. Association between Equality and Respect Score and Place of Stay

Place of Stay	Equality and Respect					Total
	Strongly Agree	Agree	Don't Know	Disagree	Strongly Disagree	
Chennai		4	10			14
		4.00%	5.80%			4.70%
Kochi		7	2	1		10
		6.90%	1.20%	4.30%		3.30%
Pune		8	7	2		17
		7.90%	4.10%	8.70%		5.70%
Kolkata		11	4	2	1	18
		10.90%	2.30%	8.70%	33.30%	6.00%
Bengaluru		11	14			25
		10.90%	8.20%			8.30%
Hyderabad	2	15	24	2		43
	100.00%	14.90%	14.00%	8.70%		14.30%
Delhi		8	12	3	1	24
		7.90%	7.00%	13.00%	33.30%	8.00%
Nagaland		37	98	13	1	149
		36.60%	57.30%	56.50%	33.30%	49.70%
Total	2	101	171	23	3	300
Chi Square: 47.458; $P < 0.05$						

Equality and Respect score of the total population showed a significant relationship between place of stay and Equality and Respect. Majority of the study population in Hyderabad expressed strongly disagreed (100.00%) followed by the youth living at Kochi and Bengaluru score in agree (6.90%) and (10.90%) respectively. Where as the Naga youth living at Chennai and Nagaland score did not know about Equality and Respect (5.80%) and (57.30%). There was a significant association between Place of Stay and Equality and Respect $P < 0.05$. The table 11.3 depicts that those residing at Hyderabad have more positive view to the Naga traditional practice and highly valued equality and respect score. This means irrespective of place of stay, Naga youth still have the sense of etiquette, equality and respect which are the key ingredients to maintain healthy relationship.

Table 11.4. Association between Equality and Respect score and Monthly Income

Monthly Income	Equality and Respect					Total
	Strongly Agree	Agree	Don't Know	Disagree	Strongly Disagree	
5000 - 10000		33 32.70%	47 27.50%	4 17.40%		84 28.00%
10000 - 15000	1 50.00%	12 11.90%	32 18.70%	1 4.30%		46 15.30%
15000 - 20000		9 8.90%	30 17.50%	5 21.70%	1 33.30%	45 15.00%
>= Rs. 20000	1 50.00%	47 46.50%	62 36.30%	13 56.50%	2 66.70%	125 41.70%
Total	2	101	171	23	3	300
Chi Square: 17.405; P > 0.05						

Equality and Respect score of the total population showed no association with Monthly Income of the population. Major population under 10000-15000 and 20000 expressed the same strongly agreed (50.00%) to Equality and Respect. Where as who comes under 5000-10000 score maximum in agree, don't know and disagree. No significant relationship was found between Monthly Income and Equality and Respect P > 0.05. This showed that the respondent who comes under the category of their monthly income 10000-150000 and 20000 give more importance to the value of the Naga culture with regard to Equality and Respect.

Table 12.0. Association between Dress and Ornaments Score and Age

Age	Dress and Ornaments					Total
	Strongly Agree	Agree	Don't Know	Disagree	Strongly Disagree	
< 25 yrs	1	34	54	28	2	119
	50.00%	39.50%	37.50%	44.40%	40.00%	39.70%
>= 25 yrs	1	52	90	35	3	181
	50.00%	60.50%	62.50%	55.60%	60.00%	60.30%
Total	2	86	144	63	5	300
Chi Square: 0.973; P > 0.05						

Dress and ornaments score of the total population showed insignificant relationship with age of the population. Major population under >25 years age group expressed don't know (62.05%) followed by agree and strongly agree (60.00%) and (60.50%) to Dress and Ornaments. Majority of the population were >25 years of age. Where as low age group score minimum to don't know and disagree. The table12.0 shows that the high age group accepts the reality that the Naga youth are more after the style of western. There was no significant relationship between Age and Dress and Ornaments P > 0.05. It is evident from the above table that overwhelming majority of the respondents has opted for western wear. This shows that changes are marked prominently in regard to western dress-code among Naga youth.

Table 12.1. Association between Dress and Ornaments Score and Gender

Gender	Dress and Ornaments					Total
	Strongly Agree	Agree	Don't Know	Disagree	Strongly Disagree	
Male	2	43	70	24	1	140
	100.00%	50.00%	48.60%	38.10%	20.00%	46.70%
Female		43	74	39	4	160
		50.00%	51.40%	61.90%	80.00%	53.30%
Total	2	86	144	63	5	300
Chi Square: 6.177; P > 0.05						

Dress and Ornaments score of the total population showed no association with Gender of the population. Major populations were male strongly agreed (100.00%) to Dress and Ornaments followed by agree, don't know, and disagree. Where as female score maximum in strongly disagree (80.00%). Majority of the population were female. No significant relationship was noticed between Gender and Dress and Ornaments P > 0.05. This table showed that the Male Naga youth have agreed to the fact of the change of modern way of dressing. This depicts that Male youth opt mostly fashionable outfits than the female members.

Table 12.2. Association between Dress and Ornaments Score and Profession

Profession	Dress and Ornaments					Total
	Strongly Agree	Agree	Don't Know	Disagree	Strongly Disagree	
Student	2	71	116	50	5	244
	100.00%	82.60%	80.60%	79.40%	100.00%	81.30%
Employed		15	28	13		56
		17.40%	19.40%	20.60%		18.70%
Total	2	86	144	63	5	300
Chi Square: 1.910; P > 0.05						

Majority of the study population were students, Major respondents of the study population were students strongly agreed (100.00%) followed strongly disagreed (100.00%) to Dress and Ornaments. Where as employed Naga youth score minimum to agree, don't know and disagree. There was no statistically significant relationship was found between Profession and Dress and Ornaments P > 0.05. The table 12.2 depicts that student Naga youth have concern and agreed to the questions on the transition taken place with regard to Dress and Ornaments. This shows that the Naga youth opted to wear fashionable way rather than to wear traditional ornaments and dresses. It is found that youth with the advent of modern civilization, dress-code seemed to have changed from being essentially an expression of one's identity to new culture and valued found their way into the present society.

Table 12.3. Association between Dress and Ornaments Score and Place of Stay

Place of Stay	Dress and Ornaments					Total
	Strongly Agree	Agree	Don't Know	Disagree	Strongly Disagree	
Chennai		4	9	1		14
		4.70%	6.30%	1.60%		4.70%
Kochi		5	3	2		10
		5.80%	2.10%	3.20%		3.30%
Pune		9	5	3		17
		10.50%	3.50%	4.80%		5.70%
Kolkata		3	14	1		18
		3.50%	9.70%	1.60%		6.00%
Bengaluru		9	11	4	1	25
		10.50%	7.60%	6.30%	20.00%	8.30%
Hyderabad	1	13	22	5	2	43
	50.00%	15.10%	15.30%	7.90%	40.00%	14.30%
Delhi	1	13	8	2		24
	50.00%	15.10%	5.60%	3.20%		8.00%
Nagaland		30	72	45	2	149
		34.90%	50.00%	71.40%	40.00%	49.70%
Total	2	86	144	63	5	300
Chi Square: 48.657; P < 0.01						

Dress and Ornaments Score of the total population showed a highly significant relationship between Place of Stay and Dress and Ornaments. Majority of the study population in Nagaland expressed disagreed (71.40%). Where as the Naga youth those living at Hyderabad and Delhi score the same (50.00%), strongly agree to Dress and Ornaments. There was a highly significant association between Place of Stay and Dress and Ornaments P< 0.01. Youth at Kochi and Pune score to agree (5.80%) and (10.50%0 respectively. It was observed that the youth staying at Hyderabad and Delhi have much concern and agreed to the modern way of dress code. On the other hand, those of whom stay at Chennai, Pune, Kolkata, and Bengaluru responded to don't know and disagree with regard to Dress and Ornaments. Despite of their stay at different places, majority of the Naga youth have accepted the reality that there is a change of wearing western dress-code and ornaments in the modern society.

Table 12.4. Association between Dress and Ornaments Score and Monthly Income

Monthly Income	Dress and Ornaments					Total
	Strongly Agree	Agree	Don't Know	Disagree	Strongly Disagree	
5000 - 10000		23	44	16	1	84
		26.70%	30.60%	25.40%	20.00%	28.00%
10000 - 15000		11	26	8	1	46
		12.80%	18.10%	12.70%	20.00%	15.30%
15000 - 20000		13	16	15	1	45
		15.10%	11.10%	23.80%	20.00%	15.00%
>= Rs. 20000	2	39	58	24	2	125
	100.00%	45.30%	40.30%	38.10%	40.00%	41.70%
Total	2	86	144	63	5	300
Chi Square: 10.204; P > 0.05						

Dress and Ornaments score of the total population showed no association with Monthly Income of the population. Major population under 20000 expressed strongly agreed (100.00%) to Dress and Ornaments followed by agree (45.30%). Where as who come under 5000-10000 score to don't know (30.60%) and strongly disagree to Dress and Ornaments (20.00%) and the same strongly disagree score responded by those who comes under 10000-15000 and 15000-20000. No significant relationship was found between Monthly Income and Dress and Ornaments P > 0.05. The table 12.4 showed that who come under 20000 and above monthly income have agreed to the change of Dress and Ornaments among Naga youth. This indicates that higher family Monthly Income have greater attitude towards the comfort, fashion, than wearing traditional attire.

Table 13.0. Association between Music and Dance Score and Age

Age	Music and Dance					Total
	Strongly Agree	Agree	Don't Know	Disagree	Strongly Disagree	
< 25 yrs	2	36	60	20	1	119
	66.70%	37.10%	39.70%	42.60%	50.00%	39.70%
>= 25 yrs	1	61	91	27	1	181
	33.30%	62.90%	60.30%	57.40%	50.00%	60.30%
Total	3	97	151	47	2	300
Chi Square: 1.431; P > 0.05						

Music and Dance Score of the total population showed insignificant relationship with Age of the population. Major population under <25 years age group expressed strongly agreed (66.70%) followed by strongly disagree, disagree and don't know to Music and Dance. Majority of the population were >25 years of age score maximum to agree (62.90%) followed by don't know and disagree. There was no significant relationship between Age and Music and Dance P > 0.05. The table 13.0 depicts that low age group have positive attribution to traditional Music and Dance. Where as the higher age group do not give much importance or find relevance to the traditional music and dance. They prefer to learn new things like songs of all sorts, dances, and fashion.

Table 13.1. Association between Music and Dance Score and Gender

Gender	Music and Dance					Total
	Strongly Agree	Agree	Don't Know	Disagree	Strongly Disagree	
Male	3	43	75	17	2	140
	100.00%	44.30%	49.70%	36.20%	100.00%	46.70%
Female		54	76	30		160
		55.70%	50.30%	63.80%		53.30%
Total	3	97	151	47	2	300
Chi Square: 8.554; P > 0.05						

Music and Dance Score of the total population showed no association with gender of the population. Major population were male strongly agreed (100.00%) followed by strongly disagree, agree and don't know to Music and Dance. Majority of the population were female score minimum to don't know, agree and disagree. No significant relationship was noticed between Gender and Music and Dance P > 0.05. This showed that male Naga youth have agreed to the disintegration of the unique cultural music, dances, folklores, and value of the tradition.

Table 13.2. Association between Music and Dance Score and Profession

Profession	Music and Dance					Total
	Strongly Agree	Agree	Don't Know	Disagree	Strongly Disagree	
Student	3	85	118	36	2	244
	100.00%	87.60%	78.10%	76.60%	100.00%	81.30%
Employed		12	33	11		56
		12.40%	21.90%	23.40%		18.70%
Total	3	97	151	47	2	300
Chi Square: 5.385; P > 0.05						

Majority of the study population were students, Major respondents of the study population were students strongly agreed (100.00%) followed strongly disagreed (100.00%) agree and don't know to Music and Dance. Where as Employed Naga youth score minimum to agree, don't know, and disagree. There was no statistically significant relationship was found between Profession and Music and Dance P > 0.05. The table 13.2 showed that the student Naga youth agreed to the questions with regard to Music and Dance. This depicts that they have almost forgotten all cultural songs, dances, folklores and the valuable oral tradition.

Table 13.3. Association between Music and Dance Score and Place of Stay

Place of Stay	Music and Dance					Total
	Strongly Agree	Agree	Don't Know	Disagree	Strongly Disagree	
Chennai		7	5	2		14
		7.20%	3.30%	4.30%		4.70%
Kochi		6	4			10
		6.20%	2.60%			3.30%
Pune		10	4	3		17
		10.30%	2.60%	6.40%		5.70%
Kolkata		7	10	1		18
		7.20%	6.60%	2.10%		6.00%
Bengaluru		13	10	1	1	25
		13.40%	6.60%	2.10%	50.00%	8.30%
Hyderabad	1	14	23	5		43
	33.30%	14.40%	15.20%	10.60%		14.30%

Delhi	1	9	13	1		24
	33.30%	9.30%	8.60%	2.10%		8.00%
Nagaland	1	31	82	34	1	149
	33.30%	32.00%	54.30%	72.30%	50.00%	49.70%
Total	3	97	151	47	2	300
Chi Square: 43.113; P < 0.05						

Music and Dance Score of the total population showed a significant relationship between Place of Stay and Music and Dance. Majority of the study population in Nagaland expressed disagreed (72.30%) followed by strongly disagree those of whom are staying at Benguluru and Nagaland (50.00%). Where as Naga youth staying at Hyderabad, Delhi, and Nagaland score the same (33.30%) followed by the agree score those at Chennai, Kochi, Pune, and Kolkata. There was significant association between Place of Stay and Music and Dance P < 0.05. The table 13.3 depicts that those youth living at Hyderabad, Delhi, and Nagaland have concern and value with regard to Music and Dance. This shows they still love to listen music, watch folk dances rather than listening to classical music and dances.

Table 13.4. Association between Music and Dance score and Monthly income

Monthly Income	Music and Dance					Total
	Strongly Agree	Agree	Don't Know	Disagree	Strongly Disagree	
5000 - 10000	1	28	45	10		84
	33.30%	28.90%	29.80%	21.30%		28.00%
10000 - 15000		18	17	11		46
		18.60%	11.30%	23.40%		15.30%
15000 - 20000		13	25	6	1	45
		13.40%	16.60%	12.80%	50.00%	15.00%
>= Rs. 20000	2	38	64	20	1	125
	66.70%	39.20%	42.40%	42.60%	50.00%	41.70%
Total	3	97	151	47	2	300
Chi Square: 9.912; P > 0.05						

Music and Dance Score of the total population showed no association with monthly income of the population. Major population under 20000 expressed strongly agreed (66.70%) followed by strongly disagree, disagree and don't know to Music and Dance. Where as who come under the category of 5000-10000 score to strongly agree (33.30%), followed by agree, don't know and disagree. No significant relationship was found between Monthly Income and Music and

Dance P > 0.05. This showed respondents who come under the income 2000 and above give more importance and value with regard to Music and Dance.

Table 14.0. Association between Behavior and Attitude Score and Age

Age	Behavior and Attitude					Total
	Strongly Agree	**Agree**	**Don't Know**	**Disagree**	**Strongly Disagree**	
< 25 yrs	1	54	60	3	1	119
	25.00%	37.50%	42.00%	37.50%	100.00%	39.70%
>= 25 yrs	3	90	83	5		181
	75.00%	62.50%	58.00%	62.50%		60.30%
Total	4	144	143	8	1	300
Chi Square: 2.492; P > 0.05						

Behavior and Attitude score of the total population showed insignificant relationship with age of the population. Major study population under <25 years age group expressed strongly disagreed (100.00%) followed by don't know and disagree to Behavior and Attitude. Where as respondent under age group >=25 yrs score maximum to agree (75.00%), agree, disagree (62.50%), and don't know (58.00%). Majority of the population were >25 years of age. There was no significant relationship between Age and Behavior and Attitude P > 0.05. This low age group identify and proud to be called born as Naga. Where as higher age group members wanted to adopt the patterns and styles of other societies.

Table 14.1. Association between Behavior and Attitude Score and Gender

Gender	Behavior and Attitude					Total
	Strongly Agree	**Agree**	**Don't Know**	**Disagree**	**Strongly Disagree**	
Male	3	71	62	4		140
	75.00%	49.30%	43.40%	50.00%		46.70%
Female	1	73	81	4	1	160
	25.00%	50.70%	56.60%	50.00%	100.00%	53.30%
Total	4	144	143	8	1	300
Chi Square: 3.233; P > 0.05						

Behavior and Attitude score of the total population showed no association with gender of the population. Major populations were female strongly disagreed (100.00%) to Behavior and Attitude. Majority of the population were female. No significant relationship was noticed between Gender and Behavior and Attitude

P > 0.05. The male members responded negatively to behavior and attitude score progressively with minimum in strongly agree group followed by don't know and maximum in disagree group, which show male members disagree to behavior and attitude of Naga where as female members agree or believe, more over want to follow the traditional culture of their own, which results high behavior and attitude score.

Table 14.2. Association between Behavior and Attitude score and Profession

Profession	Behavior and Attitude					Total
	Strongly Agree	Agree	Don't Know	Disagree	Strongly Disagree	
Student	3	120	113	7	1	244
	75.00%	83.30%	79.00%	87.50%	100.00%	81.30%
Employed	1	24	30	1		56
	25.00%	16.70%	21.00%	12.50%		18.70%
Total	4	144	143	8	1	300
Chi Square: 1.419; P > 0.05						

Majority of the study population were students, Major respondents of the study population were students strongly disagreed (100.00%) to Behavior and Attitude followed by agree, don't know, and strongly agree where as employed youth score minimum to agree, don't know, and strongly agree. There was no statistically significant relationship found between Profession and Behavior and Attitude P > 0.05. This table 14.2 showed that the student Naga have positive attitude to Behavior and attitude score. Students Naga youth respondents agree to endure their beliefs, feelings, and behavioral tendencies towards Naga cultural beliefs and practices.

Table 14.3. Association between Behavior and Attitude Score and Place of Stay

Place of Stay	Behavior and Attitude					Total
	Strongly Agree	Agree	Don't Know	Disagree	Strongly Disagree	
Chennai		9	5			14
		6.30%	3.50%			4.70%
Kochi		7	3			10
		4.90%	2.10%			3.30%
Pune		9	8			17
		6.30%	5.60%			5.70%
Kolkata		13	5			18
		9.00%	3.50%			6.00%

Bengaluru		15	9	1		25
		10.40%	6.30%	12.50%		8.30%
Hyderabad		20	22	1		43
		13.90%	15.40%	12.50%		14.30%
Delhi		11	13			24
		7.60%	9.10%			8.00%
Nagaland	4	60	78	6	1	149
	100.00%	41.70%	54.50%	75.00%	100.00%	49.70%
Total	4	144	143	8	1	300
Chi Square: 19.509; P > 0.05						

Behavior and Attitude score of the total population showed no significant relationship between Place of Stay and Behavior and Attitude. Majority of the study population in Nagaland expressed strongly agreed (100.00%) followed by Hyderabad (13.90%), Bengaluru (10.40%), Kotkata (9.00%), Delhi (7.60%), Pune (6.30%), Chennai (6.30%), and Kochi (4.90%). There was no association found between Place of Stay and Behavior and Attitude P > 0.05. This table 14.3 showed that Naga youth who are living in Nagaland are given much importance and concern towards behavior and attitude.

Table 14.4. Association between Behavior and Attitude score and Monthly Income

Monthly Income	**Behavior and Attitude**					**Total**
	Strongly Agree	**Agree**	**Don't Know**	**Disagree**	**Strongly Disagree**	
5000 - 10000		36	45	3		84
		25.00%	31.50%	37.50%		28.00%
10000 - 15000	1	24	21			46
	25.00%	16.70%	14.70%			15.30%
15000 - 20000	1	24	18	2		45
	25.00%	16.70%	12.60%	25.00%		15.00%
>= Rs. 20000	2	60	59	3	1	125
	50.00%	41.70%	41.30%	37.50%	100.00%	41.70%
Total	4	144	143	8	1	300
Chi Square: 7.259; P > 0.05						

Behavior and Attitude score of the total population showed no association with Monthly Income of the population. Major population under 20000 expressed strongly disagreed (100.00%) followed by strongly agree, agree, don't know and disagree to Behavior and Attitude. Respondent who comes under monthly income 10000-15000 and 15000-20000 score the same to agree (25.00%) No significant relationship was found between Monthly Income and Behavior and Attitude P > 0.05. This showed who comes under 20000 are agree or follow more Naga traditional practice with regard to behavior and attitude.

Table 15.0. Association between Hospitality and Age

Age	Hospitality				Total
	Strongly Agree	Agree	Don't Know	Disagree	
< 25 yrs	7	82	26	4	119
	36.80%	40.20%	37.70%	50.00%	39.70%
>= 25 yrs	12	122	43	4	181
	63.20%	59.80%	62.30%	50.00%	60.30%
Total	19	204	69	8	300
Chi Square 0.588; P > 0.05					

Hospitality score of the total population showed insignificant relationship with Age of the population. Major respondents of population under >=25 years age group expressed strongly agreed (63.20%) to Hospitality. No significant association was noticed between Age and Hospitality (P > 0.05). It was observed that the high age group Naga youth progressively agreed to their Hospitality with maximum (63.20%) score in strongly agree, followed by and disagree don't know with (50.00%) and (62.30%) respectively. Where as the low age group responded negative to Hospitality score progressively with minimum in agree group followed by maximum in don't know and disagree group, which show that lower age group disagree to Hospitality. Where as high age group Naga consider Hospitality as one of the high Naga cultural practices which result high Hospitality score.

Table 15.1. Association between Hospitality and Gender

Gender	Hospitality				Total
	Strongly Agree	Agree	Don't Know	Disagree	
Male	6	101	27	6	140
	31.60%	49.50%	39.10%	75.00%	46.70%
Female	13	103	42	2	160
	68.40%	50.50%	60.90%	25.00%	53.30%
Total	19	204	69	8	300
Chi Square 6.555; P > 0.05					

Hospitality score of the total population showed no association with Gender of the population. Major populations were female. Majority of the population were female strongly agree (68.40%) followed by don't know and disagree. Where as male respondent score minimum in strongly agree (31.60%) followed by don't know and agree. No significant relationship was noticed between Gender and Hospitality P > 0.05. This table 15.1 showed those females are more concern to have a sense of hospitality which result high hospitality score than the male respondents.

Table 15.2. Association between Hospitality and Profession

Profession	Hospitality				Total
	Strongly Agree	Agree	Don't Know	Disagree	
Student	12	171	54	7	244
	63.20%	83.80%	78.30%	87.50%	81.30%
Employed	7	33	15	1	56
	36.80%	16.20%	21.70%	12.50%	18.70%
Total	19	204	69	8	300
Chi Square 5.597; P > 0.05					

Majority of the study population were students, Major respondents of the study population were students disagreed (87.50%) followed by agree (83.80%), don't know and strongly (63.20%) to Hospitality. Where as employed score in strongly agree (36.80%) followed by don't know, agree, and disagree. There was no statistically significant relationship found between Profession and Hospitality P > 0.05. This table 15.2 depicts that student Naga have high sense or want to maintain good spirit of hospitality.

Table 15.3. Association between Hospitality and Place of Stay

Place of Stay	Hospitality				Total
	Strongly Agree	Agree	Don't Know	Disagree	
Chennai	2	11	1		14
	10.50%	5.40%	1.40%		4.70%
Kochi		6	4		10
		2.90%	5.80%		3.30%
Pune	1	12	4		17
	5.30%	5.90%	5.80%		5.70%
Kolkata	2	12	4		18
	10.50%	5.90%	5.80%		6.00%

Bengaluru		20	5		25
		9.80%	7.20%		8.30%
Hyderabad	2	26	14	1	43
	10.50%	12.70%	20.30%	12.50%	14.30%
Delhi	1	21	2		24
	5.30%	10.30%	2.90%		8.00%
Nagaland	11	96	35	7	149
	57.90%	47.10%	50.70%	87.50%	49.70%
Total	19	204	69	8	300
Chi Square 19.818; P > 0.05					

Hospitality score of the total population showed no significant relationship between Place of Stay and Hospitality P > 0.05. Majority of the study population in Nagaland expressed disagreed (87.50%) followed by agree (57.90%), don't know (50.70%), and agree (47.19%) to Hospitality. There was no significant association found between Place of Stay and Hospitality. Naga youth staying at Chennai, Kolkata, and Hyderabad agree the same score (10.50%). This depicts who are residing in Nagaland have high regard and maintain spirit of hospitality.

Table 15.4. Association between Hospitality and Monthly Income

Monthly Income	Hospitality				Total
	Strongly Agree	Agree	Don't Know	Disagree	
5000 - 10000	5	61	16	2	84
	26.30%	29.90%	23.20%	25.00%	28.00%
10000 - 15000		36	9	1	46
		17.60%	13.00%	12.50%	15.30%
15000 - 20000	3	28	13	1	45
	15.80%	13.70%	18.80%	12.50%	15.00%
>= Rs. 20000	11	79	31	4	125
	57.90%	38.70%	44.90%	50.00%	41.70%
Total	19	204	69	8	300
Chi Square 7.657; P > 0.05					

Hospitality score of the total population showed no association with Monthly Income of the population. Major population under 20000 expressed strongly agreed (57.90%) followed by disagree, don't know, and agree to Hospitality. Where as who comes under 5000-10000 minimum score in strongly, don't know and disagree. No significant relationship was found between Monthly Income and Hospitality P > 0.05. The table depicts that who comes under 20000 and above appreciates the sense of Naga hospitality which result high Hospitality score.

Table 16.0. Association between Community Spirit and Age

Age	Community Spirit					Total
	Strongly Agree	Agree	Don't Know	Disagree	Strongly Disagree	
< 25 yrs	5	42	60	12		119
	83.30%	40.00%	38.70%	38.70%		39.70%
>= 25 yrs	1	63	95	19	3	181
	16.70%	60.00%	61.30%	61.30%	100.00%	60.30%
Total	6	105	155	31	3	300
Chi Square: 6.829 ; P > 0.05						

Community Spirit score of the total population showed insignificant relationship with Age of the population. Major population under >=25 years age group expressed strongly disagreed (100.00%) followed by minimum score in strongly score (16.70%) to Community Spirit. Where as under low age group score minimum in disagree and don't know (38.79%) but scored highest in strongly agree (83.30%). Majority of the population were >25 years of age. There was no significant relationship found between Age and Community Spirit P > 0.05. This table 16.0 showed that low age groups have high sense of honesty, pay due respect to their elders to enhance the spirit of community life.

Table 16.1. Association between Community Spirit and Gender

Gender	Community Spirit					Total
	Strongly Agree	Agree	Don't Know	Disagree	Strongly Disagree	
Male	5	52	67	14	2	140
	83.30%	49.50%	43.20%	45.20%	66.70%	46.70%
Female	1	53	88	17	1	160
	16.70%	50.50%	56.80%	54.80%	33.30%	53.30%
Total	6	105	155	31	3	300
Chi Square: 4.833 ; P > 0.05						

Community Spirit score of the total population showed no association with Gender of the population. Major population were male strongly agreed (83.30%) followed by strongly disagree (66.70%), agree (49.50%), disagree (45.20%) and don't know (43.20%) to Community Spirit. Where as female score minimum in strongly agree (16.70%), followed by strongly disagree (33.30%), agree (50.50%), disagree (54.80%), and don't know (56.80%). Majority of the population were female. No significant relationship was noticed between Gender and Community Spirit P > 0.05. This shows that the Male Naga has maintain higher spirit of community life compared to the female respondents. It depicts that they are being involved in big groups or any kind of social gathering.

Table 16.2. Association between Community Spirit and Profession

Profession	Community Spirit					Total
	Strongly Agree	Agree	Don't Know	Disagree	Strongly Disagree	
Student	5	92	122	22	3	244
	83.30%	87.60%	78.70%	71.00%	100.00%	81.30%
Employed	1	13	33	9		56
	16.70%	12.40%	21.30%	29.00%		18.70%
Total	6	105	155	31	3	300
Chi Square: 6.334 ; P > 0.05						

Majority of the study population were students, Major respondents of the study population were students strongly disagreed (100.00%) followed by agree (87.60%), strongly agree (83.30%), and disagree (71.00%) to Community Spirit. Where as employed score minimum in agree, strongly agree, don't know and disagree. There was no statistically significant relationship found between Profession and Community Spirit P > 0.05. This depicts students Naga have more sense and concern with regard to Naga community life. This group of youth maintains an equal treatment to all irrespective of different background.

Table 16.3. Association between Community Spirit and Place of Stay

Place of Stay	Community Spirit					Total
	Strongly Agree	Agree	Don't Know	Disagree	Strongly Disagree	
Chennai	1	4	7	2		14
	16.70%	3.80%	4.50%	6.50%		4.70%
Kochi		7	3			10
		6.70%	1.90%			3.30%
Pune		8	8	1		17
		7.60%	5.20%	3.20%		5.70%
Kolkata		6	11	1		18
		5.70%	7.10%	3.20%		6.00%
Bengaluru		13	10	2		25
		12.40%	6.50%	6.50%		8.30%

Hyderabad	1	13	27	2		43
	16.70%	12.40%	17.40%	6.50%		14.30%
Delhi		13	9	2		24
		12.40%	5.80%	6.50%		8.00%
Nagaland	4	41	80	21	3	149
	66.70%	39.00%	51.60%	67.70%	100.00%	49.70%
Total	6	105	155	31	3	300
Chi Square: 28.388 ; P > 0.05						

Community Spirit score of the total population showed no significant relationship between place of stay and Community Spirit. Majority of the study population in Nagaland expressed strongly disagreed (100.00%) followed by strongly agree (66.70%), Hyderabad and Chennai (16.70%) to Community Spirit. Where as Kochi, Pune, Bengaluru and Delhi score agree (6.70%), (7.60%), (12.40%) respectively. There was no significant association found between place of Stay and Community Spirit P > 0.05. This table 16.3 depicts that Naga youth residing in Nagaland have much concern and maintain good spirit of community life. This reveals that Naga youth who are residing in Nagaland have higher sense to maintain and associate with the people irrespective of different social status.

Table 16.4. Association between Community Spirit and Monthly Income

Monthly Income	Community Spirit					Total
	Strongly Agree	Agree	Don't Know	Disagree	Strongly Disagree	
5000 - 10000	2	31	44	6	1	84
	33.30%	29.50%	28.40%	19.40%	33.30%	28.00%
10000 - 15000		15	25	6		46
		14.30%	16.10%	19.40%		15.30%
15000 - 20000	3	15	21	6		45
	50.00%	14.30%	13.50%	19.40%		15.00%
>= Rs. 20000	1	44	65	13	2	125
	16.70%	41.90%	41.90%	41.90%	66.70%	41.70%
Total	6	105	155	31	3	300
Chi Square: 10.210 ; P > 0.05						

Community Spirit score of the total population showed no association with Monthly Income of the population. Major population under 20000 expressed strongly disagreed (66.70%) followed by don't know, agree and disagree to Community Spirit. Respondents who come under monthly income 15000

-20000 score in strongly agree (50.0%) and 5000-10000 (33.30%). No significant relationship was found between monthly income and Community Spirit P > 0.05. This table 16.4 depicts that respondents who come under 15000-20000 have high sense to maintain the spirit of Naga community life.

Table 17.0. Association between Folklore and Art score and Age

Age	Folklore and Art					Total
	Strongly Agree	Agree	Don't Know	Disagree	Strongly Disagree	
< 25 yrs		29	41	44	5	119
		34.50%	47.70%	37.60%	41.70%	39.70%
>= 25 yrs	1	55	45	73	7	181
	100.00%	65.50%	52.30%	62.40%	58.30%	60.30%
Total	1	84	86	117	12	300
Chi Square: 4.118 ; P > 0.05						

Folklore and Art score of the total population showed insignificant relationship with Age of the population. Major population under >=25 years age group expressed strongly agreed (100.00%) followed by agree, disagree, and don't know to Folklore and Art. Where as low age group score minimum in agree (34.50%) followed by disagree and don't know. Majority of the population were >25 years of age. There was no significant relationship found between Age and Folklore and Art P > 0.05. This study shows that high age group Naga has interest and want to learn more of the Naga traditional culture with regard to Folklore and Art, which was handed by their fore parents as medium of communication.

Table 17.1. Association between Folklore and Art score and Gender

Gender	Folklore and Art					Total
	Strongly Agree	Agree	Don't Know	Disagree	Strongly Disagree	
Male	1	44	38	51	6	140
	100.00%	52.40%	44.20%	43.60%	50.00%	46.70%
Female		40	48	66	6	160
		47.60%	55.80%	56.40%	50.00%	53.30%
Total	1	84	86	117	12	300
Chi Square: 2.956 ; P > 0.05						

Folklore and Art score of the total population showed no association with Gender of the population. Major populations were female. However, male respondents score in strongly agreed (100.00%) followed by agree, don't know and disagree to Folklore and Art. Where as female score minimum in Agree followed by don't know and disagree. No significant relationship was noticed between Gender and Folklore and Art $P > 0.05$. This table 17.1 depicts that male respondents are more into the traditional culture with regard to Folklore and Art. Male members still regard the traditional cultural practices such as folklore, art and crafts are relevant and useful in the present world.

Table 17.2. Association between Folklore and Art score and Profession

Profession	Folklore and Art					Total
	Strongly Agree	Agree	Don't Know	Disagree	Strongly Disagree	
Student	1	70	73	90	10	244
	100.00%	83.30%	84.90%	76.90%	83.30%	81.30%
Employed		14	13	27	2	56
		16.70%	15.10%	23.10%	16.70%	18.70%
Total	1	84	86	117	12	300
Chi Square: 2.695 ; P > 0.05						

Majority of the study population were students, Major respondents of the study population were students strongly agreed (100.00%) followed by don't know, agree, strongly agree and disagree to Folklore and Art. Where as employed score minimum in agree (16.70%) followed by don't know, disagree, and strongly disagree. There was no statistically significant relationship found between Profession and Folklore and Art $P > 0.05$. The study showed that the student Naga give high respect and importance to the traditional practice of Folklore and Art. Where as the employed members have no longer interest in the historical rich culture of the Nagas.

Table 17.3. Association between Folklore and Art score and Place of stay

Place of Stay	Folklore and Art					Total
	Strongly Agree	Agree	Don't Know	Disagree	Strongly Disagree	
Chennai		5	3	6		14
		6.00%	3.50%	5.10%		4.70%
Kochi		4	5	1		10
		4.80%	5.80%	0.90%		3.30%
Pune		5	7	4	1	17
		6.00%	8.10%	3.40%	8.30%	5.70%
Kolkata		7	5	6		18
		8.30%	5.80%	5.10%		6.00%
Bengaluru		13	3	6	3	25
		15.50%	3.50%	5.10%	25.00%	8.30%

Hyderabad	1	10	14	18		43
	100.00%	11.90%	16.30%	15.40%		14.30%
Delhi		11	5	7	1	24
		13.10%	5.80%	6.00%	8.30%	8.00%
Nagaland		29	44	69	7	149
		34.50%	51.20%	59.00%	58.30%	49.70%
Total	1	84	86	117	12	300
Chi Square: 40.938 ; P < 0.05						

Folklore and Art score of the total population showed a significant relationship between Place of Stay and Folklore and Art. Majority of the study population in Hyderabad expressed strongly agreed (100.00%) followed those residing in Nagaland score in agree (34.50%), Chennai (6.00%), Kolkata (8.30%), to Folklore and Art. There was a significant association found between Place of Stay and Folklore and Art P < 0.05 that the Naga youth who are residing at Hyderabad are much more interest and have positive outlook with regard to Folklore and Art. This shows that many Naga youth have looked down upon their unique culture and rich material that was handed down by the fore parents.

Table 17.4. Association between Folklore and Art score and Monthly Income

Monthly Income	Folklore and Art					Total
	Strongly Agree	Agree	Don't Know	Disagree	Strongly Disagree	
5000 - 10000		25	25	30	4	84
		29.80%	29.10%	25.60%	33.30%	28.00%
10000 - 15000		9	20	16	1	46
		10.70%	23.30%	13.70%	8.30%	15.30%
15000 - 20000		10	11	21	3	45
		11.90%	12.80%	17.90%	25.00%	15.00%
>= Rs. 20000	1	40	30	50	4	125
	100.00%	47.60%	34.90%	42.70%	33.30%	41.70%
Total	1	84	86	117	12	300
Chi Square: 11.356 ; P > 0.05						

Folklore and Art score of the total population showed no association with Monthly Income of the population. Major respondents of population under 20000 expressed strongly agreed (100.00%) followed by agree, disagree, and don't know to Folklore and Art. Where as respondent who comes under monthly income 5000-10000 score in agree (29.80%) followed by 10000-15000 minimum score in agree (10.70%) No significant relationship was found between

Monthly Income and Folklore and Art P > 0.05. It was observed that those who comes under 20000 and above monthly income considers the traditional value of practicing Folklore and Art in the present context.

Table 18.0. Association between Information Technology and Age

Age	Information Technology					Total
	Strongly Agree	Agree	Don't Know	Disagree	Strongly Disagree	
<25 yrs		39	33	40	7	119
		37.50%	41.30%	40.00%	46.70%	39.70%
>=25 yrs	1	65	47	60	8	181
	100.00%	62.50%	58.80%	60.00%	53.30%	60.30%
Total	1	104	80	100	15	300
Chi Square: 1.257 ; P > 0.05						

Information and Technology score of the total population showed no significant (P>0.05) association with Age of the population table 18.0. As the majority (60.30%) of the total population fell in >= 25 years of age group, major respondents of population with >= 25 years age group strongly agreed (100.00%) to Information and Technology score. It was observed that the high age group Naga youth progressively agreed to the Information and Technology with maximum (62.50%) score in agree, followed by disagree and 'don't know with (60.00%) and (58.80%) respectively. Where as the low age group have negative fidelity score progressively with minimum in agree group followed by disagree and maximum in disagree group, which show that lower age group disagree to Information and Technology where as high age group Naga agree or believe, more over want to know about Information and Technology. This depicts that youth who comes under the age group 25 years and above have influenced on knowing modern and post-modern advancement, they considered their indigenous culture as something obsolete rather than an antique.

Table 18.1. Association between Information Technology and Gender

Gender	Information Technology					Total
	Strongly Agree	Agree	Don't Know	Disagree	Strongly Disagree	
Male	1	52	36	46	5	140
	100.00%	50.00%	45.00%	46.00%	33.30%	46.70%
Female		52	44	54	10	160
		50.00%	55.00%	54.00%	66.70%	53.30%
Total	1	104	80	100	15	300
Chi Square: 2.789 ; P > 0.05						

Information and Technology score of the total population showed no association with Gender of the population. Major population were female (53.30%) however male respondents strongly agreed (100.00%) followed by agree, disagree, don't know, and strongly to Information and Technology. Where as female score minimum in agree (50.00%), followed by disagree, don't know and strongly disagree. No significant relationship was noticed between Gender and Information and Technology P > 0.05. The study shows that Male Naga has much interest with regard to Information and Technology. It clearly depicts that more than female Naga youth, Male members are influenced to spend most of the time sitting in the computer rather than spend time with family members, friends, and in recreation.

Table 18.2. Association between Information Technology and Profession

Profession	Information Technology					Total
	Strongly Agree	Agree	Don't Know	Disagree	Strongly Disagree	
Student	1	90	64	78	11	244
	100.00%	86.50%	80.00%	78.00%	73.30%	81.30%
Employed		14	16	22	4	56
		13.50%	20.00%	22.00%	26.70%	18.70%
Total	1	104	80	100	15	300
Chi Square: 3.543 ; P > 0.05						

Majority of the study population were students, Major respondents of the study population were students strongly agreed (100.00%) followed by agree, don't know, disagree, and strongly disagree to Information and Technology. Where as employed Naga youth score minimum in agree (13.50%) followed by agree, don't know, disagree, and strongly disagree to Information and Technology. There was no statistically significant relationship found between Profession and Information and Technology P > 0.05. The table 18.2 depicts that student respondents have considered the advancement of Information and Technology. This shows that student members spent much time in watching television and other alternative entertainment.

Table 18.3. Association between Information Technology and Place of Stay

Place of Stay	Information Technology					Total
	Strongly Agree	Agree	Don't Know	Disagree	Strongly Disagree	
Chennai		6	4	3	1	14
		5.80%	5.00%	3.00%	6.70%	4.70%
Kochi		4	4	2		10
		3.80%	5.00%	2.00%		3.30%
Pune		9	2	4	2	17
		8.70%	2.50%	4.00%	13.30%	5.70%
Kolkata		11	4	3		18
		10.60%	5.00%	3.00%		6.00%
Bengaluru		14	3	7	1	25
		13.50%	3.80%	7.00%	6.70%	8.30%
Hyderabad	1	16	15	10	1	43
	100.00%	15.40%	18.80%	10.00%	6.70%	14.30%
Delhi		12	4	8		24
		11.50%	5.00%	8.00%		8.00%
Nagaland		32	44	63	10	149
		30.80%	55.00%	63.00%	66.70%	49.70%
Total	1	104	80	100	15	300
Chi Square: 44.808 ; P < 0.05						

Information and Technology score of the total population showed a significant relationship between Place of Stay and Information and Technology. Majority of the study population in Hyderabad expressed strongly agree (100.00%) followed by agree score Bengaluru (13.50%), Delhi (11.50%), Kolkata (10.60%), and Nagaland minimum score in agree (30.80%), followed by Kochi (3.80%). Where as Nagaland and Pune score minimum in strongly disagree (13.30%), (66.70%) respectively to Information and Technology. There was a significant association found between Place of Stay and Information and Technology $P < 0.05$. This table 18.3 showed that Naga youth residing at Hyderabad are agreed to the effect of Information and Technology among Naga youth, also shown that they become individualistic and remain withdrawn from society due to the intact with modern technologies.

Table 18.4. Association between Information Technology and Monthly Income

Monthly Income	Information Technology					Total
	Strongly Agree	Agree	Don't Know	Disagree	Strongly Disagree	
5000 - 10000	1	26	24	29	4	84
	100.00%	25.00%	30.00%	29.00%	26.70%	28.00%
10000 - 15000		17	9	16	4	46
		16.30%	11.30%	16.00%	26.70%	15.30%
15000 - 20000		14	14	15	2	45
		13.50%	17.50%	15.00%	13.30%	15.00%
>= Rs. 20000		47	33	40	5	125
		45.20%	41.30%	40.00%	33.30%	41.70%
Total	1	104	80	100	15	300
Chi Square: 6.446 ; P > 0.05						

Information and Technology score of the total population showed no association with Monthly Income of the population. Major respondents of population under 5000-10000 expressed strongly agree (100.00%) followed by 20000 and above in agree (45.20%), 10000-15000 (16.30%), 15000-20000 (13.50%) to Information and Technology. No significant relationship was found between Monthly Income and Information and Technology P > 0.05. The study revealed that who come under 5000-10000 agrees to the effect of Information and Technology.

Table 19.0. Association between Church and Youth score and Age

Age	Church and Youth				Total
	Strongly Agree	Agree	Don't Know	Disagree	
< 25 yrs	20	74	25		119
	48.80%	35.20%	53.20%		39.70%
>= 25 yrs	21	136	22	2	181
	51.20%	64.80%	46.80%	100.00%	60.30%
Total	41	210	47	2	300
Chi Square 8.051; P < 0.05					

Church and Youth score of the total population showed a significant relationship with Age of the population. Major respondents of population under >=25 years Age group expressed strongly disagreed (100.00%) followed by strongly agree (51.20%), followed by agree (64.80%), don't know (46.80%). Where as lower age group score minimum in agree (35.20%), strongly agree (48.80%), and don't know (53.20%) to Church and Youth. Majority of the population were >25 years of age. There was a significant relationship found between Age and Church and Youth P < 0.05. The table 19.0 depicts that high age group Naga youth give much emphasis on the growth of the Church and youth, wanted the church to organize programmes more creative to the emerging design.

Table 19.1. Association between Church and Youth score and Gender

Gender	Church and Youth				Total
	Strongly Agree	Agree	Don't Know	Disagree	
Male	19	99	22		140
	46.30%	47.10%	46.80%		46.70%
Female	22	111	25	2	160
	53.70%	52.90%	53.20%	100.00%	53.30%
Total	41	210	47	2	300
Chi Square 1.771; P > 0.05					

Church and Youth score of the total population showed no association with Gender of the population. Major population were female disagree (100.00%) followed by strongly agree (53.70%), don't know (53.20%), and agree (52.90%) to Church and Youth. Where as Male respondents score minimum in strongly agree (46.30%), don't know (46.80%), and agree (47.19%). Majority of the population were female. No significant relationship was noticed between Gender and Church and Youth P > 0.05. It was observed that female respondents have high concern and positive attitude towards the responsibility of Church and the youth. This shows more than male members, female members wanted the church to address the needs of the youth.

Table 19.2. Association between Church and Youth score and Profession

Profession	Church and Youth				Total
	Strongly Agree	Agree	Don't Know	Disagree	
Student	36	169	38	1	244
	87.80%	80.50%	80.90%	50.00%	81.30%
Employed	5	41	9	1	56
	12.20%	19.50%	19.10%	50.00%	18.70%
Total	41	210	47	2	300
Chi Square 2.533; P > 0.05					

Majority of the study population were students, Major respondents of the study population were students strongly agree (87.80%) followed by don't know

(80.90%), agree (80.50%), and disagree (50.00%) to Church and Youth. Where as the employed youth score minimum in strongly agree (12.20%), don't know (19.10%), agree (19.50%), and disagree (50.00%). There was no statistically significant relationship found between Profession and Church and Youth P >0.05. The table 19.2 depicts that student Naga have agreed and want churches to meet the needs of the present youth.

Table 19.3. Association between Church and Youth score and Place of Stay

Place of Stay	Church and Youth				Total
	Strongly Agree	Agree	Don't Know	Disagree	
Chennai	1	11	1	1	14
	2.40%	5.20%	2.10%	50.00%	4.70%
Kochi	3	6	1		10
	7.30%	2.90%	2.10%		3.30%
Pune	6	10	1		17
	14.60%	4.80%	2.10%		5.70%
Kolkata	3	15			18
	7.30%	7.10%			6.00%
Bengaluru	2	22	1		25
	4.90%	10.50%	2.10%		8.30%
Hyderabad	3	31	8	1	43
	7.30%	14.80%	17.00%	50.00%	14.30%
Delhi	8	15	1		24
	19.50%	7.10%	2.10%		8.00%
Nagaland	15	100	34		149
	36.60%	47.60%	72.30%		49.70%
Total	41	210	47	2	300
Chi Square 47.345; P < 0.01					

Church and Youth score of the total population showed a highly significant relationship between Place of Stay and Church and Youth. Majority of the study population in Nagaland expressed don't know (72.30%) followed by agree (47.60%), strongly agree (36.60%) to Church and Youth. Naga youth who are residing at Chennai and Hyderabad score maximum in disagree (50.00%) respectively. Where as youth who are staying at Kochi agree (7.30%), followed by Pune (14.60%), Kolkata (7.30%), Delhi (19.50%), and Nagaland (36.60%). Bengaluru score in disagree (10.50%). There was a highly significant association found between Place of Stay and Church and Youth P < 0.01. The table 19.3 depicts that Majority of the Naga youth irrespective of their locale of migration agrees to the need of the churches and demand more church activities and involvement upon the present Naga youth.

Table 19.4. Association between Church and Youth score and Monthly Income

Monthly Income	Church and Youth				Total
	Strongly Agree	Agree	Don't Know	Disagree	
5000 - 10000	10	57	17		84
	24.40%	27.10%	36.20%		28.00%
10000 - 15000	6	32	8		46
	14.60%	15.20%	17.00%		15.30%
15000 - 20000	4	34	7		45
	9.80%	16.20%	14.90%		15.00%
>= Rs. 20000	21	87	15	2	125
	51.20%	41.40%	31.90%	100.00%	41.70%
Total	41	210	47	2	300
Chi Square 7.192; P > 0.05					

Church and Youth score of the total population showed no association with Monthly Income of the population. Major respondents of population under 20000 expressed disagree (100.00%) followed by strongly agree (51. 20%), agree (41.40%) and don't know (31.90%) to Church and Youth. Where as those who come under 15000-20000 score minimum in strongly agree (9.80%), followed by agree (16.20%) and don't know (14.90%) No significant relationship was found between Monthly Income and Church and Youth P > 0.05. The study revealed that who comes under monthly income 20000 and above are agreed to the responsibility of churches to meet the needs and demands of the present Naga youth.

4.2.4. Student's Test Used to Compare Mean Values Between Two Groups

In this section, the statistical technique used is expressed in Student's t test. The result is presented in table 20.0, 20.1, 20.2.

Table 20.0. Mean sub and total score of different sub groups comparing Age

Parameters	Age	Mean	± SD	t value	P value
Dignity of Labour	< 25 yrs	2.95	0.70	0.773	> 0.05
	>= 25 yrs	2.88	0.73		
Education and Language	< 25 yrs	2.94	0.76	3.208	< 0.01
	>= 25 yrs	2.67	0.67		

Family System	< 25 yrs	2.61	0.67	0.875	> 0.05
	>= 25 yrs	2.54	0.67		
Generation Gap	< 25 yrs	3.36	1.01	1.602	> 0.05
	>= 25 yrs	3.18	0.95		
Naga Youth	< 25 yrs	3.43	1.05	0.756	> 0.05
	>= 25 yrs	3.34	1.01		
Equality and Respect	< 25 yrs	2.80	0.67	1.124	> 0.05
	>= 25 yrs	2.71	0.63		
Dress & Ornaments	< 25 yrs	2.97	0.79	0.421	> 0.05
	>= 25 yrs	2.93	0.75		
Music & Dance	< 25 yrs	2.85	0.74	0.431	> 0.05
	>= 25 yrs	2.81	0.71		
Behaviour & Attitude	< 25 yrs	2.57	0.60	1.062	> 0.05
	>= 25 yrs	2.50	0.58		
Hospitality	< 25 yrs	2.23	0.60	0.163	> 0.05
	>= 25 yrs	2.22	0.59		
Community Spirit	< 25 yrs	2.66	0.72	- 1.376	> 0.05
	>= 25 yrs	2.78	0.70		
Folklore & Art	< 25 yrs	3.21	0.86	0.416	> 0.05
	>= 25 yrs	3.17	0.93		
Information Technology	< 25 yrs	3.13	0.94	0.685	> 0.05
	>= 25 yrs	3.05	0.94		
Church & Youth	< 25 yrs	2.04	0.62	0.215	> 0.05
	>= 25 yrs	2.03	0.53		
Total Cultural Fidelity	< 25 yrs	2.91	0.58	1.167	> 0.05
	>= 25 yrs	2.83	0.57		

The age difference in each sub group score and total cultural fidelity score was assessed using Student's t test. The mean score for each sub group was compared and for majority of sub group scores, the < 25 years age group showed high mean score except for few sub groups (Table 20.0). The total cultural fidelity score was also high for <25 years age group. The difference in scores between age groups were negligible and hence Student's t test showed no significant difference between two age groups in all the sub groups and for total cultural fidelity score except for Education and Language score. < 25 years age responded significantly (P<0.01) high mean score, which may be due to the fact that < 25 years age group was mostly represented by the student community, who value their education and language as part of their cultural fidelity. All other scores including cultural fidelity and total scores were comparable between age groups. This may be due to the fact that Cultural fidelity is almost same among the Naga youth irrespective of Age group.

Table 20.1. Mean sub and total score of different sub groups comparing Gender

Parameters	Gender	Mean	± SD	t value	P value
Dignity of Labour	Male	2.89	0.68	- 0.547	> 0.05
	Female	2.93	0.75		
Education and Language	Male	2.81	0.75	0.775	> 0.05
	Female	2.75	0.69		
Family System	Male	2.61	0.64	1.235	> 0.05
	Female	2.52	0.69		
Generation Gap	Male	3.25	0.98	0.001	> 0.05
	Female	3.25	0.98		
Naga Youth	Male	3.29	0.95	- 1.273	> 0.05
	Female	3.44	1.09		
Equality and Respect	Male	2.66	0.56	- 2.078	< 0.05
	Female	2.82	0.71		
Dress & Ornaments	Male	2.85	0.74	- 1.981	< 0.05
	Female	3.03	0.78		
Music & Dance	Male	2.80	0.73	-0.599	> 0.05
	Female	2.85	0.71		
Behaviour & Attitude	Male	2.48	0.59	- 1.318	> 0.05
	Female	2.57	0.59		
Hospitality	Male	2.24	0.60	0.128	> 0.05
	Female	2.21	0.59		
Community Spirit	Male	2.69	0.76	- 1.087	> 0.05
	Female	2.78	0.66		
Folklore & Art	Male	3.12	0.93	- 1.113	> 0.05
	Female	3.24	0.87		
Information Technology	Male	3.01	0.94	- 1.129	> 0.05
	Female	3.14	0.95		
Church & Youth	Male	2.02	0.54	-0.341	> 0.05
	Female	2.04	0.59		
Total Cultural Fidelity	Male	2.82	0.58	- 1.091	> 0.05
	Female	2.89	0.57		

Student's test was employed even in the Gender distribution to compare different sub-scores and total scores between Male and Female population. Equality & Respect, Dress & Ornaments, and Behavior & Attitude were the scores which showed significant difference between Male and Female population. All other scores and total scores were comparable between Male and Female population. This is the fact that Cultural Fidelity is almost same among the Naga youth irrespective of the gender difference. The mean score for each sub group was compared and for majority of sub group scores, the female group showed high mean score except for few sub groups (Table 20.1). The total cultural fidelity score was high for male. The difference in scores between genders were negligible and hence Student's t test showed no significant difference between gender in almost all the sub groups and for total cultural fidelity score except for Equality & Respect, Dress & Ornaments, and Behavior & Attitude score. Female members responded significantly ($P<0.05$) high mean score, which may be due to the fact that female members were value their Equality & Respect, Dress & Ornaments, and Behavior & Attitude as part of their cultural fidelity. All other scores including cultural fidelity and total scores were comparable between genders. This result showed that Cultural fidelity is almost same among the Naga youth irrespective of gender.

Table 20.2. Mean sub and total score of different sub groups comparing Profession

Parameters	Profession	Mean	± SD	t value	P value
Dignity of Labour	Student	2.90	0.73	- 0.626	> 0.05
	Employed	2.96	0.66		
Education and Language	Student	2.79	0.73	0.554	> 0.05
	Employed	2.73	0.65		
Family System	Student	2.56	0.67	-0.321	> 0.05
	Employed	2.59	0.65		
Generation Gap	Student	3.22	0.99	- 1.212	> 0.05
	Employed	3.39	0.91		
Naga Youth	Student	3.32	1.02	-1.754	> 0.05
	Employed	3.59	1.04		
Equality and Respect	Student	2.71	0.66	-1.886	< 0.05
	Employed	2.89	0.56		
Dress & Ornaments	Student	2.94	0.78	-0.226	> 0.05
	Employed	2.96	0.71		

Music & Dance	Student	2.79	0.73	- 1.799	> 0.05
	Employed	2.98	0.65		
Behaviour & Attitude	Student	2.52	0.60	-0.377	> 0.05
	Employed	2.55	0.57		
Hospitality	Student	2.23	0.58	0.578	> 0.05
	Employed	2.18	0.66		
Community Spirit	Student	2.70	0.71	- 1.872	< 0.05
	Employed	2.89	0.68		
Folklore & Art	Student	3.16	0.90	- 1.107	> 0.05
	Employed	3.30	0.89		
Information Technology	Student	3.03	0.94	- 1.816	> 0.05
	Employed	3.29	0.93		
Church & Youth	Student	2.02	0.57	- 1.083	> 0.05
	Employed	2.11	0.56		
Total Cultural Fidelity	Student	2.84	0.58	- 1.514	> 0.05
	Employed	2.96	0.54		

The Profession difference in each sub group score and total cultural fidelity score was assessed using Student's t test. The mean score for each sub group was compared and for majority of sub group scores, the employed group showed high mean score except for few sub groups (Table 20.2). The total cultural fidelity score was high for students group. The difference in scores between Profession groups were negligible and hence Student's t test showed no significant difference between two profession group in all the sub group and for total cultural fidelity score except for Equality & Respect and Community spirit score. Employed group responded significantly (P<0.05) high mean score, which may be due to the fact that employed group valued their Equality & Respect and Community spirit as part of their cultural fidelity. All other scores including cultural fidelity and total scores were comparable between Profession groups. This may be due to the fact that Cultural fidelity is almost same among the Naga youth irrespective of Profession.

4.2.5. Analysis of Variance (one way ANOVA)

In this section, the statistical technique used is expressed in Analysis of variance (One Way ANOVA). The result is presented in Table 21.0, and 21.1.

Table 21.0. Mean sub and total score of different sub groups comparing Place of Residence

Parameters	Place of Stay	Mean	± SD	F value	P value
Dignity of Labour	Chennai	2.57	0.51	3.092	< 0.01
	Kochi	2.40	0.70		
	Pune	3.06	0.75		
	Kolkata	2.72	0.83		
	Bengaluru	2.76	0.83		
	Hyderabad	2.77	0.75		
	Delhi	2.79	0.72		
	Nagaland	3.07	0.65		
Education and Language	Chennai	2.57	0.65	0.691	> 0.05
	Kochi	2.90	0.74		
	Pune	2.76	0.75		
	Kolkata	2.94	0.73		
	Bengaluru	2.68	0.69		
	Hyderabad	2.67	0.78		
	Delhi	2.71	0.81		
	Nagaland	2.83	0.69		
Family System	Chennai	2.36	0.63	2.867	< 0.01
	Kochi	2.40	0.52		
	Pune	2.18	0.73		
	Kolkata	2.28	0.75		
	Bengaluru	2.36	0.49		
	Hyderabad	2.56	0.59		
	Delhi	2.67	0.56		
	Nagaland	2.69	0.70		
Generation Gap	Chennai	2.93	1.07	4.636	< 0.001
	Kochi	2.70	0.95		
	Pune	2.94	1.14		
	Kolkata	3.06	1.00		
	Bengaluru	2.80	1.00		
	Hyderabad	3.00	0.95		
	Delhi	3.08	0.97		
	Nagaland	3.55	0.87		

Naga Youth	Chennai	3.07	1.00	4.579	< 0.001
	Kochi	2.50	0.97		
	Pune	3.24	1.25		
	Kolkata	2.94	0.94		
	Bengaluru	3.08	1.00		
	Hyderabad	3.21	1.06		
	Delhi	3.08	1.06		
	Nagaland	3.67	0.92		
Equality and Respect	Chennai	2.71	0.47	1.929	> 0.05
	Kochi	2.40	0.70		
	Pune	2.65	0.70		
	Kolkata	2.61	0.92		
	Bengaluru	2.56	0.51		
	Hyderabad	2.60	0.66		
	Delhi	2.88	0.80		
	Nagaland	2.85	0.59		
Dress & Ornaments	Chennai	2.79	0.58	3.478	< 0.01
	Kochi	2.70	0.82		
	Pune	2.65	0.79		
	Kolkata	2.89	0.47		
	Bengaluru	2.88	0.83		
	Hyderabad	2.86	0.83		
	Delhi	2.46	0.72		
	Nagaland	3.13	0.74		

Music & Dance	Chennai	2.64	0.74	3.595	< 0.01
	Kochi	2.40	0.52		
	Pune	2.59	0.80		
	Kolkata	2.67	0.59		
	Bengaluru	2.60	0.76		
	Hyderabad	2.74	0.69		
	Delhi	2.58	0.65		
	Nagaland	3.02	0.70		
Behaviour & Attitude	Chennai	2.36	0.50	1.257	> 0.05
	Kochi	2.30	0.48		
	Pune	2.47	0.51		
	Kolkata	2.28	0.46		
	Bengaluru	2.44	0.58		
	Hyderabad	2.56	0.55		
	Delhi	2.54	0.51		
	Nagaland	2.60	0.65		
Hospitality	Chennai	1.93	0.47	1.303	> 0.05
	Kochi	2.40	0.52		
	Pune	2.18	0.53		
	Kolkata	2.11	0.58		
	Bengaluru	2.20	0.41		
	Hyderabad	2.33	0.61		
	Delhi	2.04	0.36		
	Nagaland	2.26	0.66		
Community Spirit	Chennai	2.71	0.83	1.742	> 0.05
	Kochi	2.30	0.48		
	Pune	2.59	0.62		
	Kolkata	2.72	0.57		
	Bengaluru	2.56	0.65		
	Hyderabad	2.70	0.60		
	Delhi	2.54	0.66		
	Nagaland	2.85	0.77		

Folklore & Art	Chennai	3.07	0.92	2.095	< 0.05
	Kochi	2.70	0.67		
	Pune	3.06	0.90		
	Kolkata	2.94	0.87		
	Bengaluru	2.96	1.14		
	Hyderabad	3.14	0.86		
	Delhi	2.92	0.97		
	Nagaland	3.36	0.85		
Information Technology	Chennai	2.93	1.00	3.783	< 0.01
	Kochi	2.80	0.79		
	Pune	2.94	1.14		
	Kolkata	2.56	0.78		
	Bengaluru	2.80	1.00		
	Hyderabad	2.86	0.89		
	Delhi	2.83	0.92		
	Nagaland	3.34	0.89		
Church & Youth	Chennai	2.14	0.66	3.789	< 0.01
	Kochi	1.80	0.63		
	Pune	1.71	0.59		
	Kolkata	1.83	0.38		
	Bengaluru	1.96	0.35		
	Hyderabad	2.16	0.57		
	Delhi	1.71	0.55		
	Nagaland	2.13	0.56		
Total Cultural Fidelity	Chennai	2.64	0.63	5.928	< 0.001
	Kochi	2.50	0.53		
	Pune	2.59	0.62		
	Kolkata	2.61	0.61		
	Bengaluru	2.60	0.58		
	Hyderabad	2.88	0.63		
	Delhi	2.63	0.58		
	Nagaland	3.04	0.48		

Analysis of Variance of different sub-scores comparing Place of Stay of respondents showed a highly significant difference between different Places of stay for almost all sub-scores except five sub-scores. Dignity of labor, Family system, Generation gap, Present Naga youth style, Dress and Ornaments, Music and Dance, Folklore and Art, Information Technology, Church and Youth were found to be highly significant. Total Cultural fidelity score found to be very highly significant when compared between different places of stay, of which highest scores was responded by Naga lives in Nagaland. Results suggest that Naga youth lives in Nagaland withhold all cultural aspects with traditional importance. When they migrate to other cities, they loss the original cultural loyalty and merge with the urban life. Education and Language, Equality and Respect, Behavior and Attitude, Hospitality, Community spirit showed no statistical difference between Places of stay. It was found higher mean scores for people resides in Nagaland for many sub-scores when compared to other places. The analysis revealed that Cultural Fidelity scores have a very highly significant relationship among the Naga youth and the Place of Stay.

Table 21.1. Mean sub and total score of different sub groups comparing Monthly Income

Parameters	Monthly Income	Mean	± SD	F value	P value
Dignity of Labour	5000 - 10000	2.94	0.77	0.784	> 0.05
	10000 - 15000	2.80	0.69		
	15000 - 20000	3.02	0.75		
	>= Rs. 20000	2.89	0.69		
Education and Language	5000 - 10000	2.79	0.68	2.123	> 0.05
	10000 - 15000	2.57	0.75		
	15000 - 20000	2.93	0.69		
	>= Rs. 20000	2.80	0.73		
Family System	5000 - 10000	2.51	0.57	0.598	> 0.05
	10000 - 15000	2.50	0.59		
	15000 - 20000	2.64	0.83		
	>= Rs. 20000	2.59	0.70		
Generation Gap	5000 - 10000	3.18	1.02	0.518	> 0.05
	10000 - 15000	3.22	1.01		
	15000 - 20000	3.40	0.91		
	>= Rs. 20000	3.26	0.97		
Naga Youth	5000 - 10000	3.35	0.98	0.058	> 0.05
	10000 - 15000	3.35	0.95		
	15000 - 20000	3.38	1.05		
	>= Rs. 20000	3.40	1.09		
Equality and Respect	5000 - 10000	2.65	0.57	2.194	> 0.05
	10000 - 15000	2.72	0.54		
	15000 - 20000	2.96	0.64		
	>= Rs. 20000	2.74	0.72		

Dress & Ornaments	5000 - 10000	2.94	0.72	0.855	> 0.05
	10000 - 15000	2.98	0.71		
	15000 - 20000	3.09	0.85		
	>= Rs. 20000	2.88	0.79		
Music & Dance	5000 - 10000	2.76	0.67	0.364	> 0.05
	10000 - 15000	2.85	0.79		
	15000 - 20000	2.89	0.71		
	>= Rs. 20000	2.84	0.73		
Behaviour & Attitude	5000 - 10000	2.61	0.56	1.042	> 0.05
	10000 - 15000	2.43	0.54		
	15000 - 20000	2.47	0.63		
	>= Rs. 20000	2.53	0.62		
Hospitality	5000 - 10000	2.18	0.56	0.245	> 0.05
	10000 - 15000	2.24	0.48		
	15000 - 20000	2.27	0.62		
	>= Rs. 20000	2.22	0.65		
Community Spirit	5000 - 10000	2.68	0.70	0.549	> 0.05
	10000 - 15000	2.80	0.65		
	15000 - 20000	2.67	0.80		
	>= Rs. 20000	2.77	0.71		
Folklore & Art	5000 - 10000	3.15	0.91	0.885	> 0.05
	10000 - 15000	3.20	0.78		
	15000 - 20000	3.38	0.91		
	>= Rs. 20000	3.13	0.93		
Information Technology	5000 - 10000	3.11	0.94	0.274	> 0.05
	10000 - 15000	3.15	1.03		
	15000 - 20000	3.11	0.91		
	>= Rs. 20000	3.02	0.93		
Church & Youth	5000 - 10000	2.08	0.56	0.591	> 0.05
	10000 - 15000	2.04	0.56		
	15000 - 20000	2.07	0.50		
	>= Rs. 20000	1.98	0.60		
Total Cultural Fidelity	5000 - 10000	2.83	0.58	0.333	> 0.05
	10000 - 15000	2.93	0.57		
	15000 - 20000	2.84	0.60		
	>= Rs. 20000	2.86	0.56		

Analysis of Variance of different sub-scores comparing Monthly Income of respondents showed no significant difference between different monthly income levels. Monthly income of the respondents was not found to be significant factor for Cultural Fidelity. Even though there were no statistical differences between different monthly income levels, 1000-15000 monthly income showed higher mean scores. The analysis revealed that cultural values may not change according to the respondent's monthly income. Total Cultural fidelity score found to be insignificant when compared between different monthly incomes, the analysis revealed that Cultural Fidelity scores have no significant relationship among the Naga youth and their family Monthly Income.

4.2.6. Findings of the Research Work

4.2.6.1. Relationship Between Socio-Demographic Variables and the Fidelity to Naga Culture

a) Age and Cultural Fidelity

The study found that the effect of age on Cultural fidelity is not significant. Hence, the hypothesis that age will not be significantly related to cultural fidelity is confirmed. Student's t test was employed to compare different sub-scores and total scores between different age group <25yrs >=25yrs. Education and Language score was the only score which showed highly significant difference between age group. All other scores including cultural fidelity and total scores were comparable between age group. This may be due to the fact that Cultural Fidelity is almost same among the Naga youth irrespective of age group.

b) Gender and Cultural Fidelity

The study found that the effect of gender on Cultural Fidelity is not significant. A gender - wise comparison revealed that females had significantly higher cultural scores than male. Hence, the hypothesis that gender will not be significantly related to cultural fidelity is confirmed. t test was employed even in the gender distribution to compare different sub-scores and total scores between Male and Female population. Equality & Respect, Dress & Ornaments, and Behavior & Attitude were the scores which showed significant difference between Male and Female population. All other scores and total scores were comparable between Male and Female population. This is the fact that Cultural Fidelity is almost same among the Naga youth irrespective of the gender difference.

c) Profession and Cultural Fidelity

Profession showed no independent effect on Cultural Fidelity. A profession - wise comparison revealed that Students had significantly higher cultural scores than employed. Hence, the hypothesis that profession will not be significantly related to cultural fidelity is confirmed. Student's t test was followed in the Profession distribution to compare different sub-scores and total scores between Student and Employed. Equality & Respect and Community spirit scores were the scores which showed significant difference between Student and Employed. All other scores including Cultural Fidelity and total scores were comparable between Student and Employed. This is the reason that Cultural Fidelity is almost same among the Naga youth irrespective of the Profession.

d) Monthly Income and Cultural Fidelity

The study found that the effect of monthly income on Cultural Fidelity is not significant. Hence, the hypothesis that monthly income will not be significantly related to cultural fidelity is confirmed. Analysis of Variance of different sub-scores comparing monthly income of respondents showed no significant difference between different monthly income levels. Monthly income of the respondents was not found to be significant factor for Cultural Fidelity. Even though there were no statistical differences between different monthly income levels, 15000-20000 monthly income showed higher mean scores. The analysis revealed that cultural values may not change according to the respondent's monthly income.

4.2.6.2. Relationship Between Fidelity to Naga Culture and Locale of Migration

The study revealed that locale of migration had a highly significant effect on Cultural Fidelity. Analysis of Variance of different sub-scores comparing Place of stay of respondents showed a highly significant difference between different Places of Stay. Dignity of labor, Family system, Generation gap, Present Naga style youth, Dress and Ornaments, Music and Dance, Folklore and Art, Information Technology, Church and Youth were found to be highly significant. Total Cultural Fidelity score found to be very highly significant. Even though Education and Language, Equality and Respect, Behavior and Attitude, Hospitality, Community spirit showed no statistical difference between Place of Stay. Hence, the hypothesis that there will be no significant relationship between fidelity to Naga culture and locale of migration is rejected.

a) Dignity of Labor score (Sub-scale A) and Place of Stay
   Dignity of Labor score of the total population showed a very highly significant relationship between Place of Stay and Dignity of labor ($P<0.001$).
b) Education and Language score (Sub-scale B) and place of Stay
   Education and Language score of the total population showed no significant relationship between Place of Stay and Education and Language $P > 0.05$.
c) Family system score (Sub-scale C) and Place of Stay
   Family System score of the total population showed a very highly significant relationship between Place of Stay and Family System.

There is a significant association between Place of Stay and Family System $P<0.001$.

d) Generation Gap between Parent and Naga Youth score (Sub-scale D) and Place of Stay
Generation gap between parent and children score of the total population showed a very highly significant relationship between Place of Stay and Generation gap $P < 0.001$.

e) Present Naga youth style score (Sub-scale E) and Place of Stay
Present Naga youth score of the total population showed a very highly significant relationship between Place of Stay and Naga youth. The study revealed that there is a very highly significant association between Place of Stay and present Naga youth $P < 0.001$.

f) Equality and Respect score (Sub-scale F) and Place of Stay
Equality and Respect score of the total population showed no significant relationship between Place of Stay and Equality and respect. The result of the study showed no significant association between Place of Stay and Equality and respect $P > 0.05$.

g) Dress and Ornaments score (Sub-scale G) and Place of Stay
Dress and Ornaments score of the total population showed a highly significant relationship between place of stay and Dress and Ornaments. The study found that there is a highly significant association between Place of Stay and Dress and Ornaments $P< 0.01$.

h) Music and Dance score (Sub-scale H) and Place of Stay
Music and Dance score of the total population showed a significant relationship between Place of Stay and Music and Dance. The study revealed that there is a significant association between Place of Stay and Music and Dance $P < 0.05$.

i) Behavior and attitude score (Sub-scale I) and Place of Stay
Behavior and Attitude score of the total population showed no significant relationship between Place of Stay and Behavior and Attitude. There is no association found between Place of Stay and Behavior and Attitude $P > 0.05$.

j) Hospitality score (Sub-scale J) and Place of Stay
Hospitality score of the total population showed no significant relationship between Place of Stay and Hospitality $P > 0.05$.

k) Communitarian spirit score (Sub-scale K) and Place of Stay
Community Spirit score of the total population showed no significant relationship between Place of Stay and Community Spirit. There is no significant association found between Place of Stay and Community Spirit $P > 0.05$.

l) Folklore and Art crafts score (Sub-scale L) and Place of Stay

Folklore and Art score of the total population showed a significant relationship between Place of Stay and Folklore and Art. The study revealed that there is a significant association found between Place of Stay and Folklore and Art $P < 0.05$.

m) Information Technology score (Sub-scale M) and Place of Stay

Information and Technology score of the total population showed a significant relationship between place of stay and Information and Technology. There is a significant association found between Place of Stay and Information and Technology $P < 0.05$.

n) Church and Youth score (Sub-scale N) and Place of Stay

Church and Youth score of the total population showed a highly significant relationship between place of stay and Church and Youth. There is a highly significant association found between Place of Stay and Church and Youth $P < 0.01$.

4.2.6.3. Relationship Between Naga Youth Living in and Outside Nagaland and their Fidelity to Naga Culture

The study revealed that Naga youth living in and outside Nagaland had a highly significant effect on Cultural Fidelity. It was found higher Mean scores for many sub-scores among the youth who lives outside Nagaland. The analysis revealed that Cultural Fidelity scores have a very highly significant relationship among the Naga youth living outside Nagaland. Results suggest that Naga youth lives in Nagaland withhold almost all cultural aspects with traditional importance. But Naga youth who migrate to other cities, they loss the original cultural loyalty and merge with the urban life. Hence, the hypothesis Naga youth living in and outside Nagaland will not be significantly related to cultural fidelity is rejected.

a) Dignity of Labor score and Total Cultural Fidelity score

Dignity of Labor score of the total population showed a very highly significant relationship among the Naga youth. ($P < 0.001$). Maximum score in agree are the Naga youth who are residing outside Nagaland. The pride of dignity of labor in the present tradition has rather become the pride to tell others that 'they don't know how to work.' Naga youth have moved away from cultivating work culture to technologies with the passage of time. However, Naga youth have to realize that things have changed and they cannot go back to the kind of work that their fore parents did. The pragmatic thing right now is to instill work culture through creative ways. Naga youth revealed that the hard work and sincere nature is disappearing among many Naga youth today.

b) Education and Language score and Total Cultural Fidelity score

The study found that there is no significant association between Naga youth both living in and outside Nagaland and Education and Language $P > 0.05$, which means, with urbanization and educational system in schools and colleges, the Naga youth are caught in between and have become the victims of hybrid languages. English education has adversely affected the use of tribal languages especially among the youth in the towns and cities. According to the finding, the present Naga youth needs to preserve Naga tribal languages as language is a vehicle of one's identity.

c) Family System score and Total Cultural Fidelity score

Family System score of the total population showed a very highly significant relationship between Naga youth both living in and outside Nagaland and Family System. There is a significant association among the Naga youth and Family System $P < 0.001$. It was observed that Naga youth have high value and concern on Naga Family System. Some families are closely knitted and on the other hand some are not. Families those who are closely knitted share and discuss family problems and issues in some way on the other hand, some Naga family are loosely knitted due to massive intrusion of western culture. Filial relationships are still maintained but there are strong signs of disintegration. Thus, according to the finding, the present Naga family is not closely knitted as it was in the past. It is because of the influx of modern civilizations and as well as by the advancement in technology that youth get enough entertainment programmes to spend their leisure times on it.

d) Generation Gap between Parent and Naga Youth score and Total Cultural Fidelity score

Generation gap score of the total population showed a very highly significant relationship between Naga youth both living in and outside Nagaland and Generation gap $P < 0.001$. This shows that the Naga youth have agreed to the generation gap. Generation gap between youth and parents indeed has a long gap because parents on one hand tries to inculcate their tradition and cultures, whereas youth today do not incline to it, thinking that it is not necessary for them at all. As a result many families have issues over this gap unable to link to each other. One of the reasons why this chasm emerged is because of drastic modernization and advancement in technology within the last decade. Consequently, the things that were considered appropriate ten years back have become unacceptable today. Most Naga parents are still tradition bound and are loyal to their clan, village and tribe. Whereas most Naga youth who do studies in towns and cities in Nagaland and outside do not maintain the same ties as their parents do, to their clan, village or tribe. Thus the study revealed, things youth consider basic and important appears trivial to parents.

e) Present Naga Youth Style score and Total Cultural Fidelity score

Naga youth score of the total population showed a very highly significant relationship between Naga youth both living in and outside Nagaland P < 0.001. Naga living style today is neither a 'real Naga' nor a 'modern one', because youths are sandwiched between tradition and western culture. Though, Naga culture might have taken it wrongs twists down the road, they cannot ignore the dynamic continuous process of culture which continues to include and exclude things along its way. According to the finding, Naga culture is gradually becoming foreign even for the Nagas themselves, the quest for ones roots and identity and the need to feel belonged must be considered among present Naga youth.

f) Equality and Respect score and Total Cultural Fidelity score

Equality and respect score of the total population showed no significant relationship between Naga youth both living in and outside Nagaland and Equality and Respect P > 0.05. It is generally observed that there is a decline in respect, regard and care for someone elder, comparing to the past as a part of Naga culture. Earlier Naga society was based on "Egalitarianism" where people respected each other and treated others in an appropriate way. Ruefully, such values have disappeared. However, according to the finding, both the youth living in and out outside Nagaland understand that this eroded value is not exclusive to Naga society but in almost every culture in modernity and post-modernity world. It differs from person to person, but may be generally they try to maintain equality and respect in their day today life.

g) Dress and Ornaments score and Total Cultural Fidelity score

Dress and ornaments score of the total population showed a highly significant relationship between Naga youth both living in and outside Nagaland and Dress and ornaments. The study found that there is a highly significant association among Naga youth and Dress and Ornaments P< 0.01. Dress code is purely westernized; the living style and fashion sense of youth have drastically changed with the invasion of television, newspapers, magazines, and internet. While good number of youths hunts for modern scanty dress code yet there are also some youth talented men and women who are trying to retained the originality of Naga traditional dress code in the modern trendy wears. It has found out that, Naga traditional dresses are not used because they have not been modified to suit the modern situation. Traditional ethnic dresses are used almost exclusively during tribal festivals.

h) Music and Dance score and Total Cultural Fidelity score

Music and Dance score of the total population showed a significant relationship between Naga youth both living in and outside Nagaland and Music and Dance. The study revealed that there is a significant association among the Naga youth and Music and Dance $P < 0.05$. Many Naga youth still have not come to the realization that to be someone in a society one has to be rooted in one's own culture. When it comes to enhancing the life of Naga youth through cultural items like Indigenous music and dance, it will not only enable the youth to keep in touch with their invaluable cultural heritage but also help them to generate local economy by showcasing cultural identity through indigenous music and dance. There are many avenues where Naga people can now exhibit and trade their traditional practices especially, with the government of Nagaland organizing various Youth Expos and Handloom Expos throughout the year. Cultural practices can still be practiced and can enhance the life of Naga youth. Study tells that, present Naga youths should retrospect and maintain the traditional practices in every possible way. The Nagas were rich in its folk songs, dances and folklores which have been handed down from generations to generations through oral traditions, in order to preserve those rich cultural practices the youths today must practice and preserve it.

i) Behavior and Attitude score and Total Cultural Fidelity score

Behavior and Attitude score of the total population showed no significant relationship between Naga youth both living in and outside Nagaland and Behavior and Attitude. There is no association found among the Naga youth and Behavior and Attitude $P > 0.05$. This shows that Naga youth have great concern in regard to behavior and attitude. Though it would depend on what yardstick an individual person use to define behavior and attitude, it is generally observed that Naga youth are concern to maintain good behavior and attitude. At the same time, many Naga youth do not exhibit good behavior and maintain attitude towards others; not being generous; disrespecting elders; these are some of the malady arising among the Naga youth today. This is also a reflection of the lack of proper teaching and guidance at homes. It differs from person to person, but may be generally it is true that behavior and attitude are slowly diminishing.

j) Hospitality score and Total Cultural Fidelity score

Hospitality score of the total population showed no significant relationship between Naga youth both living in and outside Nagaland and Hospitality $P > 0.05$. This shows that there is no significant association found among the Naga youth and Hospitality. According to the finding, this is truly a matter of great concern for all the Naga youth. Many Naga youth are trying to exhibit politeness, good manners, and show hospitality towards others, may not be considerate comparing to the olden living style. Due to fast changing living style, youth are becoming more individualistic and self-centeredness where the sense of showing solidarity and hospitality is slowly diminishing.

k) Communitarian spirit score and Total Cultural Fidelity score

Community Spirit score of the total population showed no significant relationship between Naga youth both living in and outside Nagaland and Community Spirit. There is no significant association found among the Naga youth and Community Spirit $P > 0.05$. Modern civilization has in many ways brought changes to the social life of the Nagas. In the early days the community life was strongly advocated in the Naga society. However, with the advent of the modern society there are some changes taken place with regard to the community life. According to the study, modern civilization might have brought some changes in the community life of the Nagas, but the spirit of communitarian is still existing or practicing among the Naga youth. More and more people are now living in mixed urban and semi urban communities under different laws and therefore it is only expected that traditional communitarian system will go through a shift, youth revealed that the Nagas are still community-oriented people.

l) Folklore and Art crafts score and Total Cultural Fidelity score

Folklore and Art score of the total population showed a significant relationship between Naga youth both living in and outside Nagaland and Folklore and Art. The study revealed that there is a significant association found among the Naga youth and Folklore and Art $P < 0.05$. Cultural practices such as, Indigenous music, folklore, Art and crafts can still be practiced and can enhance the life of Naga youth. The reason for the loss of Naga cultural music, art, folklore, etc., is because there have not been much attempt to finesse and modify them to appeal to the taste of the present modern generation. Youth should continue to innovate, refine and popularize indigenous cultural practices in order to strengthen their identity.

m) Information Technology score and Total Cultural Fidelity score

Information and Technology score of the total population showed a significant relationship between Naga youth both living in and outside Nagaland and Information and Technology. There is a significant association found among the Naga youth and Information and Technology $P < 0.05$. With globalization and technological advancement, youth's interests, hobbies, professional choices, nature of relationships are also undergoing a sea change. Youths prefer to spend considerable time in front of PC, TV, mobile, internet and other electronic gadgets. It is because of the influx of modern civilizations and as well as by the advancement in technology that the youth get enough entertainment programms. The study has revealed that, information technology is truly impacting on the lives of Naga youth.

n) Church and Youth score and Total Cultural Fidelity score

Church and Youth score of the total population showed a highly significant relationship between Naga youth living in and outside Nagaland and Church and Youth. There is a highly significant association found among the Naga youth and Church and Youth $P < 0.01$. Majority of the Naga youth agrees to the need of the church activities and involvement upon the present Naga youth. Majority of the youth wants the church to address the needs of the present Naga youth, issues and problems relating to the youth. Naga youth are also in demand both of their intellectual and spiritual needs and satisfaction, where they can participate and search for truth and also develop new skills and become more creative to the emerging design.

4.3. Suggestions for Further Research

The researcher has also recommended for further research in the light of the present findings

1. The study included subjects from the youth (20-30) only into its scope. As the present study revealed that age has no significant relationship with cultural fidelity, it will be a useful exercise to carry out a study among the youth (30 years) and above.
2. The present study included the subjects on Cultural fidelity to the migrant Naga youth. The present study revealed that place of stay has a highly significant relationship, it will be worthwhile to undertake a study incorporating psycho-social problem of the migrant and their adaptation to other metropolis culture.
3. The present study indicated that the subjects distributed to the individuals through Questionnaires were satisfactorily successful. Though this problem is solved in the present investigation, a further investigation linking within-group research will be a useful one. Within-group studies should be conducted to better understanding the nature and significance of cultural variations within groups.
4. The researcher feels that the Churches need to study with separate Cultural Counselling, using skills such as cultural change, reflection on traditional meanings and values; insight presumes a high level of cultural awareness and knowledge in their culture context.

4.4. Important Conclusion

This chapter has been an attempt to analyze the data to present the results systematically. The following are the important conclusions that emerged from the study. The hypotheses put forward are evident from the research findings; different age group, gender, profession, and monthly income are not significantly differed from each other on cultural fidelity. Locale of migration, Chennai, Kochi, Pune, Kolkata, Bengaluru, Hyderabad, Delhi, and Nagaland has a highly significant impact on cultural fidelity. Naga youth living in and outside Nagaland and cultural fidelity score found to be very highly significant. It was found higher Mean score for many sub-scores among Naga youth living outside Nagaland. Therefore, the analysis revealed Naga youth who resides in Nagaland withhold certain cultural norms and values with compared to Naga youth who migrate to different places.

It has intended to determine the nature and extent of the relationship between migrant Naga youth and cultural fidelity. The research findings provide with a sufficient and eminent ground to draw implications for pastoral care and counselling, which is another concern of the present study. Hence, the following chapter is an attempt to present pastoral care and counselling towards fidelity to Naga culture.

Chapter 5

Pastoral Care and Counselling Towards Fidelity to Naga Culture

5. Introduction

The aim of Pastoral Care[289] and Counselling[290] for the present study is to understand and support Naga youth. It has found that there seems to be a diminishing of cultural values in the contemporary Naga youth. This highlights the need that the Naga youth may be helped to improve their coping ability to Naga culture. Tradition, continuity and change should happen in a balance way among the Naga migrant. Significant elements of the old will remain necessary in the modern society; also cultural continuity along with cultural change. New customs are likely to be more readily adopted if they represent what is viewed as socially desirable and useful and if they do not clash with pre-existent and still-valued customs. Few Counselling Theories/Approaches are suggested in order to help the youth to retain important culture. Following are Person-Centered theory, Cognitive-Behavioral Theory, Gestalt Therapy, Reality Therapy, Behavior Therapy, and Group Counselling, with a view to eliciting significant insights that will be help for presenting implications for care and counselling to Naga youth.

---

289 Pastoral care is that aspect of the ministry of the Church which is concerned with the well-being of individuals and of communities. Alastair V. Campbell, "Pastoral Care, Nature of," *In A Dictionary of Pastoral Care*, edited by Alastair V. Campbell (Great Britain: SPCK, 1990), 188-190.

290 The utilization by clergy of counselling and psychotherapeutic methods to enable individuals, couples and families to handle their personal crises and problems in living constructively. Howard Clinebell, "Pastoral Counselling," *In A Dictionary of Pastoral Care*, edited by Alastair V. Campbell (Great Britain: SPCK, 1990), 198-199.

5.1. Theories of Pastoral Care and Counselling

5.1.1. Concepts and Principles of Person-Centered Theory

Carl Ransom Roger's theory of person-centered starts and ends with the subjective experiences of the individual. In his view, the subjective experiencing of reality as the basis for all the individual's judgments and behaviors, inner experience includes everything within the organism at a particular moment. Conscious experience, or awareness, is the aspect of the phenomenal field that can be symbolized such as verbalized or imagined. Unconscious experience in contrast, is experience that cannot be verbalized or imagined by the person.[291] Rogers writes of his fundamental belief in the subjective, observing that 'Human lives essentially in their own and subjective world, and even his most objective functioning, in science, mathematics, and the like, is the result of subjective purpose and subjective choice.'[292] Rogers believed that people have the capacity to change within themselves and will change in constructive ways. Briefly, they are as follows:

5.1.1.1. Actualizing Tendency

Individuals are basically trustworthy and have a tendency toward self-actualizing.[293] The actualizing tendency has both biological and a psychological aspect. The biological aspect aimed at the satisfaction of basic survival needs such as the need of water, food, and air. The psychological needs aspect involves the development of potentials that makes human beings worthwhile.[294] The person-centered formulates view about personality development, incongruence, and full functioning. The congruence permits the actualizing tendency to do its work and helps the individual to become a fully functioning person. Fully functioning persons are increasingly open to their experience, accepting of their feelings, free to make choices that are best for them and to act on those choices spontaneously, trusting of self and of human nature, capable of balanced and realistic expressions of both aggression and affection, and creative and nonconforming.[295]

Self-actualizing gradually develops from simple to complex; a person can be better actualized that ultimately allows for greater development of creativity. Person who have adequate degree of self-actualizing always keep moving forward,

291 Richard M. Ryckman, *Theories of Personality*, 403.

292 Richard Nelson-Jones, *Theory and Practice of Counseling and Therapy*, 89.

293 Charles Gelso, Bruce Fretz, *Counselling Psychology, Practices, Issues, and Intervention* (New Delhi: Cengage Learning India Private Limited, 2001), 257.

294 Richard M. Ryckman, *Theories of Personality*, 404.

295 Charles Gelso, Bruce Fretz, *Counselling Psychology, Practices, Issues, and Intervention*, 258.

such person never like to stop at a particular point. They always have faith in fulfilling their self- potential in socially approved way.[296]

5.1.1.2. Valuing Process

The concept of valuing process is central to the idea of a real or true and unique. The source of the valuing process or value placed on the various experiences seems clearly to be in the infants, who react to their own sensory and visceral evidence. As people grow older, their valuing process is effective in helping them to achieve self-actualizing to the degree that they are able to be aware of and perceive the experiencing which is going on within themselves.[297]

In the developing process, youth is making more complicated judgments about a variety of experiences relating to the issues in art, politics, career, ethics, personal relationships, cultural backgrounds, and so forth. Value judgments in these areas often change. Judgments about friends, acquaintances, politicians, doctors, teachers, clergy people, parents, and others do not remain constant. In addition, youths unlike children, are exposed to variety of opinions and come to incorporate them into their value systems, listening to what others think, must ultimately trust the wisdom of their own, if they are to grow constructively. If they trust themselves fully, they can maintain their feelings and intuitions may be wiser than their thinking or what they have learned from others.[298]

5.1.1.3. The Self-Concept

The self-concept is the self as perceived and the values attached to these perceptions to what a person refers to as 'I' or 'me'. As youth interact with the environment, more and more experience may become symbolized in awareness as self-experience. They develop a self- concept which includes both their perceptions about themselves and the varying positive and negative values attached to these self-perceptions.[299] The self-concept is primarily a social product and is acquired through social contact.

The ideal condition for development of a healthy self-concept, in Roger's view, is unconditional positive regard, deep and genuine caring by others, uncontaminated by judgments or evaluations of thoughts, feelings, or behavior with unconditional positive regard. Self –concept consists of all, those aspects of experiences which are perceived by the person in awareness. Such experiences may not sometimes be perceived accurately. [300] In the course of socialization, that some feelings and behaviors are 'appropriate' for self and others are 'inappropriate'. When

296 Arun Kumar Singh, *The Comprehensive History of Psychology*, (New Delhi: Motilal Banarsidass, 2002), 337.

297 Richard Nelson- Jones, *Theory and Practice of Counseling and Therapy*, 90.

298 Richard M. Ryckman, *Theories of Personality*, 407.

299 Richard Nelson-Jones, *Theory and Practice of Counseling and Therapy*, 92.

300 Arun Kumar Singh, *The Comprehensive History of Psychology*, 376.

these normative rules and incongruent with evaluations occurs, a person moves toward self-actualization then one can establish creative- fostering environment.

5.1.2. Basic Concepts of Cognitive-Behavioral Theory

Cognitive theory was initially developed by Aaron Beck in the early 1960s. Cognitive theoretical underpinnings come from three main sources. First is the phenomenological approach to psychology, which posits that the individual's view of self and personal world is central to how they behave. Second are structural theory and depth psychology. Third, the early work of cognitive psychologists like, Allport, Piaget and George Kelly's concepts on cognitive and behavior therapists. Aoaron Beck writes "cognition" is defined as that of function that involves inferences about one's experiences and about the occurrences and control of future events. Humans need to adapt to changing environmental circumstances. Cognition includes the progress involved identifying and predicting complex relations among events for the purposes of adaptation. Human have the capacity both for primal and or higher-level cognitive processing.[301] Some of the major antecedent forces of the cognitive psychology may be discussed as under.

5.1.2.1. The Nature of Constructs

For Kelly, constructs are ways of organizing experiences in terms of similarities and constructs. He believed that constructs are not identical to the verbal labels used to express them. Constructs are actual discriminations people make on an experiential level between varieties of experiences. Constructs are arranged hierarchically within a particular person's cognitive world; that is, one construct may subsume one or more other constructs. For example, a person's seen by others as a 'moralizer' may actually use a super ordinate construct of 'good versus bad' to control many other concepts: a 'good' person might be intelligent, cooperative, kind, ambitious, and sincere; a 'bad' person might be stupid, competitive, cruel, unambitious, and insincere.[302] Kelly has posited, hierarchical system of cognition populated by personal constructs derived from experience that now controls to determine the ways in which the person will react to incoming stimuli or information. There is also a room to within the system for change because the super ordinate concepts are free and often permeable. Change in these permeable constructs would then produce changes in the subordinate construct system.

5.1.2.2. Schemas

Schemas are structures that consist of people's fundamental beliefs and assumptions. Schemas are meaning-making cognitive structures. There are two categories of meaning: first, the objective or public meaning of an event, which may have few significant implications for the individual; and second, its personal

301 Richard Nelson-Jones, *Theory and Practice of Counseling and Therapy*, 312.

302 Richard M. Ryckman, *Theories of Personality*, 341.

or private meaning. Meaning assignment controls the psychological systems, such as behavioral, emotional, attention and memory, so that the individual can activate strategies for adaptation. Schemas are relatively stable cognitive patterns that influence, through their beliefs, how people select and synthesize incoming information. They are developed early in life from personal experiences and identifications with significant others and reinforced by further learning experiences. People categorize their experiences through a matrix of schemas.[303]

5.1.2.3. Structuralism

The development of cognitive psychology has been, to a greater extent had made it clear that the subject –matter of psychology was conscious experience. They also had shown that perception was the most correct way of knowing about the world. Modern cognitive psychologists have emphasized upon the study of perception and have considered it to be a very important mental function. These structuralisms had emphasized that introspection was the best method of analyzing the conscious experience.[304]

5.1.2.4. Social-Cognitive Model

According to the social-cognitive model, the environment affects behavior depends on how the person perceives and interprets these environmental events and stimuli, rather than on the environmental events themselves. These perceptions and interpretation are fundamentally cognitive. For example, one's behavior itself affects how the environment responds, and the reinforcements that are received.[305] The social-cognitive model has fueled the integration of cognitive and behavioral approaches. Behavior therapy, has increasingly used the methods of cognitive therapy, and thus focuses on the internal cognitions that underlie human problems and conflicts. When cognitive and behavioral approaches are combined based on the social-cognitive model, the person is seen more as the fundamental agent of change, rather than as a passive recipient of stimuli, as in earlier models of behavioral treatment.[306]

5.1.3. Gestalt Theory

The Perls, Fritz, and Laura developed Gestalt theory in the 1940s, with emphasis on the importance of healing through the recognition of "blocks" to fully experiencing the "here and now". Gestalt theory, an existential approach, focuses on creating a therapeutic environment in which the client gets "in touch" with unfinished issues by "presenting," re-experiencing, and integrating such experiences into current awareness. Gestalt theory recognizes that clients tend to

303 Richard Nelson- Jones, *Theory and Practice of Counseling and Therapy*, 312.

304 Arun Kumar Singh, *The Comprehensive History of Psychology*, 397.

305 Charles Gelso, Bruce Fretz, *Counselling Psychology, Practices, Issues, and Intervention,* 229.

306 Charles Gelso, Bruce Fretz, *Counselling Psychology, Practices, Issues, and Intervention,* 230.

compartmentalize their lives, "hiding" disowned or unacceptable parts from the conscious self. The ultimate goal of therapy is the integration of these parts and movements toward independence, maturity, and self-actualization.[307]

5.1.3.1. Part-Whole Psychology

The German noun Gestalt means form or shape. Other terms for gestalt include pattern, configuration or organized whole.[308] Thus, perceptual wholes are more than the sum of its parts. Such wholes emerge and have their characteristics of the parts. The whole as given in experience has two major characteristics. First, these perceptual wholes are unfilled wholes and not cluster of sensations. It means the original characteristic whole will be lost. Second, such perceptual wholes are separate and distinct from background. Therefore, they are segregated whole and not simply wholes.[309] The major thrust of the experimental work of the gestalt psychologists was to show that humans do not perceive things in isolation but organize them through their perceptual processes into meaningful wholes.

5.1.3.2. The Homeostasis and Balance

The basic tendency of every organism is to strive for balance. The organism is continuously faced with an imbalance that is disturbing through either external or internal factor. Life is characterized by a continuous interplay of balance and imbalance in the organism. Homeostasis is the process by which the organism satisfies its needs by restoring balance when faced with a demand or need that upsets its equilibrium.[310]

Life is basically an infinite number of unfinished situations or incomplete gestalts, with no sooner than one gestalt being completed than another comes up. The homeostatic process is the means by which the organism maintains itself and the only law which is constant is the forming of gestalts- wholes, completeness. A gestalt is an organic function, an ultimate experiential unit. With the introduction of the concept of the homeostatic process, it was possible to see gestalt formation as a primary biological drive, with the gestalt being the basic experiential unit having such properties as figure and ground and completeness or incompleteness.[311]

5.1.3.3. Growth and Maladjustment

The theory of personality that does exist is more clusters of loosely connected ideas that have evolved from the clinical experience of gestalt practitioners, rather than an overall theory of personality. Careful examination of the gestalt

---

307 Ed E. Jacobs, Robert L. Masson, Riley L. Harvill, *Theory and Practice of Group Counselling* (New Delhi: Cengage Learning Private Limited, 2010), 225.

308 Richard Nelson-Jones, *Theory and Practice of Counseling and Therapy*, 118.

309 Arun Kumar Singh, *The Comprehensive History of Psychology*, 268.

310 Richard Nelson- Jones, *Theory and Practice of Counseling and Therapy*, 120.

311 Richard Nelson- Jones, *Theory and Practice of Counseling and Therapy*, 121.

literature, does suggest several themes related to personality development and to healthy versus unhealthy functioning.[312] The personality theory of gestalt consists of many polarities, or opposites. Example, strength and weakness, activity and passivity; in healthy functioning these polarities are integrated such that they work in harmony, but in unhealthy functioning the polarities develop into splits, or dichotomies, throwing the person into a state of conflict.[313] In so-called here and now therapy, the individual is a hedonist who is concerned only with his/her own ego needs. The preoccupation with the past and the future is largely given up, so that one lives one's experience in the now. Values and standards are part of the immediate experience, and taking the responsibility to be oneself and live in the present may help the person to creative potential.

5.1.4. Reality Theory

Reality theory, based on the work of William Glasser, proposes that human beings are responsible for making choices about the behavior and that such choices are intended to meet five basic needs: survival, love and belonging, power, freedom, and fun. William's original work in reality theory has evolved into what he terms choice theory, with the focus on the importance of interpersonal relationships in the satisfaction of human needs. His theory considers conduct such as "angering" and "depressing" as active choices, which can be altered in favor of more constructive behaviors.[314]

Choice theory focuses little on the past and relies much on the present to play an active role in helping the members to make better choices and to develop more positive plans of action. When using reality therapy, the ultimate goal is for members to accept responsibility for their behavior and to make better choices. In order to facilitate change, the member must understand their inseparable, distinct components of behavior: acting, feeling, and thinking.

5.1.4.1. Basic Needs and Feelings

Choice theory sees humans as driven by basic needs that are genetic in origin. All human behavior represents an attempt to control the world to best satisfy these needs. People have no rest from their needs. Once aware of a need they have no choice but to attempt to satisfy the need and, when satisfied, other needs emerge. Human life is a constant struggle to satisfy these different needs and to solve the ever-present conflicts between them. He stresses that their sources are still biologic and their genetic instructions no less urgent than the genetic instructions for the physical need to survive and reproduce.[315] The needs are survival: which

312 Charles Gelso, Bruce Fretz, *Counselling Psychology, Practices, Issues, and Intervention,* 262.

313 Charles Gelso, Bruce Fretz, *Counselling Psychology, Practices, Issues, and Intervention,* 263.

314 Ed E. Jacobs, Robert L. Masson, Riley L. Harvill, *Theory and Practice of Group Counselling,* 211.

315 Richard Nelson-Jones, *Theory and Practice of Counseling and Therapy,* 176.

people's genes instruct the old brain to carry out all the survival needs. Love, loving sex and belonging: this need of love and belonging may be satisfied by marital partners, family, friends, groups, and even pets. Probably, failure to meet love and belonging needs is the prime cause of human misery. Power: power is ultimately a sense of self –worth and can be met by valuing oneself independently of external recognition. Freedom: people need freedom to choose how to live, express themselves freely, and associate with whom they choose. Fun: the need for fun or enjoyment is as fundamental a need as the other needs, the need for fun and enjoyment also includes being interested and having interests.[316]

5.1.4.2. Total Behavior

In choice theory, behavior is how people choose to attempt to control the world to satisfy the needs rather than a response to stimulation. Behavior is more than conduct or action. William expresses concept of behavior as total behavior, the whole, 'always consists of the four components: acting like walking, running, and eating. Thinking, like voluntary generating thoughts, involuntary generating thoughts. Feeling like pleasurable, and painful thoughts, and the physiology associated with all actions, thoughts, and feelings that generates components of total behavior.[317] Reality theory is active, directive, practical, and behavioral. The focus is on what people are doing and thinking, because these components of behavior guide and assist people in deciding on a constructive plan of responsible behavior change that will lead to effective control of their lives.[318]

5.1.4.3. Maintenance

William sees all clients at the start of therapy as choosing some form of self-destructive behavior that represents their misguided attempts to regain control over their poorly controlled and frustrating lives. People who are depressed, guilty, angry and have headache insufficiently realize both what their needs are and that they can make better choices about satisfying them than they currently do.[319] Reality theory engage people in a processes of questioning the wisdom of their choices and assist people to relate better by developing the habit awareness of themselves as persons who can make good or poor choices.

5.1.5. Behavior Theory

The work of the Russian physiologist Ivan Pavlon on the conditioned on reflex,[320] experiments served as an objective and scientific method for development and

---

316 Richard Nelson-Jones, *Theory and Practice of Counseling and Therapy*, 177.

317 Richard Nelson-Jones, *Theory and Practice of Counseling and Therapy*, 179.

318 Gerald Corey, *Case Approach to Counseling and Psychotherapy* (Belmont, California: Brooks Publishing Company, 1991), 230.

319 Richard Nelson-Jones, *Theory and Practice of Counseling and Therapy*, 183.

320 Richard M. Ryckman, *Theories of Personality*, 454.

modification of behavior.[321] In the course of his work, he discovered that the animals salivated not only when food was actually in their mouths but also when it was shown to them by the experimenter. He called this phenomenon a "psychic secretion."[322] His step was to control the conditions under which such secretions occurred, that salivation could be brought under the control of specific stimuli such as a light or a bell. The fact that such respondent conditioning can account for a variety of behaviors, Burrhus Frederick Skinner was impressed by the procedure Pavlon used to bring the behavior under control.[323] These two interrelated events, rise of behaviorism and the development of the experimental study of learning did pave the way toward behavioral therapy.

5.1.5.1. Classical Conditioning

Pavlon considered that instincts and reflexes were alike in being inevitable responses of the organism to internal and external stimuli. 'Reflex' was the preferred term since it had been used from the beginning with a scientific connotation. The whole nervous activity of animals is based on inborn reflexes, which may be either excitatory or inhibitory. Such reflexes are regular causal connections between certain definite external stimuli acting on the organism and its necessary reflex reaction. The inborn reflexes alone are inadequate to ensure the continued existence of the organism, with the more specialized interaction between the animal and the environment provided through the medium of the cerebral hemispheres.[324] Learning a conditioned response has come to be termed classical or respondent conditioning, and this has become essential to the founding of behavior therapy.

5.1.5.2. Operant Conditioning

Operant conditioning principles of reinforcement and punishment are the most powerful influences determining behavior.[325] The term 'operant' emphasizes the fact that behavior operates on the environment to generate consequences. Thus, the consequences define the properties with respect to which responses are viewed as similar. The probability of a response is increased after both positive and negative reinforcement. Positive reinforcements consist of presenting something, such as food, water or sexual contact, in a situation. Negative reinforcements consist of removing something, such as a bright light or an electric shock, from the situation. Thus, the difference between positive and negative reinforcement hinges on whether it is the presence or absence of a given reinforcer that increases

321 Arun Kumar Singh, *The comprehensive History of Psychology*, 192.

322 Richard M. Ryckman, *Theories of Personality*, 454.

323 Richard M. Ryckman, *Theories of Personality*, 455.

324 Richard Nelson- Jones, *Theory and Practice of counseling and Therapy*, 246.

325 Charles Gelso, Bruce Fretz, *Counselling Psychology, Practices, Issues, and Intervention*, 227.

the probability of a response. The with-drawal of a positive reinforcer has the same effect as the presentation of a negative reinforce.[326]

5.1.5.3. Discrimination

The stimuli preceding the behavior are important because they provide the occasion under which reinforcement is likely to occur if the behavior is performed. Thus, people learn discrimination. They learn that in the presence of certain stimuli or in situations their behavior is likely to be reinforced, whereas the same behavior in the presence of other stimuli or in other situations is not likely to be punished. People learn the appropriate behavior through oral or written instructions. Instructions, directions, examples, and models are all used to facilitate the development of responses.[327]

5.1.6. Group Theory

A word 'group' can be defined as "any aggregate of individuals among which some degree of interdependence exists." A therapeutic group may be defined as an "aggregate of interdependent individuals whose interaction is in pursuit of some shared goal or goals." Therapeutic group is always more than the sum of its individual parts because the group itself takes on its own life, its own psyche so to speak, and its own personality.[328] Therapeutic groups can include a wide range of interventions such as group counselling, group psychotherapy, skill practice, and feedback.

5.1.6.1. Group Counselling and Group Psychotherapy

Group counselling tends to be more oriented toward prevention than psychotherapy. Also group counselling is more likely to focus on the conscious concerns of the client, to include attention to educational and vocational issues as well as personal issues, to occur in educational settings in contrast to medical or clinical settings, and to be used with clients within the normal range rather than with severely troubled persons. Group counselling is, on the whole, briefer than group therapy. Group therapy, on the other hand, may continue for several years and is more likely than counselling to seek deep personality change in clients.[329]

In counselling and therapy groups, the leader must be keenly aware of how members feel about each other and the leader. Members may resent others for being too quiet, too open, or too together.[330] It is important for leaders to realize that they must attend too much more than just the verbal exchange among members. Some of these currents are lack of trust, lack of commitment, conflicts

---

326 Richard Nelson-Jones, *Theory and Practice of Counseling and Therapy*, 251.

327 Richard M. Ryckman, *Theories of Personality*, 464.

328 Charles Gelso, Bruce Fretz, *Counselling Psychology, Practices, Issues, and Intervention,* 249.

329 Charles Gelso, Bruce Fretz, *Counselling Psychology, Practices, Issues, and Intervention,* 349.

330 Ed E. Jacobs, Robert L. Masson, Riley L. Harvill, *Theory and Practice of Group Counselling*, 36.

between members, strong alliances between members, and attention-seeking behavior.[331]

5.1.6.2. Skill Practice

Members can practice new skills and behaviors in a supportive environment before trying them in real-world situations. The range of new behaviors to explore is nearly infinite, members can practice learning how to make friends, being more assertive, talking to a significant people in their lives, and asking for a raise. They may share personal facts about themselves, confront others when they talk to others, about their family, and about their practices and cultures. Assertiveness, communication, parenting, and cultural enrichment are all examples of groups where members might experiment with new behavior.[332]

5.1.6.3. Feedback

Groups provide an opportunity for members to receive feedback. Group feedback often is more powerful than individual feedback because when only one person is giving feedback, the receiver can dismiss that person's viewpoint. When more people are saying the same thing, it is difficult to deny the accuracy of what is being said. In group, behavior rehearsal is a major component. The suggestions, reactions, and perceptions of others can be valuable. Members will have the opportunity to hear both first impressions and updated impressions.[333]

5.2. Implications for Pastoral Care and Counselling Towards Fidelity to Naga Culture

5.2.1. Person-Centered Approach

The first approach reviewed is the person-centered counselling. It is a humanistic approach that deals with the ways in which individuals perceive themselves consciously rather than how a counsellor can interpret their unconscious thoughts or ideas. The person-centered approach ultimately sees human beings as having an innate tendency to develop towards their full potential. The counsellor in this approach works to understand an individual's experience from their point of view. The counsellor must positively value the client as a person in all aspects of their humanity, while aiming to be open and genuine. This is vital in helping an individual to feel accepted and better understanding their own feelings- essentially helping them to reconnect with their inner values and sense of self-worth. This reconnection with their inner resources enables them to find their own way to move forward.[334]

---

331 Ed E. Jacobs, Robert L. Masson, Riley L. Harvill, *Theory and Practice of Group Counselling*, 37.

332 Ed E. Jacobs, Robert L. Masson, Riley L. Harvill, *Theory and Practice of Group Counselling*, 13.

333 Ed E. Jacobs, Robert L. Masson, Riley L. Harvill, *Theory and Practice of Group Counselling*, 13.

334 http://www. Person-Centered Therapy-Counselling Directorywww.counselling-directory.org. UK > Person-centered therapy(Accesses, April 20, 2016).

Person-centered counsellors can use Rogerian[335] empathy to help them to experience and explore their cultural and racial concerns. The person-centered concept of empathy can be expanded to include cultural empathy. Person-centered counsellors who see themselves and their clients as cultural beings can encourage non-western clients to share their experiences by such methods as listening carefully for and responding to culturally relevant cues, and also by openly acknowledging that they are from a different cultural context of their concerns. The basic assumptions of the Person-centered Counselling and Therapy include 'actualization' –the tendency towards the fulfillment of potential and 'wholeness' –that represents the sole motivational construct in Person-centered psychology. Person-centered Counselling regards persons as potentially fully functionally creative, social and congruent. The approach believes in the capacity of each individual client to become more self-directed in a relationship. Clients have, within themselves the resources for personal change. The Counsellor facilitates change.

The Client-Centered Therapy can be effectively made use of in counselling the Naga youths. There are various cultural factors that don't exist anymore in this modern society which were conducive in fostering a qualitative individual, family and communal living. With advancement of time and with expansion of living outside territory, the closeness that a community shared as a close knit village would undeniably deteriorate. Cultural aloofness is a problem maladjusted among Naga youths. The core condition of therapeutic and personality change in the client-centered therapy namely empathic understanding, congruence and unconditional positive regard has significant role in cultural counselling, regarding persons as potentially fully functioning, self actualizing their cultural identity, values and norms.

Actualization is the sole motivational construct in person-centered psychology. A function of the actualizing tendency differentiates a portion of one's experience into an awareness of self and the organization of a self-concept.[336] The self-concept, or self-structure, is a persistent pattern of perception in relation to the environment, culture, values, goals and ideals. Naga youth, in contemporary times, is exposed to several conflicting, distracting, difficult and stressful situations. Youth generally tended to rely on the advice, wisdom and judgment of their elders.

In modern times, owing to their exposure to other cultural milieu through mass media, books, and to some extent migrating to other metropolitan cities, they

335 Carl Rogers developed Person-Centered Counselling, also known as Client-Centered and Non-directive Approach, in the United States of America in the 1930s. Rogers formulated his 'core conditions' for therapeutic and personality change namely empathic understanding, congruence and unconditional positive regard.

336 D. John Antony, *Psychotherapies in Counselling* (Tamilnadu: Anughaha Publications, 2003), 234.

are often tempted to imitate and emulate other modes and patterns of behavior.[337] Because of several socio-economic and cultural changes, a significant group of youth is becoming estranged and alienated from the traditional settings of their life. Therefore, Rogers theory of person-centered approach would be resourceful, capable of self-understanding and self-direction, able to make constructive changes, and able to live effective and productive lives.

5.2.2. Cognitive-Behavioral Approach

Cognitive behavioral Therapy is a form of psychotherapy. It was originally designed to treat depression, but is now used for a number of mental disorders. It works to solve current problems and change unhelpful thinking and behavior. This technique acknowledges that there may be behaviors that cannot be controlled through rational thought, but rather emerge based on prior conditioning from the environment and other external and/or internal stimuli. Ivan Pavlon believed that conscious thoughts could influence a person's behavior all on its own.[338] The cognitive-behavioral counselling approaches provide another example of how it is possible to extend existing. Regarding rational emotive behavior therapy, Ellis includes racial prejudice in his list of prejudice-related irrationalities. In REBT, clients' cultural and racial irrational beliefs and preferential and rational terms, similarly, in Beck's cognitive therapy, questioning by skilled counsellors can help clients to identify their underlying cultural and racial automatic thought and perceptions for the future.[339] The attitude held by culturally skilled counsellors include being sensitive to their own cultural heritage, being comfortable with the differences of clients from other cultures and races, and recognizing the limitations of their competence and expertise. Counsellors should know about their cultural and racial heritage and how this affects the counselling process, understand how oppression, racism and discrimination may affect them personally and in their work, and realize the impact of how they communicate on culturally different clients. Skills required include seeking out relevant educational and training experiences, actively understanding oneself as a cultural and racial being, and seeking an identity that transcends race.[340]

Cognitive-behavioral counselling is also another important and relevant counselling approach that can be applied to the Naga youth. Due to the advancement and progress in the educational level and adopting various languages, Naga culture is gradually becoming foreign even for the Nagas

337 S. Narayana Rao, *Counselling Psychology* (New Delhi: Tata McGraw-Hill Publishing Company Limited, 1984), 42.

338 Cognitive behavioral therapy-Wikipedia, the free encyclopedia https://en.m.wikipedia.org>wiki>cognitive behavioral therapy (Accesses, April 21, 2016).

339 Richard Nelson-Jones, Richard Nelson- Jones, *Practical Counseling and Helping skills*, 5th edition (London: Sage Publications, 2005), 432.

340 Richard Nelson-Jones, *Practical Counseling and Helping Skills*, 435.

themselves, Nevertheless, there is a gradual renaissance of sort growing at least among conscious people who, even from the personal pervading philosophical question of who am I and where do I come from, the quest for ones roots and identity and the need to feel belonged, or from the general discontent over the current social and cultural conditions, or from the intellectual awakenings and pursuits. The cognitive- behavioral counselling will help them recognizing their attitudes, behavior, and patterns, which was leading to its obsolete state and also the decline of their interest, fondness, respect, and the ability to relate to their cultural elements. Cognitive-behavioral approach would help the Naga youth to acknowledge their socio-cultural conditioning and take specific actions to change their life.

5.2.3. Gestalt Therapy Approach

Gestalt Therapy is the third approach considered. Gestalt Therapy is an existential/ experiential form of psychotherapy that emphasizes personal responsibility, and that focuses upon the individual's experience in the present moment, the therapist-client relationship, the environmental and social contexts of a person's life, and the self-regulating adjustments people make as a result of their overall situation. Gestalt Therapy focuses on process what is actually happening over content (what is being talked about). Gestalt Therapy is a method of awareness practice (also called "mindfulness" in other clinical domains), by which perceiving, feeling, and acting are understood to be conducive to interpreting, explaining, and conceptualizing the hermeneutics of experience. The client learns to be aware of what he or she is doing and that triggers the ability to risk a shift or change. The objective of Gestalt Therapy is to enable the client to become more fully and creatively alive and to become more free from the blocks and unfinished business that may diminish satisfaction, fulfillment, and growth, and to experience with new ways of being.[341]

There are opportunities to sensitivity and creatively use Gestalt methods, if they are timed appropriately, with culturally diverse populations. One of the advantages of drawing on Gestalt experiments is that they can be tailored to fit the unique way in which an individual perceives and interprets his or her culture. Gestalt therapists approach each client in an open way and without preconceptions. Gestalt therapy is particularly effective in helping people in integrating the polarities within themselves. Many bicultural clients experience an ongoing struggle to reconcile what appear to be diverse aspects of the cultures in which they live. There are many opportunities to apply Gestalt experiments in creative ways with diverse client populations. In culture where indirect speech is the norm, nonverbal behaviors may emphasize the unspoken content of verbal communication. These clients may express themselves nonverbally more

341 Gestalt therapy-Wikipedia, the free encyclopedia https://en.m.wikipedia.org>Gestalt therapy, (Accesses, April 20, 2016).

expressively than they do with words. Gestalt therapists may ask clients to focus on their gestures, facial expressions, and what they are experiencing within their own body. Moreover, Gestalt therapists attempt to fully understand the background of their client's culture. They are concerned about how and which aspects of this background become central or figured for them and what meaning clients place on these figures.[342]

Gestalt Therapy is used in cultural counselling, Naga youth could be helped to change by way of aiding them to open-up their different thinking, ways of life, their adaptation to new trends of culture. The living style and fashion, the way they wear modern dress and ornaments have drastically changed due to migration to other metropolitan cities and also with the invasion of information technology like television, newspapers, magazines, and internet. Traditional values and practices seem to be diminishing on the present living style of Naga youth. This therapy would help the Naga youth to bring those values and practices to the present and lived as much as possible. In a way they enact the past event as though they are living it now. Gestalt therapy is particularly effective in helping Naga youths to integrate the polarities within themselves.

5.2.4. Reality Therapy Approach

The fourth approach is the Reality Therapy.[343] It focuses on what Glasser calls psychiatry's three Rs: realism, responsibility, and right and wrong; rather than symptoms of mental disorders. Reality therapy maintains that the individual is suffering from a socially universal human condition rather than a mental illness. It is in the unsuccessful attainment of basic needs that a person's behaviors move away from the norm. Since fulfilling essential needs is part of a person's present life. The reality therapy approach to counselling and problem-solving focuses on the here-and –now actions of the client and the ability to create and choose a better future. Typically, clients seek to discover what they really want and how they are currently choosing to behave in order to achieve these goals.[344]

The core principles of choice theory/reality therapy have much to offer in the area of cultural counselling. In cross-cultural therapy it is essential that counsellors respect the differences in worldview between themselves and their clients. Counsellors demonstrate their respect for the cultural values of their clients by helping them explore how satisfying their current behavior is both to

---

342 Gerald Corey, *Theory and Practice of Counseling and Psychotherapy* 6th ed (Australia: Brooks/ Cole, 2001), 222.

343 Reality therapy is the method of Counselling that Dr. Glasser has been teaching since 1965. Reality therapy is firmly based on choice theory and its successful application is dependent on a strong understanding of choice therapy. www.wglasser.com.> the-glasser approach, (Accesses, April 14, 2016).

344 Reality therapy- William Glasser Institute www.wglasser.com> the glasser approach, (Accesses, April 20, 2016).

themselves and to others. Once clients make this assessment, they can formulate realistic plans that are consistent with their cultural values. It is a further sign of respect that the counsellor refrains from deciding what behavior should be changed. Though skillful questioning on the counsellor's part, ethnic minority clients can be helped to determine the degree to which they have an acculturated into the dominant society. It is possible for them to find a balance, retaining their ethnic identity and values while integrating some of the values and practices of the dominant group. Again, the counsellor does not determine this balance for clients but challenges them to arrive at their own answer. With this focus on acting and thinking rather than on identifying and exploring feelings, many clients are less likely to display resistance to counselling.[345]

This Reality Therapy attempts to understand and help Naga youths concerned about the challenge. The challenge is to understand their place and role within the systems they live, that is, the family, groups, the culture and the beliefs, and meaning and behavior that they construct to explain their world of intimate relationships. Urbanization and the scattering of people from their respective villages mean that traditional rules and regulations, activities, celebrations, etc., that bound the village together have become obsolete and ineffective. More and more people are now living in mixed urban and semi urban communities under different laws, which has greatly influence in the spirit of maintaining communitarian life, equality and respect, behavior and attitude, and hospitality. Therefore, it is only expected that traditional systems will go through a shift. Regardless of what had been practiced in the past traditional ways of living, one can re-evaluate one's current reality and choose to satisfy their living more effectively now and in the future. Reality therapy demonstrates their respect for the cultural values of their clients by helping them explore how satisfying their current behavior is both to themselves and to others.

5.2.5. Behavior Therapy Approach

Behavior Therapy is considered as fifth approach. Behavioral Therapy is focused on human behavior and looks to eradicate unwanted or maladaptive behavior. Typically this type of therapy is used for those with behavioral problems or mental health conditions that involve unwanted behavior, example of this include addictions, anxiety, phobias and obsessive-compulsive disorder (OCD).

Behavioral Therapy is an action-based therapy that looks to foster positive behavior change. In behavioral therapy, the past is still important as it often reveals where and when the unwanted behavior was learned, however it looks more so at present behavior and ways in which it can be rectified. There are two key principles that form the foundations of behavioral therapy-classical conditioning and operant conditioning.

345 Gerald Corey, *Theory and Practice of Counseling and Psychotherapy*, 249.

Classical conditioning: Behavioral Therapy that is based on classical conditioning uses a number of techniques to bring about behavior change. Originally this type of therapy was known as behavior modification. Operant conditioning: Operant conditioning uses techniques such as positive reinforcement, punishment and modeling to help alter behavior. The premise behind behavioral therapy is that behavior can be both learned and un-learned. This goal is to help the individual learn new, positive behaviors which will minimize or eliminate the issue.[346]

Behavior Therapy has some clear advantages over many other theories in working with cultural populations. Because of their cultural and ethnic backgrounds, some clients hold values that are contrary to the free expression of feelings and the sharing of personal concerns. Behavioral counselling does not place emphasis on experiencing catharsis. Rather, it stresses changing specific behaviors and developing problem-solving skills. Clients who are looking for action plans and behavioral change are likely to cooperate with this approach; they can see that it offers them concrete methods for dealing with their problem of living. Behavior Therapy focuses on environmental conditions that contribute to a client's problem. Social and political influences can play a significant role in the lives of people of color through discriminatory practices and economic problems. Strength of behavioral procedures is that they take into consideration the social and cultural dimensions of the client's life. The behavioral approach has moved beyond treating for a specific symptom or behavioral problem. Instead, it stresses a thorough evaluation of the person's life circumstances to ascertain not only whether the target behavior is amenable to change but also whether such a change is likely to lead to a significant improvement in the client's total life situation. In designing a change program for clients from diverse backgrounds, effective behavioral practitioners conduct a functional analysis of the problem situation. This assessment includes the cultural context in which the problem behavior occurs, the consequences both to the client and to the client's socio-cultural environment, the resources within the environment that can promote change, and the impact that change is likely to have on others in the client's surroundings.[347]

Behavior Therapy approach developed insights, and working in the transference and counter-transference toward understanding and growth of Naga youths. The basic assumptions in therapy may help Naga youths to come to the realization that to be someone in a society one has to be rooted in one's own culture. When it comes to enhancing the life of Naga youth, cultural items like indigenous music, folklore, art and crafts would be two-fold blessing. It will not only enable the youth to keep in touch with their invaluable cultural heritage

346 Behavioral Therapy Counselling Directory. www.counselling-directory.org.uk> behavioral therapy, (Accesses, April 21, 2016).

347 Gerald Corey, *Theory and Practice of Counseling and Psychotherapy*, 286.

but also help them to generate their cultural identity through indigenous music, folklore theatre, animation and movies, and homegrown crafts. Behavior Therapy stresses changing specific behaviors and developing problem-solving skills and therefore, Naga youths have to realize that with the passage of time things have changed and they cannot go back to the kind of work their fore parents did. The pragmatic thing right now is to instill work culture through creative ways.

5.2.6. Group Counselling

The last approach considered is Group Counselling. Group counselling is a form of therapy where people with similar experiences/issues come together with a professional therapist. The therapist runs the sessions, but generally everyone contributes in some way, listening to others and talking themselves. Open agenda group sessions can be an effective form of help for a range of problems, providing an opportunity to explore how they relate to others and benefit from their experiences and support. These groups are a more effective form of help than individual counselling for many people. Groups can provide an opportunity to explore how they relate to others, to see themselves through their eyes, to benefit from their experiences and support while offering them their own.[348]

Face to face interaction between the counsellee and counsellor has been considered as counselling in which the counsellor helps in resolving the counsellee's problem(s). There are practical situations, however, in which a counsellee directly involves other members who may be his/her family or members of his/her group. In such a situation individual counselling may not be quite effective. Group counselling thus becomes a practical means of helping to resolve problems by harnessing the social process of group dynamics, social facilitation, and so on. Counsellors are often confronted with individuals with similar problems. This method is called group therapy, and it helps if persons realize that others have difficulties similar to their own. The aim of group counselling facilitating features in the former. A Conducive environment is created, resistances are lowered and the release of individual tensions is facilitated.[349]

Group therapy provides useful counselling to the Naga youths, churches, and society as a whole. In Naga society certain common cultural values have been identified, including the emphasis on specified role within family, church and society. One of the major problems that the Naga youths are facing is the generation gap between parents and children. This generation gap is more pronounced in families where parents are not educated. Most Naga parents are still tradition bound and are loyal to their clan, village and tribe. Whereas most Naga youths who do studies in towns and cities in Nagaland and outside do not maintain the same ties as their parents do, to their clan, village or tribe. This is an

348 Group counselling/university of Oxford https/www.ox.ac.uk>students>welfare, (Accesses, April 21, 2016).

349 S. Narayana Rao, *Counselling Psychology*, 42.

area of conflict as found in the study. Also, most churches do not understand the demands and needs of the youth from their peers and society. Therefore, group therapy/counselling is an urgent need to be applied to the Naga youths, family, church, and society as a whole with regard to the value of cultural fidelity. This group therapy approaches may help them to explore, understands, and balanced their relationships to live a harmonious life and an opportunity to draw on traditional values and practices.

5.3. Counselling Intervention

The most important finding of the present study is migrant Naga youth has a highly significant influence on cultural fidelity. This implies that Naga youth may be helped to improve adjustment on acculturation while, retaining traditional cultural practices. As people become increasingly enmeshed in the lifestyle accruing from the scientific age, the psychological consequences and behavior become more complex. As people begin to realize the potential for a fuller life that modern technology can provide, they also become aware of the inadequacies of many existing institutions and practices, beliefs and codes of conduct accepted by themselves and their fore parents at an earlier age. As a consequence, while more people hope for a better life, there is simultaneously a feeling of frustration and anxiety that they themselves may not be able to experience this better life which they feel should be available to them. They search for new anchors, new guidelines for plans of action that hold promise for realizing some of their dreams and aspirations.[350]

The goal of counselling is to help individuals overcome their immediate problems and also to equip them to meet future problems. Rapid social change brought about by industrialization and urbanization has led to several perplexing problems. The pace of this change is ever on the increase, thus making adjustment a continuous process of grappling with new situations. Counselling, to be meaningful, has to be specific for each client since it involves his unique problems and expectations. The goals of counselling may be described as immediate, long range, and process goals. A statement of goals is not only important but also necessary for a meaningful evaluation of the usefulness or otherwise of any activity, including counselling. It establishes a congruency between what is demanded or sought and what is possible or practical.

Specific counselling goals are unique to each client and involve a consideration of the client's expectations as well as the environmental aspects. Apart from the specific goals there are, however, two categories of goals which are common to most counselling situations. These are identified as long-range and process goals. The latter have great significance. They shape the counsellee and counsellors' inter-relations and behavior. The process goals comprise facilitating procedures for enhancing the effectiveness of counselling. The long-range goals

350 S. Narayana Rao, *Counselling Psychology*, 2.

are those that reflect the counsellor's philosophy of life and could be stated as: To help the counsellee become self-actualizing, to help the counsellee attain self-realization, to help the counsellee become a fully-functioning person.

The immediate goals of counselling refer to the problems for which the client is seeking solutions, here and now. The client fails to utilize his/her capacities fully and efficiently and, therefore, is unable to function efficiently. The counsellee could be helped to gain fuller self-understanding through self-exploration and be able to appreciate his/her strengths and weaknesses. The counsellor could provide necessary information, however exhaustive, may not be useful to the client unless he/she has an integrative understanding of himself/herself vis-a-vis his/her personal resources and environmental constrains and resources.[351]

Naga youth need sound values and meanings to be healthy. Growth toward Spirit-centered wholesome must include growth in life-guiding values and ethical commitments. The epidemic of moral confusion and value distortions in their society are the seedbed within which bred many of the psychological, psychosomatic, interpersonal, and spiritual problems that bring people to counselling and therapy. The widespread collapse of old authority-centered and institutionally-validated value systems has left millions of people feeling as though they are drifting in mid-ocean in a small boat without a rudder, a compass, or a chart during a storm. Many who seek pastoral help with personal problems are suffering from distorted, immature, or vacuous consciences. Often they are unaware of the ethical roots of their pain. In Naga society, ministers need to develop effective skills as guides to their people on their journey through complex and confusing ethical and values issues. This aspect of pastoral care and counselling is one of the most needed and most often neglected in Naga society.

Following are the consideration of some relevant counselling approaches to the migrant Naga youth with regard to their fidelity to the Naga culture.

5.3.1. Value Based Counselling[352]

Insights regarding fidelity to Naga culture cannot be significantly imparted into individuals. Youth as discussed above, has influence to their exposure to other cultural milieu and are tempted to imitate other modes and patterns of behavior. In olden days, the elders through their stories told the younger generations about values and morals to be kept. This has been currently taken over by the other educational programmes.

---

351 S. Narayana Rao, *Counselling Psychology*, 50.

352 Value-based counselling is becoming more interested in today's society. Owing to rapid economic and social progress, there are significant changes in human's environment affecting many of their attitudes. S. Narayana Rao, *Counselling and Guidance*, 2nd ed. (New Delhi: Tata McGraw-Hill Publishing Company Limited, 1991), 283. Among young adult Naga, several changes are taking place in the social life; their attitude towards tradition has a radical change. Therefore, value-based counselling would provide substantial value systems.

The task of formulating an ideology or philosophy of life values begins when, with intellectual maturing, youth are confronted by life's meaning and purpose. The function of ideology is to give meaning to the vague inner states of selfhood, to bring order out of the multiplicity of historical events, and to offer a compelling vision of what life can be. It connects the past with the present and projects an image of future existence. It contains idealism and a hope not only for one's own fulfillment but for the promise of a new society as well. It is in shaping a vision of life that youth begin to identify with the forces of history that have intersected with their personal experience and to find solidarity with their community and all of humanity. This enables them, despite the contradictions of value systems, to make commitment to society's cultural conservation and its evolutionary development. They thus move toward youth with a sense of devotion and fidelity. Failure to shape such a vision of life leaves youth without direction and subject to whim and change.[353] Therefore, the present research provides the pastoral counsellor with an insight of value based counselling to impart the importance of values among migrant Naga youth.

5.3.2. Modern Trends Counselling[354]

Modern counselling has been defined as assisting an individual to develop insight and ability to adjust to successive events in his/her life through appraisal of his/her capacities, aptitudes and interest; helping him/her to understand motivations, emotional reactions and compensatory behavior; and helping him/her to attain a degree of personal integration whereby he/she can most effectively use his/her potentialities and make the greatest contribution to the society in which he/she lives.[355]

Urbanization has brought together people of every kind in the city and people have a lot of opportunities to fall in love with any different cultural background.[356] This background is partly the outcome of the customs and culture of the community as a whole, and partly depends upon the various social groups to which the person belongs. Every community has its objects, ideals, knowledge, habits, values, and attitudes and there are usually customary and standardized ways of doing things which are common to those sharing a particular culture. A person learns these from the previous generation and in this way is expected to

353 Paul B. Irwin, *The Care and Counseling of Youth in the Church* (Philadelphia: Fortress Press, 1980), 18.

354 Modern trends in counselling concern the appropriate model for counselling. In the early part of the present century the medical model of remediation was popular. This, however, is rapidly giving place to preventive approaches. The modern trend is to take advantage of several agencies and institutions to bring about desirable counselling outcomes. S. Narayana Rao, *Counselling and Guidance*, 2nd ed., 282.

355 Kathleen Heasman, *An Introduction to Pastoral Counselling* "(N.p.: n.p.,n.d)," 2.

356 D. John Antony, *Types of Counselling* (Nagercoil: Anughaha Publications, 1996), 105.

be able to cope with his/her own environment and with his relationships with other people.[357] These things will also vary according to the position or role which a person holds in his/her family. The first and foremost place for the purpose is home.[358] Modern Counselling should help the migrant Naga youth in these respects and so make it possible for them to exercise their choice with a greater degree of maturity and wider knowledge about the relevant circumstances.

Now the older generation has little comprehension or understanding of the world in which youth live, they themselves often find it difficult to adjust to their own world. This has its effect not only upon family relationships, but upon all groups where the generations meet. The counsellor is inevitably called upon to interpret the outlook of one generation to another.[359]

There are many facets of changes in the Naga society, which are taking place in the traditional Naga culture. The researcher has observed in the course of the present investigation and findings that the traditional practices and values, which have been accepted almost without question for many generations, are now being criticized and thrown aside. The coming of the Christianity, modernization, urbanization, and advancement in technology has produced an entirely new perspective with regard to making progress in the life of the Naga youth in varied ways. On the other hand, the patterns and techniques of the old rich cultural traditions no longer fit reality. Therefore, the results of the present investigation as described provide the need of the modern trends in counselling among migrant Naga youth with regard to their faithfulness and fidelity to the Naga culture.

5.3.3. Culture-Centered Counselling[360]

The culture-centered approach to counselling is focused on the context where all behaviors are learned and displayed. Values and worldviews are not themselves the culture but have been constructed as ways to find meaning in each cultural context. At the same time, they influence the context in which they were learned or being applied.[361]

Rapid increases in urbanization around the world have caused many changes in village and family habits, patterns, or rules. There are several social divisive forces which have been trying to capture the Naga youth. Today, there is also an erosion of traditional values which has caused the vacuum in the shape

357 Kathleen Heasman, *An Introduction to Pastoral Counselling*, 10.

358 Gideon Sobhanam, *United to Adjust: A Sacramental Theology of Marriage for Marital Counselling* (Delhi: ISPCK, 2007), 191.

359 Kathleen Heasman, *An Introduction to Pastoral Counselling*, 12.

360 Culture-centered approach that all behaviors are learned and displayed in a cultural context. Each culture is complicated and dynamic. The search for accuracy is directed toward assessing and understanding each client in his/her own complicated and dynamic cultural context. Paul B. Pedersen, *Culture-Centered Counselling Interventions*, 23.

361 Paul B. Pedersen, *Culture-Centered Counselling Interventions*, 23.

of cultural values and morality. As a result, Naga youth is in a crisis of cultural identity, clashing with the traditional values, norms with modernity. Most youth lie somewhere between these two extremes and have the feeling that, they should be more definite in their views and yet fear to be so. This tends to breed a state of anxious confusion often expressed outwardly by a show of bravado. Adding to this, there is a dearth of models of idealism and commitment and there arises an overwhelming sense of hopelessness and indifferences. Hence, it is necessary to understand the Naga youth and the efficacious ways of ministering to them from culture-centered perspective, which would be helpful to the accurate practice of counselling.

5.4. Church's Approach to Youth Ministry

Ross Snyder, writing in "Young People and Their Culture", observes that much of today's culture leaves youth with "a sense of grayness, emptiness, meaningless, confusion, and despair." He urges the church's adult leadership to join with their youth in creating a culture that makes it possible "for each person to grow a rich and resolute inwardness," an inwardness that enables one to be self-directing and creative rather than "inward sawdust." There is a deep hunger for this kind of life, says Snyder, and the church must be about the business of bringing it into existence.[362]

The culture concept of ministry finds corroboration in a theory of education that takes account of the dynamic and holistic character of learning. That is to say, educational procedure is not confined to traditional classroom instruction with its focus upon the acquisition of knowledge, important as this function remains, but changes the total self in a total environment. Learning to become a fully functioning, self-affirming, effective, and decisive person means to be involved in multiple creative experiences and a participant in the culture. For the church, that culture is best described as a covenant-caring community. Ministry is the facilitator of such a community.[363]

The local church's approach to youth ministry was greatly affected by the sociological and cultural times. Youths across the nation began to demonstrate that they cared greatly about issues related to the world in which they lived. Those who were involved in youth ministry realized that the youth in their care needed far more their leaders than mere entertainment. In fact, many rejected entertainment as an unworthy activity for church youth ministry. Instead, they looked to their church youth leaders to provide biblical responses to issues such as war, racial discrimination, social injustice, ecological concerns, and much more.[364] Zelhou Keyho in his research on 'Church and Youth' found out that, the Naga youth,

362 As Cited by Paul B. Irwin, *The Care and Counseling of Youth in the Church*, 21.

363 Paul B. Irwin, *The Care and Counseling of Youth in the Church*, 22.

364 Kenneth R. Garland, "The Christian Education of Youth," *Foundations of Ministry*, edited by Michael J. Anthony (Grand Rapids: Baker Books, 1992), 160.

surrounded by youth in the church with whose life perceptions they cannot relate, are having difficulty finding their role in the church. Youth has had a difficult time discovering a role they and the larger church community can mutually affirm to be legitimate. At times, the roles that the youth of the church wanted have not been opened to them. At other times, the roles that the church wanted them to fill have been exploitive and demanding. Lack of proper communication and understanding have given the youth mixed signals on whether or not the church wants any part of them. And because of this, church in the last two decades have witnessed youth leaving the church. There exists an undeniable tension between the "church" and the "youth." Even though there has been much talk about revitalizing youth ministry and youth leadership development in the church, unfortunately, they have not seen significant change in the attitude of the church leaders towards youth ministry. The church knows that the youth are the future of the church yet its ministry occupies the back seat. No serious thought is given to the improvement of the department. This is evident in the hiring of youth leaders and the management of the department in the church. Because of this, the youth in the church have felt that the church is not serious about them. There is a lack of communication between the church and the youth. They know-all-attitude of the adults in the church has been a communication block for the youth. Unless they know the youth in their culture they can neither communicate the gospel effectively nor develop a successful youth ministry. Youth ministry should also be seen mission field of the church and therefore, the church, in order to formulate an effective youth ministry. First, youth ministry in the church takes the culture of the youth into consideration. Second, youth ministry in the church should be the outcome of listening to the needs of the youth. Third, youth ministry should only be confirmed within the four walls of the church. Fourth, youth in the church cannot be taken for granted.[365]

The church needs to recapture this awareness of her identity. When it comes to youth it is not sufficient to correct the image the youth has of the church. Church must create the kind of atmosphere within the church where youth can find space and experience their identity. [366] The church and the Pastoral counsellor need to ascertain the factors leading to the change of culture. Only then, they will be able to communicate and guide the youth effectively. The church can play a significant role in retaining some of the traditional cultural elements for the development of Naga society. The immediate task of the Naga church should be to make the Nagas more firmly rooted in their own culture and traditions before they are transported into other cultures and traditions. Naga youth should be taught to know, learn and appreciate their culture, traditions and values.[367]

---

365 Zelhou Keyho, "Church and Naga Youth," *Doing Youth Ministry in a Naga Context*, ed, 125.

366 M. Antony P. Rajan, *Pastoral care of Adolescents and Young Adults*, 38.

367 Mar Pongener, *Morung Speaks*, 180.

5.5. General Conclusion

The statement of the problem, fidelity to Naga culture among the youth who are staying outside Nagaland seems to be declining, giving rise to the necessity for the present work as it focuses on the few pertinent hypotheses concerning the content of culture. The concept of culture has a long history in the human sciences. However, in the light of the study the prominent and the widely shared conception suggests that culture is a collective product, constituted by the values, beliefs, symbols, behavior, and lifestyles which are transmitted across generation through oral tradition.

In Naga context, culture reflects the value- seeking process of human beings, design for living, and a composite of meanings and associated traditions which define, inform, and constitute the range of understanding and influence of day-to-day living.

Today the innate nobility, like simplicity, honesty, truthfulness, dignity of labor, community spirit, behavior and attitude, hospitality, and respect for others, have become myth rather than reality. Hence, the Naga youth are under the threat of fumbling situation. All these said problems are mainly because of polarization of the cultural fidelity, values and ethos.

Hence, the hypotheses put forward are evident from the research findings, that different age groups, gender, profession, and monthly income are not significantly differed from each other on cultural fidelity. However, locale of migration like Chennai, Kochi, Pune, Kolkata, Bengaluru, Hyderabad, Delhi, and Nagaland has a highly significant impact on cultural fidelity and moreover, Naga youth living outside Nagaland and cultural fidelity score found to be very highly significant.

Thus, the impacts of migration, modernization, social change, urbanization, education, information technology have resulted among the migrant Naga youth to loss the original cultural loyalty and fidelity. The influences of diverse culture have impacted on the life of Naga youth in various aspects such as, dress code, language, music and dance, art crafts and family relationships. Consequently, they have permeable identity crisis, ego boundary, and personalized relationships, contrast to Naga social values and virtues.

Therefore, it is necessary to apply for an appropriate pastoral care and counselling to understand and prepare the youth to rediscover rich Naga traditional cultural values. An attempt is made to find cultural horizons and allow youth to take into account the fact that they are in a new emerging hybrid situation. Hence, approaches such as, person-centered, cognitive, gestalt, reality, behavioral, and group counselling have emerged from this study to address the serious challenges among migrant Naga youth to revitalization and reclaiming of traditional Naga cultural values and practices.

Bibliography

Encyclopedia & Dictionaries

Campbell, Alastair V. "Pastoral Care, Nature of." *In A Dictionary of Pastoral Care.* Edited by Alastair V. Campbell. Great Britain: SPCK, 1990, 188-190.

Clinebell, Howard. "Pastoral Counselling." *In A Dictionary of Pastoral Care.* Edited by Alastair V. Campbell. Great Britain: SPCK, 1990, 198-199.

Gathercoal, K. A. "Life Span development." *Baker Encyclopedia of Psychology & Counseling.* Edited by David G. Benner & Peter C. Hill. Grand Rapids: Baker Books, 1999, 690-694.

Book

Aghamkar, Atul V. "Tribal Migration to the Cities." *Tribes in Transition: Indian Christians Reflect on the Original Inhabitants of the Land.* Edited by, F. Hrangkhuma and Paul Hiebert. Bangalore: SAIACS Press, 2004.

Aier, Wati. *Alcohol and Alcoholism: A Better Guide for the Nagas.* Dimapur, India: Book House, n.d.

Aier, Wati. "Reconstructing A Theology For Naga Youth." *Doing Youth Ministry in a Naga Context.* Edited by Soren Oestergaard & Adelo Mero. Dimapur: NBYF, 2004.

Anand, V. K. *Nagaland in Transaction.* New Delhi: Associated Publishing House, 1967.

Anthony, D. John. *Psychotherapies in Counselling.* Tamil Nadu, India: Anugraha Publications, 2003.

Antony, D. John. *Types of Counselling.* Nagercoil: Anughaha Publications, 1996.

Ao, Shashinungla. "Oral Tradition and Historical Discourse." *Tribe Culture Art .* Edited by Vanlalnghak Siby K. George. Guwahati, Assam: DVS Publishers, 2001.

Arimpoor, Joe. *Indian Youth in Perspective: A Research Study.* Tirupattur: Department of Social Work, Sacred Heart College, 1983.

Bediako, Kwame. "Gospel and Culture: Some Insights for Our Time from the Experience of the Earliest church." *Understanding Tribal for Effective Education*. Edited by Joseph Anikuzhikattil, George Palackapillil, Joseph Puthenpurakal. New Delhi: Commission for Education and Culture, CBCI Centre, 2003.

Bennett, John and Melvin Tumin. *Social Life*. New York: Alfred A. Knopf, 1948. Cited in Alfred L. Kroeber and Klyde Kluckhohn. *Culture: A Critical Review of Concepts and Definitions*. Cambridge, Mass: Papers of the Peabody Museum of America Archaeology and Ethnology, Harvard University, 1952.

Breakwell, Glynis M. et al., *Research Methods in Psychology*. New Delhi: Sage Publication, 2007.

Bremeld, Theodore. *Philosopies of Education in Cultural Pespectives*. Newyork: Dryden, 1955.

Chaudhary, Nandita. *Listening to Culture*. New Delhi: Sage Publications, 2004.

Choudhury, Nabanita. "Women Migration in Asia and the Pacific: A Portrayal." *Migrating Women: Opportunities and Vulnerabilities*. Edited by Asis Kumar Pain. Agartala: The Icfai University Press, 2008.

Clinebell, Howard. *Basic Types of Pastoral Care and Counseling*. Nashville: Abingdon Press, 1984.

Cohen, S. *Folk Devils and Moral panics*. London: Paladin, 1972.

Corey, Gerald. *Theory and Practice of Counseling and Psychotherapy* 6th ed. Australia: Brooks/Cole, 2002.

Corey, Gerald. *Case Approach to Counseling and Psychotherapy*. Belmont, California: Brooks Publishing Company, 1991.

Dollard, John and Allison Davis. *Children of Bondage*. Washington, D.C.: American Council on Education, 1940.

Dozo, P. *The Cross over Nagaland*. Guwahati, Assam: Christian Literature Centre, 1983.

Dozo, P. *The Growth of the Baptist Church in Chekhesang Naga Tribe*. Kohima, Nagaland: NMM, 1978.

Dressler, David and Donald Carnes. *Sociology: The Study of Human Interaction* 2nd Ed. Newyork: Alfred A. Knopf, Inc., 1973.

Durkheim, Emile. *Education and Sociology*. Translated by, D. Fox. Sherwood. Glencoe: The free press, 1956.

Earnest, Jaya. *Adolescent and Young Refugee Perspective on Psychosocial Wellbeing*. Melbourne: Common Ground Publishing, 2006.

Elwin, Verrier. *Nagaland*. N.P: RDAS, 1961.

Erikson, Erik. *Identity, Youth And Crises*. New York: Norton & Co, 1968.

Garland, Kenneth R. "The Christian Education of Youth." *Foundations of Ministry*. Edited by Michael J. Anthony Grand Rapids: Baker Books, 1992.

Gelso, Charles and Bruce Fretz. *Counselling Psychology, Practices, Issues, and Intervention*. New Delhi: Cengage Learning India Private Limited, 2001.

Grunlan, Stephen A. & Marvin K. Mayers. *Cultural Anthropology: A Christian Perspective*. 2nd ed. Grand Rapids, Michigan: Zondervan Publishing House, 1988.

Guglar, Joseph. *On the theory of Rural-Urban Migration: the Case of Sub-Saharan Africa*. Cambridge: University Press, 1969.

Hall, G. S. *Adolescence: it's Psychology, and its Relations to Physiology, Anthropology, Sociology, Sex, Crime, Religion and Education* (2vols). New York: Appleton, 1904.

Hall, Simon. "Discipleship-Making: A Practical Theology of Adolescent Spirituality." *Doing Youth Ministry in a Naga Context*. Edited by Soren Oestergaard & Adelo Mero. Dimapur: NBYF, 2004.

Heasman, Kathleen. *An Introduction to Pastoral Counselling*. "(N.p.: n.p.,n.d)."

Herskovitz, Melvin. *Man and His Works*. New York: Alfred A. Knopf, 1948. Cited by Kroeber and Kluckhohn. *Culture: A Critical Review of Concepts and Definitions*. Cambridge, Mass: Papers of the Peabody Museum of America Archaeology and Ethnology, Harvard University, 1952.

Horam, M. "Naga Religion: A Case Study." *in Religion and Society of the North-East India*. New Delhi, India: Vikas Publishing House, 1980.

Hutton, J. H. *The Sema Nagas*. London: Oxford University Press, 1967.

Hutton, J. H. *The Angami Nagas*. London: Oxford University Press, 1969.

Imchen, C. L. "The Nagas and the Legacy of Civilizing Mission of the Western World." *Understanding Tribal Cultures for Effective Education*. Edited by Joseph Anikuzhikattil, George Palackapillil, Joseph Puthenpurakal. New Delhi: Commission for Education and Culture (CBCI Centre), 2003.

Imchen, Narola. *Women in the History of Christianity*. Jorhat: Tribal Development and Communication Centre, 2014.

Imchen, Panger. *Ancient Ao Naga Religion and Culture*. New Delhi: Har-Anand Publication, 1993.

Imsenperong. "Theological Reflection on Migration." *Mapping the Context: An Interdisciplinary Exploration*. Edited by Imsenperong, Menjiwapong Jamir, Walotemjen. Kohima, Nagaland: Published by the Authors, 2011.

Imsopangla. "A Liberative of Inheritance: A Critique of the Ao Naga Customary Law of Inheritance." *Side by Side*. Edited by Limatula Longkumer & Talijungla Longkumer. Kolkata: ESPACE, 2013.

Irwin, Paul B. *The Care and Counseling of Youth in the Church*. Philadelphia: Fortress Press, 1975.

Jacobs, Ed E. Robert L. Masson, Riley L. Harvill. *Theory and Practice of Group counselling*. New Delhi: Cengage Learning Private Limited, 2010.

Jala, Dominic. "Youth and the Challenges of the Twenty-first Century." *Society and Culture in North-East India: A Christian Perspective*. Edited by Saral K. Chatterji. Delhi: ISPCK, 1996.

James, Lovely Awomi. "North East Christianity and Traditional Religio-Cultural Elements: Implications for Theology of Religions today." *Issues Confronting Church and Society Today.* Edited by, Lovely Awomi James & Razouselie Lasetso. Jorhat: ILEMA-ETC & WSC-ETC, 2017.

James, Lovely Awomi. *Tribal Theology, Reviewing the Naga Traditional Worldview*. New Delhi: Christian World Imprints, 2017.

Jamir, L. Imsutoshi. *Communication in Action: The Pattern of Naga Cultural Shift*. Mokokchung, Nagaland: Tribal Development and Communication Centre, 2000.

Jamir, I. Asenla. "Naga Traditional Media and its Usefulness." *Communication and Naga Culture*. Edited by L. Imsutoshi Jamir, C. Alitemjen Longkumer. Dimapur: TDCC, 2007.

Jamir, L. Imsutoshi. "Methodological Challenges for the Tribal Cultural Studies." *Communication and Naga Culture*. Edited by L. Imsutoshi Jamir & C. Alitemjen Longkumer. Dimapur: The Tribal Development and Communication Center (TDCC), 2007.

Jamir, L.Imsutoshi. *Sites in Tribal Cultural Studies.* Mokokchung: TDCC Publications, 2015.

Jamir, Sentimeren. "The Naga Folk Songs: Its Relevance in Church Worship." *Communication and Culture.* Edited by L. imsutoshi Jamir and C. Alitemjen Longkumer. Dimapur, Nagaland: TDCC, 2007.

Jones, Richard Nelson. *Practical Counseling and Helping Skills*, 5th Edition. London: Sage Publications, 2005.

Jones, Richard Nelson. *Theory and Practice of Counseling and Therapy*, 5th Edition. New Delhi: Sage Publications India Pvt Ltd, 2006.

Joseph, M. T. "Migration and Identity Formation: A Case Study of Dalit Assertation in Aurangabad, Maharashtra." *Migration and Mission in India*. Edited by L. Stanislaus SVD and Jose Joseph SVD. Delhi: Ishvani Kendra/ ISPCK, 2007.

Joshi, Hargovind, ed. *Nagaland Past and Present*. New Delhi: Akansha Publishing House, 2001.

Joshi, S. C. *Migration to a Metropolis*. Jaipur: RBSA Publishers, 1994.

Kakar, Sudhir, ed. *Identity And Adulthood.* Delhi: Oxford University Press, n.d.

Kappen, S. *Towards a Holistic Cultural Paradigm*. Tiruvalla: Christava Sahitya Samithy, 2003.

Keitzar, Renthy. *Triumph of Faith in Nagaland.* Kohima, India: NBCC, 1987.

Keyho, Zelhou. "Church and Naga Youth." *Doing Youth Ministry in a Naga Context.* Edited by Soren Oestergaard & Adelo Mero. Dimapur: NBYF, 2004.

Kraft, Charles H. *Christianity in Culture.* New York: Orbis Books, 1979.

Kroeber, A. L. *Anthropology.* Rev. ed. New York: Harcourt, Brace and Company, 1948.

Kumar, B. B. *Naga Identity.* New Delhi: Concept publishing Company, 2005.

Lanunungsang, A & N. Talitemjen Jamir. *Naga Society And Culture.* Jorhat: Nagaland University Tribal Research Centre Department of Sociology, 2005.

Lasetso, Razouselie. "Introduction: Shaping a Relevant Theology for the Indigenous People of North East India." *Tribal Christian Theology.* Edited by Razouselie Lasetso, Yangkahao Vashum. Jorhat, Assam: Eastern Theological College, 2007.

Lasetso, Razouselie. "Keynote Address: Restoring, Maintaining, Preserving, and Transmitting Cultural Values for Generations to Come." *Doing Tribal Christian Theology with Tribal Resources: Cultural Resources from North East India.* Edited by Razouselie Lasetso, Eyingbeni Humtsoe. Jorhat, Assam: Eastern Theological College, 2009.

Laungani, Pittu. "Culture and Identity: Implications for Counseling." *Counselling in a Multicultural Society.* Edited by, Stephen Palmer & Pittu Laungani. London: Sage Publications, 1999.

longchar, A. Wati. *The Traditional Worldview and Modernity.* Jorhat, Assam: ETC, 1995.

Longchar, Wati. "Revisiting Tribal Theology In Changing Context Today." *Tribal Christian Theology.* Edited by Razouselie Lasetso, Yangkahao Vashum. Jorhat, Assam: Eastern Theological College, 2007.

Longkumer, C. Alitemjen. "Impact of Rock Music Culture Towards Naga Culture." *Communication and Naga Culture.* Edited by L. Imsutoshi Jamir & C. Alitemjen Longkumer. Dimapur: The Tribal Development and Communication Center (TDCC), 2007.

Longkumer, Limatula. *"Christianity and Naga Women." in Transforming Theology for Empowering Women, ed.* R. L. Hnuni. Jorhat: TSC, ETC, 1999.

Longkumer, Limatula. *Chirstian Education For Transformation: Foundations, Approaches and effective Teaching,* Kolkata: ESPACE, 2017.

Longkumer, Limatula. *Christian Education for Adults in Tribal Context.* Jorhat: Published by the Author, 1998.

Longkumer, Limatula. *Women in Theological Education: Pedagogical Issues.* Bangalore: Board of Theological Education of the Senate of Serampore College, 2012.

Lotha, Abraham. "Nagas' Conversion to Christianity and Modernity in Colonial India." *Nagas Today Indigenous Discourse*. Edited by Zuchamo Yanthan, et al., Delhi: Published by Naga Students' Union, 2010.

Lotha, Yanbemo. *Making A Theology of Naga Community*. Dimapur, Nagaland: Abeni Lotha, 2005.

Macionis, John J. *Sociology*. Eaglewood Cliffs: Prentice Hall Inc., 1980.

Malinowski, Bronislaw. *A Scientific Theory of Culture*. Chapel Hill: University of North Carolina Press, 1994.

Manohar, Moses P. "Towards A Theology of Creativity of Ecumenical Youth Ministry." *NCC Review 113/10* (November, 1993).

Marbaniang, Nazarine V. "Youth Participation in Socio-Political Awareness in the North-East." *Society and Culture in North-East India: A Christian Perspective*. Edited by Saral K. Chatterji. Delhi: ISPCK, 1996.

Marcel, Gabriel. "Obedience and Fidelity." *On Being Responsible*. Edited by, James M. Gustafson and James T. Laney. Great Britain: SCM Press Ltd, 1969.

Mead, Margaret. *Cooperation and Competition among Primitive Peoples*. NewYork: McGraw-Hill, 1937.

Menamparampil, T. "The Phenomenon of Culture." *Understanding Tribal for Effective Education*. Edited by Joseph Anikuzhikattil, George Palackapillil, Joseph Puthenpurakal. New Delhi: Commission for Education and Culture, CBCI Centre, 2003.

Menamparampil, Thomas. *The Challenge of Cultures*. Bombay: St Pauls, 1996.

Mero, Adela. "The Naga Home and Youth." *Doing Youth Ministry in a Naga Context*. Edited by Soren Oestergaard & Adelo Mero. Dimapur: NBYF, 2004.

Mero, Coppe. "Current Social Issues Among The Naga Youth." *Doing Youth Ministry in a Naga Context*. Edited by Soren Oestergaard & Adelo Mero. Dimapur: NBYF, 2004.

Michael, S. M. *Christianity and Cultures: Anthropological Insights for Christian Mission in India*. Delhi: ISPCK, 2015.

Misra, Girishwar and Ajit K. Mohanty. *Perspectives on Indigenous Psychology*. Edited by Girishwar Misra and Ajit K. Mohanty. New Delhi: Concept Publishing Company, 2002.

Moon, Tasoni. *Naga Work Culture: A Theological Reflection*. Dimapur, Nagaland: Published by the Author, 2004.

Moore, Wilbert E. *Social Change*. New Delhi: Prentice-Hall of India Limited, 1965.

Murry, Ezamo. "Bible and Culture: A Model of Christian Acculturation of Tribal Culture." *Doing Tribal Christian Theology with Tribal Resources: Cultural*

Resources from North East India. Edited by Razouselie Lasetso, Eyingbeni Humtsoe. Jorhat, Assam: Eastern Theological College, 2009.

Muuss, Rolf E. *Theories of Adolescence*. New York: Random House, 1964.

Nayar, Pramod K. *An Introduction to Cultural Studies*. New Delhi: Viva Books, 2009.

Nelson-Jones, Richard. *Practical Counseling and Helping Skills*. 5th Edition. London: Sage Publications, 2005.

Nida, Eugene A. *Customs and Customs*. New York: Harper and Brothers, 1954.

Nuh, V. K and Wetshokhrolo Lasuh, eds. *The Naga Chronicle*. New Delhi: Regency Publications, 2002.

Nuh, V. K. *A Theological Reflection On Naga Society*. Kohima, Nagaland: Research Wing, Council of Naga Baptist Churches, 1996.

Nuh, V. K. *My Country, My People: Focus in Nagaland*. Kohima, Nagaland: Vision Press, 1988.

Nuh, V. K. *Nagaland Church and Politics*. Kohima, Nagaland: V. K. Nuh & Bros, 2002.

Nuh, V. K. *Struggle for Identity in North-East India: A Theological Response*. Guwahati: Spectrum Publications, 2001.

O, Sullivan. et al., *Key Concepts in Communications and Cultural Studies*. London: Rout ledge, 1994.

Ottaway, A. K. C. *Education and Society-An Introduction to the Sociology of Education*. London: Routledge and Kegan Paul, 1953.

P. Rajan, M. Antony. *Pastoral Care of Adolecents and Young Adults*. Bangalore: Asian Trading Corporation, 2004.

Pakem, B, ed. *Nationality, Ethnicity and Cultural Identity in North-East India* . Guwahati: R. Kumar for Omsons Publications, 1990.

Panda, Minati and Ajit K. Mohanty. "Socio-Cultural Construction of Mind and Language." *Culture Cognition and Behaviour*. Edited by Aradhana Shukla. New Delhi: Concept Publishing Company, 2009.

Pandey, Gaya. *Developmental Anthropology*. Delhi: Concept Publishing Company, 2008.

Panikkar, K. M. *The Features of Indian Culture*. Chowpatty: Bombay-7: Bharatiya Vidya Bhavan, 1967.

Pedersen, Paul B. *Culture-Centered Counselling Interventions*. London: Sage Publications, 1997.

Philip, P. T. *The Growth of Baptist Church in Nagaland*. Guwahati, Assam: Christian Literature Centre, 1983.

Pimomo, Paul. "From Naga Village to the Global Village: The Common Good and Human Rights." *Nagas Today Indigenous Discourse*. Edited by Zuchamo Yanthan, et al., Delhi: Published by Naga Students' Union, 2010.

Pongener, Mar. *Morung Speaks.* Jorhat, Barkataki and Company Private Limited, 2011.

Pongener, Mar. *Morung Speaks: Cultural Values and Elements for the Enrichment of Naga Christian Community.* Jorhat, Assam: CTC and TDCC, 2011.

Ponraj, S. D. *An Introduction to Missionary Anthropology.* Rev. ed. Chennai: Mission Educational Books, 2010.

Rao, C. N. Shankar. *Sociology: Principles of Sociology with an Introduction to Social Thought.* New Delhi: S. Chand & Company, 2009.

Rao, S. Narayana. *Counselling Psychology.* New Delhi: Tata McGraw-Hill Publishing Company Limited, 1984.

Rao, S. Narayana. *Counselling and Guidance.* 2nd ed. New Delhi: Tata McGraw-Hill Publishing Company Limited, 1991.

Rawat, H. K. *Sociology: Basic Concepts.* New Delhi: Rawat Publications, 2007.

Rawson, Do, Graham Whitehead and Mohan Luthra. "The Challenges of Counselling in a Multicultural Society." *Counselling in a Multicultural Society.* Edited by, Stephen Palmer & Pittu Laungani. London: Sage Publications, 1999.

Redfield, Robert. *The Folk Culture of the Yucatan.* Chicago: University of Chicago Press, 1941.

Reuter, Edward and R. E. Park , ed. *Race and Culture.* New York: McGraw-Hill, 1939.

Ryckman, Richard M. *Theories of Personality*, 5th Edition. Belmont, California: Cole Publishing company, 1993.

Sanchez, Bernadetle and Yari Colon. "Race, Ethnicity, and Culture in Mentoring Relationships." *Handbook of Youth Mentoring.* Edited by David L. DuBois, Michal J. Karcher. London: Sage Publications, 2005.

Saraswathi, S. *Youth in India.* New Delhi: Indian Council of Social Science Research, 1988.

Savi, Akhrieno. "Intercultural Bible Reading- A Case Study." *Tribal Christian Theology.* Edited by Razouselie Lasetso, Yangkahao Vashum. Jorhat, Assam: Eastern Theological College, 2007.

Sema, Boholi Z. *Parent-Children Relationship among the Naga Society Towards Family Enrichment.* Dimapur: Shikhu Scholastic Press, 2012.

Sema, Hokishe. *Emergence of Nagaland: Socio-Economic and Political Transformation and the Future.* New Delhi: Vikas Publishing House, 1986.

Shah, B.V. "Education and Social Change among Tribals In India." *Tribal Communities and Social Change.* Edited by Pariyaram M. Chacko. New Delhi: Sage Publications, 2005.

Sharma, Anita and Dalip Malhotra. *Personality and Social Norms.* New Delhi: Concept Publishing Company, 2007.

Shelton, Charles M. *Pastoral Counseling with Adolescents and Young Adults*. New York: The Crossroad Publishing Company, 1995.

Shikhu, Inato Yekheto. *A Rediscovery and Rebuilding of Naga Cultural Values*. New Delhi: Regency Publications, 2007.

Shimray, R. R. *Origin and Culture of Nagas*. New Delhi: Somsak Publication, 1985.

Shishak, Tuisem A. "Nagas and Education: Back to Basic." *Nagas Today Indigenous Discourse*. Edited by Zuchamo Yanthan, et al., Delhi: Published by Naga Students' Union, 2010.

Shukla, Aradhana. "Culture and Our Understanding." *Culture Cognition and Behaviour*. Edited by Aradhana Shukla. New Delhi: Concept Publishing Company, 2009.

Silverman, David. *Interpreting Qualitative Data*. New Delhi: Sage Publications Data, 2006.

Singh, Arun Kumar. *The Comprehensive History of Psychology*. New Delhi: Motilal Banarsidass, 2002.

Singh, Sadhu. *Research Methodology in Social Science*. Bombay: Himalaya Publishing, 1983.

Sobhanam, Gideon. *United to Adjust: A Sacramental Theology of Marriage for Marital Counselling*. Delhi: ISPCK, 2007.

Takatemjen. *Studies on Theology and Naga Culture*. Jorhat, Assam: Published by the Author, 1997.

Tanner, Kathryn. *Theories of Culture*. Minneapolis: Fortress Press, 1997.

Thanzauva, K. *Theology of Community: Tribal Theology in the Making*. Aizawl, Mizoram: Mizo Theological Conference, 1997.

Thomas, M. M and R.W. Taylor, ed. *Tribal Awakening*. Bangalore: Christian Institute for the Study of Religion and Society, 1965.

Thomas, M. M. *Nagas Towards A.D. 2000 and Other Selected Addresses and Writings*. Madras: Centre for Research on New International Economic Order, 1992.

Thong, Joseph S. *Head-Hunters Cultures*. Kohima, Nagaland: Khinyi Woch, Chunlika Tseminyu, 1997.

Thong, Joseph S. *Glimpses of Naga Legacy And Culture.* Edited by Phanenmo Kath. Kottayam, Kerala: Society for Naga Students' Welfare, Kerala, 2011.

Thong, Tezenlo. *Progress and its Impact on the Nagas A Clash of Worldviews*. England: Ashgate Publishing Limited, 2014.

Warner, W. L, et al., *Who Shall Be Educated.* Newyork: Harper, 1944.

Weingberg, A. A. "Migration and Belonging: A Study of Mental Health and Personal Adjustment in Israel." *In People in the Move: Studies on International*

Migration. Edited by Laszek A. Kosinsk and R. Mansell Brothers. London: Methuen and Co. Ltd, 1975.

Wezah, Yiepetso. *Tribal Ethical Values and Practices-a Search for a Better World.* Dimapur, Nagaland: Lhiweko-u Wezah, 2015.

Journals

Carr, L. J. "Situational Psychology." *American Journal of Sociology* 51 (1945).

Deheragoda, Kishan. "Impact of Globalization on the Third World Cultures." *Dialogue* (NS) 24/ (1997).

Dewey, John. *Education and Social Change*. Social Frontier, 2 (May 1973).

Groody, Daniel G. "Dying to live: Theology, Migration, and the Human Journey." *Reflection* 95/2 (Fall 2008).

Gruz, Gemma Tulud. "Between Identity and Security: Theological Implications of Migration in the Context of Globalization." *Theological Studies* 69/2 (2008).

Lazar, S. "Impact of Globalization on Culture." *NCC Review* 119/1 (January, 1999).

Mathson, Nebu. *Impact of Globalization on the Indian Youth: A Review of the Response of NCCI.*

Moses, Y. "Youth in India Today." *NCC Review* 119/10 (November, 1997).

Vallabaraj, Jerome. "Introducing Youth Ministry Prespectives." *Kristu Jyoti 19/1* (March, 2003).

Victor, Vinod. "Contemporary Challenges of Youth Ministry." *NCC Review* 119/9 (October, 1999).

Zetter, Roger. "Labeling Refuhees: The forming of Transformation of a Bureaucratic Identity." *Journal of Refugee Studies* 4 (1991).

Webliography

http://www.Iom.Int/jahia/jahia/cache/offence/pit/1674?entryID=932. Accesses, September 13, 2011.

http://www.iom.int/jahia/about-migration/facts-and-figures (Accessed, August 3, 2012. According to statistic collected by Gemma Tulud Gruz, migrants constitute 2.9% of the world's countries and out of which 60% of the migrants live in developed countries and out of which 75% of them are living in only 28 destination for migrants but the statistic shows that as of 2005 Europe shares 34% of the migrant population followed by North America 23%, Asia 28%, africa 9%, Latin america 3% and Oceania 3%.

Person-Centered Therapy-Counselling Directory www.counselling-directory.org. UK> Person-centered therapy. Accesses, April 20, 2016.

Cognitive behavioral therapy-Wikipedia, the free encyclopedia https://en.m.wikipedia.org>wiki>cognitive behavioral therapy. Accesses, April 21, 2016.

Gestalt therapy-Wikipedia, the free encyclopedia https://en.m.wikipedia.org> Gestalt therapy. Accesses, April 20, 2016.

Reality therapy. www.wglasser.com.> the-glasser approach. Accesses, April 20, 2016.

Reality therapy-William Glasser Institute www.wglasser.com> the glasser approach. Accesses, April 20, 2016.

Behavioral Therapy Counselling Directory. www.counselling-directory.org.uk> behavioral therapy. Accesses, April 20, 2016.

Group counselling/university of Oxford https/www.ox.ac.uk> students> welfare. Accesses, April 21, 2016.

www.un.org/esa/socdev/documents/youth/fact-sheets/youth-definition. Accesses, December 26, 2017.

www.easternmirrownagaland.com/thinkers-reason-why-naga-youth-areleaving -Nagaland. Accesses, December, 27, 2017.

https://en.wikipedia.org/wiki/quantitative-research. Accesses, December 26, 2017.

https:/wwwmy.vanderbilt.edu/perkins/files/2011/09/perkins-etal-2011. psychosocial-studies-of-migration. Accesses, Dec 29, 2017.

http://www.google.co.in.definition+of+the+term+social+media. Accesses, Dec 29, 2017.

Appendix

Cultural Fidelity Scale for Nagas

Socio Economic Status Scale

a. Age:______________

b. Gender:___________

c. Class/ Profession/ Occupation:__________________________________

d. Place of Stay:____

e. Family monthly Income: _______________________________________

The following are some statements concerning your perception on the Naga Youth and their Fidelity to Naga culture. There are response numbered from 1 to 5. You are to choose the option which fits to your perception.

Response options:

1. Strongly Agree, 2. Agree, 3. Don't know, 4. Disagree, 5. Strongly Disagree

1. I do all kinds of work for my personal and household requirement.
   1. Strongly Agree, 2. Agree, 3. Don't know, 4. Disagree, 5. Strongly Disagree
2. The present Naga youth is aptly described by someone as "sitting and eating job". I consider myself under this category.
   1. Strongly Agree, 2. Agree, 3. Don't know, 4. Disagree, 5. Strongly Disagree
3. I feel ashamed to do manual work.
   1. Strongly Agree, 2. Agree, 3. Don't know, 4. Disagree, 5. Strongly Disagree
4. I am proud to be called a hard working person.
   1. Strongly Agree, 2. Agree, 3. Don't know, 4. Disagree, 5. Strongly Disagree
5. I am more fluent in speaking English/Nagamese than speaking my own mother tongue.
   1. Strongly Agree, 2. Agree, 3. Don't know, 4. Disagree, 5. Strongly Disagree

6. I love to speak and more fluent with my own mother tongue than speaking in any other languages.
   1. Strongly Agree, 2. Agree, 3. Don't know, 4. Disagree, 5. Strongly Disagree
7. I still value the functions of Morung as an institution for imparting ethics of social, religious, political, and economic value to the members.
   1. Strongly Agree, 2. Agree, 3. Don't know, 4. Disagree, 5. Strongly Disagree
8. Our Family members never come together on certain arguments.
   1. Strongly Agree, 2. Agree, 3. Don't know, 4. Disagree, 5. Strongly Disagree
9. There is strong emphasis in our family with regard to right and wrong.
   1. Strongly Agree, 2. Agree, 3. Don't know, 4. Disagree, 5. Strongly Disagree
10. Our Family members are closely knitted to each other.
   1. Strongly Agree, 2. Agree, 3. Don't know, 4. Disagree, 5. Strongly Disagree
11. There is a wide gap between me and my parents.
   1. Strongly Agree, 2. Agree, 3. Don't know, 4. Disagree, 5. Strongly Disagree
12. I consider my parents as old fashioned.
   1. Strongly Agree, 2. Agree, 3. Don't know, 4. Disagree, 5. Strongly Disagree
13. My parents never allow me to do things by myself.
   1. Strongly Agree, 2. Agree, 3. Don't know, 4. Disagree, 5. Strongly Disagree
14. My parents allow me to things by myself.
   1. Strongly Agree, 2. Agree, 3. Don't know, 4. Disagree, 5. Strongly Disagree
15. I sneak out to the theater to watch movies.
   1. Strongly Agree, 2. Agree, 3. Don't know, 4. Disagree, 5. Strongly Disagree
16. Watching television is my daily living routine.
   1. Strongly Agree, 2. Agree, 3. Don't know, 4. Disagree, 5. Strongly Disagree
17. I have lost the will power to reassert my own identity.
   1. Strongly Agree, 2. Agree, 3. Don't know, 4. Disagree, 5. Strongly Disagree
18. I love everything that is "Western" and hate everything that is "Naga".
   1. Strongly Agree, 2. Agree, 3. Don't know, 4. Disagree, 5. Strongly Disagree
19. I am always looked up or honored by my family background/position.
   1. Strongly Agree, 2. Agree, 3. Don't know, 4. Disagree, 5. Strongly Disagree
20. I am happily associated with the people in spite of my low socio-economic status.
   1. Strongly Agree, 2. Agree, 3. Don't know, 4. Disagree, 5. Strongly Disagree
21. I give equal treatment to different classes of people.
   1. Strongly Agree, 2. Agree, 3. Don't know, 4. Disagree, 5. Strongly Disagree
22. I often give respect to people according to their status.
   1. Strongly Agree, 2. Agree, 3. Don't know, 4. Disagree, 5. Strongly Disagree

23. I feel proud when I wear traditional dress.
    1. Strongly Agree, 2. Agree, 3. Don't know, 4. Disagree, 5. Strongly Disagree
24. I prefer to wear Naga traditional dresses and pretty ornaments most of the time.
    1. Strongly Agree, 2. Agree, 3. Don't know, 4. Disagree, 5. Strongly Disagree
25. I opt to wear for the most fashionable outfits rather than wearing old traditional dresses.
    1. Strongly Agree, 2. Agree, 3. Don't know, 4. Disagree, 5. Strongly Disagree
26. I don't like to wear traditional dresses.
    1. Strongly Agree, 2. Agree, 3. Don't know, 4. Disagree, 5. Strongly Disagree
27. I regard western music as more authentic and authoritative than the rich old folk music.
    1. Strongly Agree, 2. Agree, 3. Don't know, 4. Disagree, 5. Strongly Disagree
28. I think Folk songs can still be a communication medium in the Naga Society as well in the church worship service.
    1. Strongly Agree, 2. Agree, 3. Don't know, 4. Disagree, 5. Strongly Disagree
29. I have forgotten my own cultural songs, dances, folklores, and the most valuable oral traditions.
    1. Strongly Agree, 2. Agree, 3. Don't know, 4. Disagree, 5. Strongly Disagree
30. I love listening to indigenous music, watch folk dances rather than listening to classical music and dances.
    1. Strongly Agree, 2. Agree, 3. Don't know, 4. Disagree, 5. Strongly Disagree
31. I am proud to be born as a Naga.
    1. Strongly Agree, 2. Agree, 3. Don't know, 4. Disagree, 5. Strongly Disagree
32. I want to learn new knowledge and wanted to do things differently.
    1. Strongly Agree, 2. Agree, 3. Don't know, 4. Disagree, 5. Strongly Disagree
33. I want to adopt the patterns and life styles of other societies.
    1. Strongly Agree, 2. Agree, 3. Don't know, 4. Disagree, 5. Strongly Disagree
34. I want to identify myself with the popular demand of the day.
    1. Strongly Agree, 2. Agree, 3. Don't know, 4. Disagree, 5. Strongly Disagree
35. I want to maintain a good spirit of hospitality.
    1. Strongly Agree, 2. Agree, 3. Don't know, 4. Disagree, 5. Strongly Disagree
36. I am honest, and pay due respect to my elders.
    1. Strongly Agree, 2. Agree, 3. Don't know, 4. Disagree, 5. Strongly Disagree
37. Self-centeredness and Individualistic feeling are fast emerging among the contemporary Naga youth.
    1. Strongly Agree, 2. Agree, 3. Don't know, 4. Disagree, 5. Strongly Disagree
38. I love to work together.
    1. Strongly Agree, 2. Agree, 3. Don't know, 4. Disagree, 5. Strongly Disagree

39. I don't like being involved in big groups or any kind of social gatherings.
    1. Strongly Agree, 2. Agree, 3. Don't know, 4. Disagree, 5. Strongly Disagree
40. I enjoy having feasts of merit.
    1. Strongly Agree, 2. Agree, 3. Don't know, 4. Disagree, 5. Strongly Disagree
41. I think traditional cultures practices like Arts and crafts are no more relevant and useful in the present world.
    1. Strongly Agree, 2. Agree, 3. Don't know, 4. Disagree, 5. Strongly Disagree
42. I am no longer interested in the historical rich culture of the Nagas.
    1. Strongly Agree, 2. Agree, 3. Don't know, 4. Disagree, 5. Strongly Disagree
43. I always looked up for own unique culture and rich material.
    1. Strongly Agree, 2. Agree, 3. Don't know, 4. Disagree, 5. Strongly Disagree
44. My life is often shaped by what I see in television.
    1. Strongly Agree, 2. Agree, 3. Don't know, 4. Disagree, 5. Strongly Disagree
45. Knowing modern and post-modern advancements I consider our indigenous culture as something obsolete, rather than an antique.
    1. Strongly Agree, 2. Agree, 3. Don't know, 4. Disagree, 5. Strongly Disagree
46. I spent most of my time, sitting in the computer, rather than spent time with friends, families and in recreation.
    1. Strongly Agree, 2. Agree, 3. Don't know, 4. Disagree, 5. Strongly Disagree
47. I am actively involved in Church/Fellowship activities.
    1. Strongly Agree, 2. Agree, 3. Don't know, 4. Disagree, 5. Strongly Disagree
48. I want the Church to address to the needs of the present Youth.
    1. Strongly Agree, 2. Agree, 3. Don't know, 4. Disagree, 5. Strongly Disagree
49. I want the church to provide a platform where I can search for truth.
    1. Strongly Agree, 2. Agree, 3. Don't know, 4. Disagree, 5. Strongly Disagree
50. I want church to develop new skills and become more creative to the emerging design.
    1. Strongly Agree, 2. Agree, 3. Don't know, 4. Disagree, 5. Strongly Disagree